Presented to

CELEBRATING
Springfield

CELEBRATING
Springfield
A PHOTOGRAPHIC PORTRAIT

RIVERBEND BOOKS
A division of BOOKHOUSE GROUP, INC.

CELEBRATING
Springfield

EDITOR . . . . Rob Levin

PUBLISHER . . . . Barry Levin

ASSOCIATE PUBLISHER . . . . John Lorenzo

SPRINGFIELD AREA CHAMBER OF
COMMERCE PROJECT DIRECTOR . . . . Ann Elwell

DESIGN MANAGER . . . . Ann Fowler

SENIOR EDITOR . . . . Renée Peyton

ASSOCIATE EDITOR . . . . Rena Distasio

PROJECT DIRECTOR . . . . Muriel Diguette

PHOTO EDITORS . . . . Jill Dible, Ann Fowler

WRITERS . . . . Kimberly DeMeza, Rena Distasio,
    Grace Hawthorne, Amy Meadows, Regina Roths, Gail Snyder

COPY EDITOR . . . . Bob Land

BOOK DESIGN . . . . Compoz Design

JACKET DESIGN . . . . Kevin Smith

PREPRESS . . . . Vickie Berdanis

PHOTOGRAPHERS . . . . Thomas S. England, Eric Francis
                Scott Indermaur, Lisa Means, Alan S. Weiner

RIVERBEND BOOKS
A division of BOOKHOUSE GROUP. INC.

Published by Riverbend Books
an Imprint of Bookhouse Group, Inc.
818 Marietta Street, NW
Atlanta, Georgia 30318
www.riverbendbooks.net
404.885.9515

Library of Congress Cataloging-in-Publication Data
Celebrating Springfield : a photographic portrait / [editor, Rob Levin].
p. cm. ISBN 978-1-883987-30-5
1. Springfield (Mo.)--Pictorial works. 2. Springfield (Mo.)--Description
and travel. 3. Springfield (Mo.)--Economic conditions. 4. Business
enterprises--Missouri--Springfield. I. Levin, Rob, 1955- II. Title.
F474.S7C45 2007
977.8'780440222--dc22
2007005390

When Springfield celebrates something important, it tends to do it with a bang. As soon as the sun goes down on the annual Firefall Fourth of July celebration, out come the fireworks and the eighty-two-member Springfield Symphony Orchestra. Known as the Concert in the Sky®, the extravaganza is one of the few choreographed fireworks displays in the country that is accompanied by a live orchestra. ❖

Up, up, and away, floating on the breeze, watching the world drift by. There is no better way to see and enjoy the beauty of the Ozarks. In your magic balloon you can not only appreciate the rich texture of the land- scape, but you can smell the fresh, clean air and maybe even hear the song of a bird. The Ozarks around the Springfield area present an outdoor wonderland that includes numerous crystal-blue lakes, hiking trails, fish- ing streams, parks, and an ever-changing panorama of seasons and col- ors. Ballooning is a popular sport that gives both pilots and passengers a chance to view the world from a new perspective . . . and the best part is that traffic is never a problem.

Contents

CELEBRATING

Springfield

would not have been possible without the support of the following sponsors:

BKD, LLP • Blackwell Sanders Peper Martin, LLP • Christian Health Care • Commerce Bank • Convoy of Hope

• CoxHealth • Drury University • Ferrell-Duncan Clinic, Inc. • Guaranty Bank • Hamra Enterprises • Hawthorn Park Hotel

• Headache Care Center / Primary Care Network • Ozarks Coca-Cola Dr Pepper Bottling Co. • Paul Mueller Company

• Power of the Web.com • Springfield Public Schools • Springfield–Greene County Parks Department • St. John's

Health System • The Maiman Company • The Signature Bank • University Plaza Hotel and Convention Center

BLACKWELL SANDERS

DRURY

Guaranty Bank

ST. JOHN'S

POWERFUL MEDICINE

Foreword

Springfield: It's Our Time to Celebrate

Every now and then in the life of a great city, there comes a time to celebrate. Springfield, Missouri, has been quietly waiting for its moment—but we can't hold back any longer. Let's light the fireworks!

Springfield, the third-largest city in Missouri, is embracing a renaissance never before seen in its long and colorful history.

Center City Springfield is aptly named, because it's where our celebration begins. Recent developments like art galleries, loft apartments, fine restaurants, and a pulsing nightlife keep the city's beat. Our new Springfield Cardinals Double-A baseball team invites spectators to spend a summer evening at a ballpark that's received national recognition for its design.

Downtown's Jordan Valley Park, with its fountains, trails, outdoor concerts, and ice park, has inspired further expansion and new development. Perhaps most exciting is an innovation center at the edge of Jordan Valley that promises to bring nanotechnology and related research, along with the jobs to support them.

All this has come about in just the last six years.

But the celebration is also about our people. Genuine and hard-working, Springfieldians are the heart of our city. They have a vision of what they want Springfield to be, and the energy to make those dreams happen. Residents love Springfield because it's a big city that remembers its small-town roots. It may have a common name, but Springfield has an uncommon spirit.

Nicknamed "Missouri's Economic Engine," Springfield is a regional health-care hub and home to top-notch schools and universities. We're known for a workforce that embodies midwestern sensibilities and values.

Our celebration spills over to the lovely Ozarks region that surrounds the city. Newcomers and natives alike discover unforgettable experiences in the natural beauty of our lakes, rivers, and mountains. Is it any wonder that the "granddaddy" of all sporting goods stores was born here?

On the pages of this book, you'll join our celebration. In these faces and places, you'll see why those of us who love Springfield agree, "Everywhere should be like this!" ❖

James B. Anderson
President
Springfield Area Chamber of Commerce

Photo by Thomas S. England

Jim Anderson, president, Springfield Area Chamber of Commerce

Photo by Scott Indermaur

A passion for music and for bringing that music to audiences has been a hallmark of the Springfield Symphony Orchestra since its establishment in 1933. Its musical season includes six classical performances per year, as well as three pop series performances, like this one at Jordan Valley Park as part of the Artsfest Fine Arts Festival. Since its founding, the Springfield Symphony has also supported a series of outreach programs that enrich the musical experience of youth through-out Southwest Missouri and which offer high-quality musical performances free to the public. ❖

Photo by Rod Reilly

Enjoying SPRINGFIELD

"We can leave our house and have our boats in the water in fifteen minutes," says Marla Calico. That's one reason she and husband Jeff Geyman enjoy kayaking. Lake Springfield is one of three access points of a new water trail, a cooperative partnership of the Missouri Conservation Department, Ozark Greenways, Springfield–Greene County Parks Board, and Ozark Mountain Paddlers. Dedicated in the summer of 2006, the water trail is designed to promote the availability of water recreation right here in the city, as well as a subtle reminder of the importance of preserving water quality. "Kayaking is a nice way to relax," says Calico. "We often go out, paddle for an hour, grab a burger on the way home, and are back home within a couple of hours." ❖

Even the name "Springfield" suggests natural vibrancy. History intermingles with modern conveniences here, nature thrives within the city limits, recreation opportunities are as important and as diverse as the economy, and the plateau geography gives way to enjoyable seasons for year-round outdoor pleasure.

Springfield is located in Greene County, an area of approximately 675 square miles. And though Springfield is definitely a thriving environment in which to work, it is also a well-known place for play, with bodies of water and nature conservation areas right in town, and other fishing, hunting, camping, and hiking areas a stone's throw from municipal boundaries.

Parks and greenways are plentiful in Springfield, scattered all around town in places such as Phelps Grove, Jordan Valley, and Nathanael Greene. Some provide simple spaces of tranquility; others offer a view of life on a pioneer homestead. Attractions such as "destination" libraries of the Springfield–Greene County Libraries District; the conservation museum, Wonders of Wildlife; and the Dickerson Park Zoo allow for hands-on education. Springfield even has the country's only ride-through cave to explore.

Springfield's everyday life is full of enrichment too. The revitalized downtown area is a popular after-work and weekend destination with a choice of theatres, art galleries, restaurants, and shops. Center City plays host to fun festivals for all things creative, including the musical C-Street Jam, a Loftwalk, and the famous First Friday Art Walk. What's more, Hammons Field, a state-of-the-art baseball stadium that hosts the Double A Springfield Cardinals, sits right downtown, drawing fans in for nine innings, and the usual before- and after-game fun.

No wonder that family-friendly, business-friendly Springfield can boast that it offers a "chamber-of-commerce kind of day" nearly every day of the year. Springfield gives everyone a lot to enjoy. ❖

Photo by Scott Indermaur

Dalton Borders (front) of Mansfield, Missouri, and Jeffrey Swain of Springfield take their best shot in a game of tug-of-war at Firefall, Springfield's annual Fourth of July extravaganza. Tens of thousands show up for a day of music and a night of fireworks, all taking place in a field near the Springfield-Branson National Airport. Started in 1982 by a couple of friends as an Independence Day celebration, the event has expanded to a lineup of bands, sky-divers, hot air balloons, and more. Music of all kinds is an important part of the event. Below, Kathleen Standage of Springfield and Sue Engel of Marshfield, Missouri, rock out to the on-stage tunes provided by both local and national bands. ❖

Photo by Scott Indermaur

DICKERSON PARK ZOO: A SPRINGFIELD FAMILY TRADITION

Seeing eye to eye is what the residents of Springfield and of Dickerson Park Zoo do best. Visitors to the park can stand on a platform and feed the giraffes while looking eye to eye. This engaging feature was part of a $5.8 million expansion made possible by a voter-approved countywide parks sales tax referendum in 2001.

The expansion allowed the zoo to complete Missouri Habitats, a hilly, forested example of Missouri wilderness, and to open Tropical Asia with new facilities for elephants, tigers, and gibbons. "One of the most exciting things is that we now have a new display yard and facilities for our elephants," said Mike Crocker, zoo superintendent and executive director of Friends of the Zoo. "We participate in several Species Survival Plans® (SSP); the most recognizable one is with our Asian elephants. We have two males—not many zoos have them because they are difficult to manage—and four females, plus baby Nisha, who was born in 2006. Several zoos have sent their cows here for breeding. Our males have sired calves for zoos throughout the country. Haji, a calf born here in 1999, was the first elephant calf conceived by artificial insemination." The zoo has also developed successful breeding programs for cheetahs and maned wolves.

"Zoo Education Broadens Realization of Animals (Z.E.B.R.A.) classes encourage youngsters to become interested in conservation," said Crocker.

◄ *Pinky and C.C. are the elder members of Dickerson Park Zoo's elephant herd.*

Photo by Lisa Means

"People are fascinated by elephants, which are the most popular animal at the zoo," said Crocker. "Second on the list are primates like the gibbons."

There is much more to Dickerson Park Zoo. The zoo family includes South American exhibits with Chilean flamingos, maned wolves, tamarins, macaws, toucans, and the always entertaining squirrel and spider monkeys. Missouri Habitats is home to black bears, coyotes, red foxes, white-tailed deer, bobcats, raccoons, river otters, and mountain lions, all native to Missouri. Guests traveling to the Australian area will see red kangaroos, emus, wallabies, black swans, and other birds.

On a visit to the African area, in addition to cheetahs and giraffes, guests encounter kudu, crowned cranes, zebras, lions, warthogs, and monkeys. The Hearld and Marge Ambler Diversity of Life exhibits house the popular reptile and amphibian collection, which is among the unique features at the zoo.

One will also see alligators, meerkats, Aldabra tortoises, hippopotamus, and bald eagles. Three islands in Dickerson Park Lake are home to a variety of lemurs, primates from Madagascar. A miniature train ride transports guests around the lake for views of the lemurs in their summer homes.

"Education is a fundamental part of our mission, and Zoo Education Broadens Realization of Animals (Z.E.B.R.A.) classes encourage youngsters to become interested in conservation," said Crocker. "They hold the key to the future preservation of the diversity of life on this earth."

Dickerson Park Zoo, accredited by the Associations for Zoos and Aquariums and recipient of the 1997 Edward Bean Award for Excellence, enjoys a positive place in the cultural fabric of the community, and by all indications, it will continue to be treasured as one of the city's beloved family traditions. ❖

Photo by Lisa Means

*Andrea Coble climbed to the ►
elevated deck to give
daughter Emilee the
opportunity to feed a giraffe
and get a view of the
Dickerson Park Zoo from the
giraffe's lofty point of view.
The platform is a favorite of
adults and children of all
ages who visit the Baringo
giraffes in the African exhibit
area. An update of a zoo
master plan was completed
in 1996. Through the use of
public and private funding,
plans are under way to
complete the master plan
by 2010.*

The annual Artsfest on Walnut Street brought out a crowd to enjoy a weekend of activities in Center City. Events began on Friday night with ArtsFiesta! celebrating Springfield's relationship with its sister city Tlaquepaque, Mexico, and featuring a concert by the Mariachi Juvenil Tapatio de Tlaquepaque. Right, Tedd Hamaker brought his children Joe, Lena, and Dan, who all seem to be having a great time. On Saturday, the Springfield Symphony (above) performed at Jordan Valley Park for the first time. The pops program included popular classics as well as American favorites. A grant from the Community Foundation of the Ozarks and other sponsors made the free concerts possible. ✤

Photo by Scott Indermaur

For more than twenty-five years, residents and visitors have looked forward to the annual Artsfest, one of the premier outdoor festivals in Southwest Missouri. It's a great place to see new art forms, buy gifts, enjoy the outdoors, and be entertained royally.

Photo by Scott Indermaur

Photo by Scott Indermaur

For more than twenty-five years, the Springfield Regional Arts Council has issued an invitation, and an average of thirty-five thousand people have turned out for a wonderful event called Artsfest on Walnut Street. There is definitely something for everyone: music, food, fun, and arts of every shape and kind, and in every medium, including clay, metal, mixed media, painting, photography, drawing, fiber, paper, glass, jewelry, wood, and printmaking. The event usually draws up to 150 artists from twenty states. For the kids, and the more adventurous adults, there are hands-on projects such as Foam Fun, which are part of Art-Town Downtown. Events run the gamut too, from Tent Cinema to the Artsfest Dog Parade. ❖

Photo by Scott Indermaur

Photo by Scott Indermaur

Photo by Scott Indermaur

Photo by Thomas S. England

▲ *A Hiland employee carefully surveys the refrigerated cooler inventory inside the main storage cooler, to ensure that proper rotation is observed in the numerous stacks of fresh dairy products immediately prior to loading and shipping to grocery and institutional accounts.*

HILAND DAIRY: A SPLASH OF FRESHNESS

Hiland Dairy's employees are single-minded. All 1,231 humans and more than one hundred thousand dairy cows focus on one thing, and one thing only: quality. It's been that way since two dairy farmers began milking their fifty cows and selling milk door-to-door back in 1938, and it remains that way today.

This clear concentration on quality is at the heart of Hiland Dairy's success as the only locally operated dairy in Springfield, and the largest supplier in Missouri, Arkansas, Kansas, and Oklahoma. "As a farmer-owned cooperative, Hiland Dairy reflects the values of the people of the Midwest," says Gary Aggus, president. "Our dairy farmer owners' primary interest is the dairy industry. They want us to succeed in providing healthy, nutritious products for our

> "Our dairy farmer owners' primary interest is the dairy industry. They want us to succeed in providing healthy, nutritious products for our customers."

customers." That's why when customers hear Hiland Dairy's marketing message—"A Splash of Fresh Flavor"—they know it's far more than a slogan. "Our products are the best sales and marketing tools we have, because they represent quality, day in and day out," he adds.

Of course, it goes without saying that quality is critical in the food industry, but Hiland Dairy takes it one step further by exceeding state and federal production standards. In fact, Hiland Dairy consistently receives awards and recognition for its products from Quality Chekd Dairies, Inc., an organization of dairy processors who achieve the highest levels of quality and food safety in their products and processes. With members worldwide, Quality Chekd validates its members' performance through third-party product testing and frequent audits. Among the awards received by Hiland Dairy are "Excellence in Milk Quality," "Excellence in Ice Cream Quality," and "Excellence in Cultured Products Quality"—which spans the array of dairy items produced and sold. As such, Hiland Dairy has earned the right to bear the Quality Chekd trademark—a big red check mark.

The company also knows the importance of being a good neighbor and an active community member. Hiland Dairy enthusiastically supports local and regional causes, events, and organizations that seek to help make their communities better places to live. The "Quality Brigade" takes this message on the road, attending all types of events, donating a variety of healthy, fresh dairy products and ice cream for tasting. The Quality Brigade is selected from employee volunteers with various backgrounds (office, transportation, maintenance, production, and sales) who are willing to share with the community Hiland's continuing commitment to quality.

In the past thirty years, growth has been steady for Hiland Dairy, primarily through acquisitions. The dairy operates seven manufacturing plants and twenty-five distribution sites in Missouri and surrounding states. In the competitive world of the dairy industry, this growth is often difficult to accomplish, particularly when competing against much larger dairies. Aggus cites as keys to success low employee turnover, the willingness of the owners to reinvest capital in facilities and employee training, and an emphasis on being an efficient, low-cost producer—all efforts to remain single-mindedly focused on quality above all. ❖

Photo by Alan S. Weiner

A Splash of Fresh Flavor! ▶
Hiland Dairy maintains one of the nation's safest dairy transportation fleets, comprising more than one thousand vehicles delivering refrigerated products throughout the Midwestern states of Missouri, Oklahoma, Kansas, Arkansas, and Texas.

Photo by Scott Indermaur

The Double A Springfield Cardinals may be the new boys in town, having arrived in 2005, but baseball fans have welcomed them with open arms. To many, the presence of an affiliate of the St. Louis Cardinals makes summers in Springfield that much sweeter. To the athletes, the opportunity to play to a home crowd at the $32 million Hammons Field is pure fun. And the players really get a kick out of signing autographs. Minor league baseball is a real success story for the athletes, the fans, and the cities they represent. There's an intimate connection between team and town, between players and people—a bond that is often stronger and more personal than in the big leagues. After all, both sides know this is the stepping-stone in many a successful career, and there's nothing like saying "I knew him when . . ." ✤

Photo by Rod Reilly

Photo by Scott Indermaur

Photo by Rod Reilly

Photo by Scott Indermaur

CREATING IMPACT: TURN ON THE POWER OF THE WEB FOR YOUR BUSINESS

Packy Savvenas knows all about harnessing the power of untapped potential. His company, Power of the Web.com, is not only founded on that principle; its purpose is to help businesses do the same.

Power of the Web.com is a concept-driven Web development/flash design and marketing firm that knows how to harness the power of the Web for its clients. The story of how Power of the Web.com went from dream, to startup, to award-winning success in a timeframe that can be compared to that of "high-speed access" is a story worth telling.

First, note that while the creative

> "I study the client's business carefully and develop the concept around who they are and what they want to portray," says Savvenas.

genius behind Power of the Web, Packy Savvenas, is now designing Web sites that repeatedly garner international industry awards, he has no formal training in design. And while he admits to being an electronics and computer guru for as long as he can remember, he knew how to tinker and build hardware, but not how to write in the language of Web sites. So how did he start Power of the Web.com? More importantly, why?

"My inspiration came from a painting of my sister. She was asked to model for an artist creating a poster for the U.S. Olympic Team. We are Greek American,

◄ *There's power behind the efficient and dynamic Power of the Web team: (left to right) Packy Savvenas, Josh Abbott, Bill Gilbert, and Billy Gilbert.*

Photo by Thomas S. England

and he thought she represented the perfect blend of the country represented and the country hosting the Olympics," explains Savvenas. The final creation was so moving that it stirred a latent talent. "My parents tell me that I showed talent as an artist as a child, but I never pursued it further. They encouraged me to tap the potential by asking me to build a Web site for their business—Manolis Jewelers." Long on determination, but short on know-how, Savvenas set out learning all he could about Web design online, and within a year he delivered. His final design for Manolis— also his first Web site—has won dozens of international awards.

Springfield entrepreneurs Bill and Billy Gilbert recognized Savvenas's unique combination of passion, talent, and drive and offered to invest in Power of the Web, giving Savvenas the financial power and independence to grow the business. Today, Power of the Web is making an impact in the industry with clients on the left coast, the right coast, and right here in the middle. "Their work is so cutting-edge," says Kasey Gillham, office manager for Gregg Stancer Realty. "I was really surprised that they were local and doing that kind of work." The commercial realty business sought out Power of the Web to design a Web site that would compete with national and international commercial Realtors. "We needed something that would tell our clients, and our potential clients, that although we are located in a smaller market, we mean business. Packy just took the ball and ran with it, giving us incredible results," Gillham adds.

Continued on page 28

The Foot Doctors PC is a ► *client that understands the power of a great Web site, and understands also that Power of the Web principal and award-winning designer Packy Savvenas is only happy with a perfect product and a satisfied client.*

Photo by Thomas S. England

◀ Fishing is one of the reasons Packy Savvenas loves Southwest Missouri. He looks for every opportunity to take clients out to catch some fish and perhaps a little creative spark.

Continued from page 27

Understanding that a well-developed and up-to-date Web site is a fundamental requirement for building marketplace legitimacy and customer confidence is just one of the reasons that Power of the Web seems to get it right for their clients from the start. A perfectionist who also has a background in sales, Savvenas applies a concept-driven approach to the work. "I study the client's business carefully and develop the concept around who they are and what they want to portray," says Savvenas. "I ask the right questions, I listen to their voice, I look at the way they dress, and even the way their office looks. That way, I know exactly what they want. In fact, the first design I present to the client is almost always approved."

Power of the Web designed and ▶ donated the Web site for Boys & Girls Town of Missouri.

Photo by Thomas S. England

◄ Power of the Web began when Packy's parents, who own Manolis Jewelers, asked him to design a Web site for the business. The rest, as they say, is history.

Great design is paramount, but Power of the Web also helps its clients focus on maximizing the power of the Internet through search engine optimization, content management systems friendly enough that clients can manage them on their own, as well as coordinated print marketing materials that harmonize with the Web site. "If a site doesn't look good, or doesn't function well, the customer won't stay more than a second," says Savvenas. "We completely understand this, and that's why we're only happy with a perfect product for each and every client." And it's that focus on fulfilling potential that is the hallmark of Power of the Web.com. ❖

Photo by Thomas S. England

Client GSR Realty enjoys ► meeting with Power of the Web at the Mud Lounge, where the coffee is always fresh.

A peaceful place, Nathanael Greene Park is meant for reflection and relaxation. Dedicated in 1976 and named after Revolutionary War hero and Greene County namesake General Nathanael Greene, the park is home to the Master Gardener's Demonstration Garden, Close Park, the Japanese Stroll Garden, the Gray-Campbell Farmstead, as well as the South Creek Greenway Trail. Between the natural flora and the cultivated varieties of plants, the elements of Nathanael Greene Park remind us to slow down and take time to smell the roses. ❖

Hamra Defines Success by Giving Back

Hamra Enterprises is synonymous with building communities. When the successful Springfield-based restaurant and hospitality company adds a Wendy's Hamburger Restaurant, a Panera Bread Bakery-Cafe, a Baymont Inn & Suites, or a Holiday Inn Express and Suites to a community, it does so with a sole purpose. "In every town that we're in, it's about making a contribution to that community," says Sam F. Hamra, chairman and CEO of Hamra Enterprises. Today, the privately owned family business employs more than twenty-six hundred employees in restaurants and hotels across four states.

Hamra—through his businesses and with the support of his wife, June—is known for giving more than he receives and helping others to achieve success.

It's a simple story: Hamra Enterprises buys land and builds and operates restaurants and hotels. Behind the Hamra Enterprise name is Sam F. Hamra, a Springfield attorney whose reputation as a dynamic community advocate nearly overshadows his reputation as a legal expert and entrepreneur. Since he opened the first Wendy's Restaurant in Springfield in 1976, Hamra—through his businesses and with the support of his wife, June—is known for giving more than he receives and helping others to achieve success. Hamra Enterprises as of 2006 consists of Wendy's of Missouri, Inc.

◀ *Behind every successful business of Hamra Enterprises are employees dedicated to making a contribution to the community. More than twenty-six hundred employees in total are supported by the corporate team.*

(twenty-four Wendy's restaurants); Chicago Bread LLC (twenty-eight Panera Bread cafés); Boston Bread LLC (fifteen Panera Bread cafés); and hotels in Springfield and Dallas. Sam and June's son, Mike Hamra, is president of Chicago Bread LLC and Boston Bread LLC. Chuck Ocarz is president and COO of Wendy's of Missouri, Inc., and Steve Davidson serves as executive vice president of Hamra Enterprises.

Sam serves on the boards of CoxHealth, St. Jude Children's Research Hospital, and the Truman Library, having previously served as charter president of the Rotary Club of Springfield Southeast, and the Missouri Sports Hall of Fame board. In 2003, he received Missouri University's Distinguished Service Award, and the Law School's Citation of Merit. He was elected to the Missouri Academy of Squires in 2004. Sam and June were recipients of the "Missourian Award" in 2001.

June graduated from the Eastman School of Music and received her master's degree and taught voice at the University of Missouri. She served on the Board of Regents at SMS (now Missouri State University), the Missouri Arts Council, and the President's Advisory Committee on the Arts for the John F. Kennedy Center for the Performing Arts. In 2001, she received Missouri University's Faculty-Alumni Award and the College of Arts and Science Distinguished Alumni Award.

However, June and Sam feel their most significant community involvement has been in the adoption program for foster children, which is a perfect tie-in to the founder of Wendy's—Dave Thomas —who was an adopted child. Wendy's of Missouri's pioneer program is a syndicated television series, the Adoption Series, For Your Life, hosted by June Hamra, which features June interviewing foster parents and foster children who are waiting for a forever family in a permanent home. Its

Photo by Thomas S. England

Photo by Thomas S. England

Sam and June Hamra are ▶ *known for their big hearts. The couple have focused their lives on service, advocacy, and philanthropy.*

Continued on page 34

Continued from page 33

success is measured not only with a seal of approval from the Missouri Division of Children's Services, but also by the television program being shown in Springfield, Kansas City, Jefferson City, and Columbia. The real success is measured in the smiles of the many children who have been adopted as a direct result of the program. From an original goal of matching one child with one family, the Adoption Series, For Your Life, has far exceeded expectations with the adoption of twenty featured foster children this past year.

The Wendy's Web site is so full of vital information on child advocacy that it might be easy to forget that it is a business Web site, and that's just the way Sam Hamra wants it—giving back more to the community than he receives. ❖

▲ *Hamra Enterprises supports foster children in many ways. Wendy's of Missouri pioneered a syndicated television series to educate the public on the adoption process. Here a few of the adoptive children enjoy a tasty Frosty with June Hamra and Hamra Enterprises administrative assistant, Tonya Branstetter, as "Wendy."*

Hamra Enterprises executive ▶ assistant Judy Self gladly accepts Wendy's drinks from Wendy's president and COO Chuck Ocarz.

Springfield attracts a variety of visitors with just as varied interests, and facilities such as the University Plaza Hotel and Convention Center provide a welcome place to stay and meet. The hotel, a John Q. Hammons property, has earned a reputation for exceeding the expectations of its guests, whether they are traveling for leisure or business. With thirty-nine thousand square feet of meeting space, the hotel can accommodate everything from small planning sessions to large, extended day conventions. The executive staff meets regularly to ensure that the hotel remains a place where style and hospitality go hand in hand. ❖

Photo by Lisa Means

Photo by Alan S. Weiner

Photo by Alan S. Weiner

Photo by Alan S. Weiner

Each third weekend in September, Springfield celebrates its relationship with sister city Isesaki, Japan, with a colorful festival honoring Japanese social and cultural traditions. Sponsored by the Springfield Sister Cities Association and the Springfield–Greene County Park Board, the festival was established in 1996 and takes place at the city's Japanese Stroll Garden. Located in Nathanael Greene Park, the seven-and-a-half-acre garden was developed starting in 1986 in conjunction with the city of Isesaki, which donated various trees and money to construct the tea hut. Proceeds from the festival go toward the garden's upkeep. And while the garden is open to visitors from April through October, the festival really showcases its beauty. Events include games, chopstick lessons, martial arts demonstrations, and traditional Japanese music and dance. Attendees may also participate in a Japanese tea ceremony and purchase authentic Japanese silk works, origami, bonsai, orchids, and food. The festival closes each day with a spectacular candlelight walk, which lasts from dark until ten o'clock in the evening. ❖

Maxon's Diamond Merchants: Exquisite Jewelry, Unequaled Service

Few things are as enduring and endearing as fine jewelry. Since 1972, Maxon's Diamond Merchants has built an equally enduring reputation for quality, integrity, and exceptional customer service. Rick and Jane McElvaine, co-owners and American Gem Society Certified Gemologists, bought the store from the original owner and added their own style and expertise.

"Joe Maxon traveled to New York to buy diamonds, but now we purchase diamonds from international cutting centers. Our bigger buying power and better technology make the process more global," said Rick.

That kind of selectivity and fore-thought go into every aspect of service at Maxon's. "Our whole operation is service-oriented," Rick explained. "Our customers are accustomed to seeing familiar faces and having our staff call them by name. We routinely offer to clean their jewelry—for free, of course—and re-polish it so it looks brand new. We cultivate long-term relationships and are always pleased when new customers come to us through referrals."

"One way we've created this bond is by offering the very best in services and fine jewelry repairs," said Jane. "Jay Casey, our shop foreman, who has thirty years of experience, is a perfectionist. Rick considers him one of the best crafts-men in the nation, and I agree. Using the

> "Our customers are accustomed to seeing familiar faces and having our staff call them by name."

◄ *Rick and Jane McElvaine, co-owners of Maxon's Diamond Merchants, and American Gem Society Certified Gemologists, have established a long history of selectivity and service with their clientele. Here they work with customers Mary Beth and Charlie O'Reilly, founders of the Breast Cancer Foundation of the Ozarks, as Mary Beth tries on a diamond Riviera necklace.*

latest tools and laser welder technology, he routinely exceeds customers' expectations."

"We not only repair estate jewelry, but we offer an important selection for resale. Maxon's has long been known for offering interesting antique jewelry and period jewelry, which reflects a certain era like Art Deco or Victorian. Many customers come in on a regular basis to see what's new in old jewelry," Rick said.

Because Maxon's has a market for estate jewelry, it is uniquely positioned to give customers fair value for pieces they want to trade. "We redesign pieces for customers whose tastes may have changed," Jane said. This process begins with careful communication, followed by the presentation of a design sketch, and finally, the execution of the design by one of Maxon's craftspersons. "Customers love being involved in this creative process," she adds.

Maxon's offers the latest designs by Jean Francois Albert, John Atencio, Jewels by Star, Precision Set, and Simon G. "Another distinction is that we have been an official Rolex jeweler since 1972, which is a testament to our high standards," said Rick.

Customers are not the only ones who benefit from Maxon's experience and expertise. "We do a lot of educational programs for art groups, local schools, and clubs," Rick explained. "And, of course, we always bring jewelry and gemstones for hands-on experiences," Jane added. "Springfield has been good to us, and we give back in donations, merchandise, and time. We are particularly involved with the Breast Cancer Foundation of the Ozarks."

By offering exquisite jewelry and unequaled customer service, it is easy to understand how Maxon's established an impeccable reputation for quality. ❖

Photo by Alan S. Weiner

Photo by Alan S. Weiner

As a means of giving back to ► the community, Maxon's Diamond Merchants have been involved in fund-raising for the Breast Cancer Foundation of the Ozarks (BCFO) for many years. Co-owners Rick and Jane McElvaine donated the diamond Riviera necklace, modeled by employee Amy Pope, to be used as part of the Hooked on Dance event. Ellen Hammock, director of BCFO, agrees that the necklace and the donation are both stunning.

Photo by Lisa Means

Wonders of Wildlife will wow visitors of all ages. Part natural history museum, part aquarium, the facility encourages interactive exploration of the outdoors indoors with more than 225 species of live animals in natural habitats. Its official name is the National Fish and Wildlife Museum and Aquarium, but the quarter-million people who visit each year have come to know it simply as "Wonders of Wildlife," and it's easy to see why. Every inch of the ninety-two-thousand-square foot space is designed to educate, inform, and entertain visitors regarding the value of fish and wildlife. In addition, Wonders of Wildlife helps people understand our nation's heritage of hunting and fishing, while also encouraging conservation of our precious outdoor resources. Aptly situated next door to the original Bass Pro Shops, the unique facility is the vision-come-true of Bass Pro Shops founder John L. Morris. Wonders of Wildlife is accredited by the American Zoo and Aquarium Association, and an affiliate program of the Smithsonian. ❖

Photo by Lisa Means

Out is in at one of Southwest Missouri's most popular attractions, where wildlife can be observed and enjoyed indoors.

Photo by Lisa Means

Photo by Lisa Means

Photo by Rod Reilly

On the first Friday of every month, the Downtown Arts District in Springfield comes alive with the First Friday Art Walk, a program of the Springfield Regional Arts Council. During this popular event, the artists of Springfield play host to those who take the self-guided tour of new works exhibited in the local galleries. Accompanied by the sounds of live music, attendees of this art adventure can browse the works of skilled artisans, including sculpture, pottery, photography, and paintings. Visitors take full advantage of the extended hours in such galleries as the Springfield Hot Glass Studio, where they can watch master glass blowers form exquisite vases, ornaments, and figures. When they need to rest, attendees can drop in for some shopping or entertainment at one of the many local retail boutiques, restaurants, coffeehouses, nightclubs, and theaters in this diverse and accessible urban setting. ✤

Photo by Lisa Means

Photo by Rod Reilly

Photo by Rod Reilly

SPRINGFIELD BREWING: ENJOY THE FINE ART OF GOOD TASTE

One of the few breweries in the world built, operated, and owned by a brewery equipment fabrication company, Springfield Brewing Company was established in 1997 by Paul Mueller Company for the purposes of researching and developing brewery equipment. Today, it is one of the city's most noted restaurants and brewpubs.

The focal point of the operations is a state-of-the-art computer-automated brew-house that was custom designed and built by Springfield-based Paul Mueller Company, a premier stainless steel engineering and manufacturing company founded in 1940. The brewery has all the proper equipment—namely four-roll malt mill, mash mixer, lauter tun, in-line wort aeration, uni-tank fermentation tanks, two-stage beer filter, water purification system, and kegging and bottling equip-

Years of knowledge and skill have gone into the creation of the company's selection of beers produced under the Mueller name.

ment—to brew and package a wide range of delicious beers.

Putting all that technology to work is the job of brewers Ashton Lewis and Cecil Manning III. Years of knowledge and skill have gone into the creation of the company's selection of beers produced under the Mueller name, including Mueller Wheat, Pale Ale, and Lager. In addition, the company brews quarterly seasonal specialties, along with an ever-changing selection of Brewmaster's Specials that celebrate the world's diverse beer styles. Springfield Brewing Company has also won many medals at the world's largest beer festival, the Great American Beer Festival, held annually in Denver since 1982. Since 2000, their beers, including wheat, lager, and märzen, have won gold, silver, and bronze medals in multiple beer categories.

◀ Downstairs at Springfield Brewing Company is the restaurant's primary formal dining area. Upstairs, patrons can enjoy a drink and a meal on the outside patio, play a game of pool, or relax in the cigar room. The area also holds the restaurant's private banquet room. Live music can be heard Wednesday through Sunday starting at 10 p.m. There is also live jazz from 6:00 to 9:00 at night on Fridays and Saturdays.

To accompany its fine beers, Springfield Brewing is also a full-service restaurant. Open seven days a week for lunch and dinner, it features a selection of beautifully prepared appetizers, salads, pastas, pizzas, and burgers, with seating indoors or out at the rooftop beer garden. The brewery also has a private cigar room, and banquet facilities for up to three hundred. For entertainment, the brewery offers six pool tables, live music Wednesday through Sunday, and video games.

From its location in the heart of downtown, Springfield Brewing continues to make a positive impact on the local and regional economy. The brewery's reputation for crafting excellent beers makes it a destination not only for locals, but also traveling microbrew aficionados and tourists. As a showcase for Paul Mueller Company's equipment, the brewery hosts visitors from all over the world interested in the wide array of stainless-steel products designed and manufactured by Mueller less than two miles from the brewery.

The brewery also pumps its own dollars into the local economy by purchasing whenever possible its supplies and foodstuffs from local and regional providers. In fact, an overwhelming majority of the company's contracts are held locally or regionally, with companies like The Bake House, Har-Bell Athletic, and Springfield Grocer.

The company's participation in local community initiatives also continues to grow. Not only does Springfield Brewing donate its products to various fund-raising functions, but it also hosts many yearly fund-raising events, including functions that benefit local organizations like the Springfield Area Chamber of Commerce and the James River Basin Partnership.

Great beer. Great food. Great community leadership. Mix it all together, and you've got the recipe for Springfield Brewing Company's success. ❖

Photo by Scott Indermaur

Photo by Scott Indermaur

Ashton Lewis, Springfield ▶ Brewing Company's master brewer, takes a beer sample from one of the brewery's fermentation tanks for evaluation. "Beer is a product of art and science," says Lewis. "We craft a wide range of beers to satisfy local beer connoisseurs using the brewer's art. Springfield Brewing Company is fortunate to have extremely fine equipment, enabling us to express our brewing vision in a beautiful and very brewer-friendly facility."

The Library Station, a new "destination library" in the Springfield–Greene County Library District, replaces the picture of dusty bookshelves with the promise of adventure. The thirty-six-thousand-square-foot facility inspires the involvement of all visitors, such as Angela Lynn pictured here with her daughter Bailey. The planes-trains-and-automobiles theme throughout provides a visual history of U.S. transportation, including the image of the famous Route 66—from Chicago to Los Angeles—traced on the floor. And Springfield claims a special role as the city that gave the route its numerical moniker. What could be more inviting to children than to enter their own special section by walking through the replica of a covered bridge? And for the adults, high-tech online services, genealogy search assistance, special displays, and meeting facilities are available. ❖

photo by Scott Indermaur

When Linus Campbell takes a break from his busy custom homebuilding company, Campbell Homes, he gets away from it all by piloting his own powerchute plane over the Springfield, Missouri, countryside. A powerchute pilot pulls on the throttle until a canopy behind him fills with air and lifts the craft into the clouds. The throttle and rudder foot pedals control altitude and allow directional changes. To land, the pilot pushes the throttle slowly forward. It's an increasingly popular, cheaper, and, some say, safer method for taking to the skies compared to other small airplanes. His clients credit him for his craftsmanship and down-to-earth friendliness. "You will come to know Linus as a friend, an honest businessman, gentleman, and family man," said client Mona Casady.✤

Photo by Lisa Means

Voted by the *Springfield News-Leader* as the city's Best Romantic Place to dine, Bijan's Sea and Grill places a modern twist on old-world ambience. Upstairs, there's a cigar and martini bar where the signature drink is the Chambord-based Romeo y Julieta, which is guaranteed to put you in the mood for love—not to mention a really great dinner. That happens in the restaurant downstairs, which is famous for its inventive steak, pasta, and seafood dishes, including Bijan's signature cashew- and pecan-encrusted Chilean sea bass. Top it all off with one of the restaurant's decadent desserts or after-dinner drinks, and you'll purr all the way home. ❖

Photo by Lisa Means

Springfield offers a nice balance of city and country, of sports and arts, of business and pleasure, and Hawthorn Park is one of the premiere places to stay. With more than two hundred sleeping rooms and ten thousand square feet of convention space, the Hawthorn Park is ideal for meetings of any size and for business travelers, as well as for visitors coming to enjoy what awaits in the city and the surrounding Ozarks. ❖

Photo by Scott Indermaur

Located between Springfield and Branson, Missouri, Lambert's Café II is the second in a series of three. Southern fare, including chicken-fried steaks, fried chops, fried chicken, and all the fixins, entices an almost constantly full house—so much so that the restaurant's signature item is "throwed rolls," pictured here as waiter Matt Eubankes tosses one of the tasty morsels to diner Leza Curtin. "The first Lambert's got so crowded they couldn't get through to pass the rolls. Somebody yelled, 'Just throw the darn things!' and that's where it all started," explained Woody Wilson, general manager. Customers can have as many rolls as they can catch; apparently that's a lot. Lambert's bakes about 520 dozen of the five-inch-diameter rolls every day. ❖

Photo by Thomas S. England

THE GENERAL COUNCIL OF THE ASSEMBLIES OF GOD: UNITING CHURCHES

The Assemblies of God international headquarters houses the denomination's ministries and its publishing arm.

In 1914, a group of three hundred preachers and laymen from across the nation gathered in the Midwest to discuss a growing need for unity among Pentecostal congregations scattered across the country. One outcome from that meeting was the General Council of the Assemblies of God, an organization that unites churches in a cooperative fellowship.

The church moved its headquarters to Springfield in 1918. From there, the General Council of the Assemblies of God supports an organization of over 2.8 million members and adherents in over 12,200 churches across the nation.

While each congregation operates independently, the Fellowship is united in its commitment to a threefold mission: to worship, to disciple, and to evangelize. This mission provides the basis for living for the glory of God, growing in spirit and character while helping others reach their potential, and reaching out with compassion to bring others to salvation.

The headquarters publishes twelve tons of church literature each day and oversees ministries, including aggressive missions programs in the United States and two hundred other countries.

> The Fellowship is united in its commitment to a threefold mission: to worship, to disciple, and to evangelize.

In addition to evangelism and missions, growth for the organization stems from a commitment to training of ministers and leaders. This occurs in well over one thousand Bible schools overseas as well as in nineteen colleges and a seminary in the United States—four of these located in Springfield.

The Assemblies of God is one of the fastest-growing denominations, with an 18.5 percent increase during the past decade. ❖

Photo by Thomas S. England

Visitors and residents like Susan Wade and her son Damon frequently take advantage of a beautiful day to go for a bike ride along the Ozark Greenways. These linear parks protect undeveloped ribbons of natural habitat, usually through urban areas. The Ozark Greenways is managed by a nonprofit group of private citizens in Springfield who are working to preserve and enhance the Ozarks' natural heritage for public use and enjoyment. Greenways typically follow stream corridors or abandoned railroad rights-of-way. In addition to bike riders, walkers, runners, in-line skaters, wheelchairs, and baby strollers are also common sights on the hard-surfaced paths with minimal grades. The Greenways are not only beautiful, they also promote fitness and alternative transportation in a safe setting, provide habitat for wildlife in urban areas, and protect critical floodplains from development. ❖

Photo by Thomas S. England

Completed in 2006, the $10 million Cooper Tennis Complex is a shining example of the importance Springfield places on recreational activities. Initial construction in 1994 was made possible by a five-hundred-thousand-dollar donation from local philanthropist Harry Cooper, but the complex has turned into a state-of-the-art-facility, thanks to the city's ongoing support of both amateur and professional tennis. As part of the Springfield–Greene County Park Board, the complex features twelve indoor and sixteen outdoor courts, plus a twenty-five-hundred-square-foot stadium court. Springfield is represented on the professional circuit by the World Team Tennis pro franchise team, the Springfield Lasers, and has served as host city for the FedCup, Missouri Valley Championships, the Volvo Regional, and the USTA-sanctioned Pro Classic. In 2000, the USTA also named Cooper Tennis Complex as its facility of the year. ❖

Photo by Alan S. Weiner

Photo by Alan S. Weiner

Photo by Alan S. Weiner

There's always something exciting to experience at Discovery Center of Springfield. This interactive, hands-on museum is thirty thousand square feet of fun and learning about science and technology, math and health, culture and communications, and the world we call home. There's the Exploratory Lab, where themed investigations range from the power of centrifugal force to a study of the microscopic world. Over in Discovery Town, kids can learn about the grown-up world through activities centered around money, food, careers, and more. And anyone can create energy in the EnergyExchange, where explorers can use their own power or machines to convert potential energy into kinetic, mechanical, or electrical forms. The EnergyExchange also houses the WaterTable, a place of liquid learning about water, waves, a water wheel, and more. ✦

Photo by Rod Reilly

David Peery of Pleasant Hope, Missouri, can tell you. So can David Riggs. If the perfect fishing spot is a secret to be carefully guarded, then there are plenty of secrets being kept in Springfield. With its abundance of aquatic playgrounds, Southwest Missouri is an angler's happy place. A turn and an easy drive in just about any direction will reveal a lake famous for its resident bass, an Ozark stream, or even a well-stocked trout pond. Right in town, Springfield Lake on the James River also offers good fishing for catfish and crappie, as well as bass. ❖

WILLOW BROOK FOODS: BRINGING A LOT TO THE TABLE

Willow Brook Foods, one of the country's largest food processors, calls Springfield "home." In fact, Willow Brook's corporate headquarters is located near the heart of downtown Springfield.

Willow Brook Foods is a producer and marketer of further processed meat and poultry products with annual sales of nearly $250 million. Through brands such as Lifestyle Premium Deli, Schweigert, Harvest Provisions, and Gourmet Recipe, Willow Brook Foods provides a wide variety of protein products, including deli meats, sausages, wieners, and precooked wings and chicken tenders. Willow Brook

"As one of Springfield's largest employers, we value our relationship with the people, the city, and the area," says company president Mike Briggs.

cooks, processes, slices, and distributes these products for local, national, and even international use.

Locally owned and operated, Willow Brook has three production facilities in Springfield, as well as facilities in Minnesota, Oklahoma, and Arkansas. The company traces its Springfield roots back to 1927, where it began as a small, local turkey processor for the Missouri Farmers Association. Today, Willow Brook's poultry operation makes it the fifteenth-largest turkey producer in the United States.

"As one of Springfield's largest employers, we value our relationship with the

◄ *Willow Brook employees, each of whom is committed to excellence and to producing high-quality products, gather in the kitchen to showcase some of their popular offerings. Willow Brook Foods provides a wide variety of protein products, including deli meats, sausages, wieners, and precooked wings and chicken tenders.*

people, the city, and the area," says company president Mike Briggs. "We've benefited from being in Springfield, and we believe Springfield has benefited from Willow Brook Foods."

The company keeps growing. In 2005, the company partnered with Springfield Underground to form Precision Slicing, a state-of-the-art slicing facility. The facility incorporates the most current food safety and technology in Springfield Underground's unique "cavern" facility.

As a food company, Willow Brook is able to make a positive impact on the community at the most fundamental and beneficial levels. Willow Brook products are donated to the Salvation Army; the Kitchen, a local homeless shelter; and Ozarks Food Harvest, an area food bank.

"We make daily donations to help those in need," said Briggs. "Some of the people we've helped over the years have come to work for us and have become some of our most productive and valued employees. We think that's a good investment." Willow Brook is also a major sponsor for the annual Turkey Trot, a charitable run/walk event held on Thanksgiving morning in Springfield.

"At Willow Brook, we believe in 'bringing a lot to the table,'" says Briggs. "Whether that means the safest equipment for our employees to work with; the tastiest, quality products for our customers; or providing a meal for a local family in need, we intend to exceed the expectations." ❖

Photo by Eric Francis

Photo by Eric Francis

At Willow Brook Foods, ▶ *the goal is to deliver quality products to customers throughout the world. Locally owned and operated, Willow Brook has three state-of-the-art production facilities in Springfield, as well as locations in Minnesota, Oklahoma, and Arkansas.*

The Rothschild's or Baringo giraffe is the tallest animal on earth. Males can reach up to twenty feet tall and weigh up to 3,000 pounds. Females are slightly smaller. A giraffe's neck is approximately seventy-eight inches long, and although they have the same number of bones in their necks as humans do, their necks weigh up to 550 pounds. Giraffes adapt well to living in facilities like the Dickerson Park Zoo, basically because they are sociable, tolerant animals. Or maybe it's because they're as curious about their young visitors as the children are about them. It never hurts to look a new friend in the eye when you're trying to figure out who they are. The giraffe's long eyelashes, which are certainly worth a closer look, are not only beautiful, but they protect the animal's eyes from dust and sand. ❖

Photo by Lisa Means

Photo by Lisa Means

Photo by Lisa Means

Photo by Lisa Means

Since 1922 when the Dickerson Park Zoo was developed with the help of WPA labor, the park has always depended on its friends to keep it going. With the zoo thriving today as a valuable cultural asset to the Springfield community, it is hard to believe that in 1975 it was on the verge of being closed. That's when a support group, now known as Friends of the Zoo (FOZ), came to the rescue. They developed a membership base, launched education programs, and garnered the support of donors. The zoo continues to grow and improve with a master plan in place that will take it through 2010. ❖

There are so many reasons to look forward to the Ozark Empire Fair. There's fair fare, like the corndogs Jereme Barrera and Josh Mattson sell. There's the spinning, twirling, stomach-flipping thrill of the rides on the midway. The E-Plex offers an air-conditioned oasis from the summer heat, and plenty of exhibits. And then there are the animals, the mainstay of any county fair. After all, agriculture is the foundation on which county fairs are built. ❖

Time to shriek.
Time to feast.
Time to be a kid again.
Fairs find the fun
hidden in all of us.

Photo by Rod Reilly

Photo by Rod Reilly

Photo by Rod Reilly

Photo by Rod Reilly

▲ *The City of Springfield's multimillion-dollar annual capital improvements program addresses infrastructure needs like roads, sidewalks, and neighborhood improvements. Public Works employees John Erwin (left) and Joe Hamp use a pothole patcher to place asphalt for a street repair.*

CITY OF SPRINGFIELD: WORKING WITH THE COMMUNITY

"Make no little plans; they have no magic to stir men's blood. . . . Make big plans; aim high in hope and work. . . ." —Daniel Burnham, 1907

This quote serves as the mantra for Vision 20/20, the citizen-driven plan guiding Springfield's future.

It's not that Springfield isn't already a great place to live. It is. Known as the "Queen City" of the Southwest Missouri Ozarks, the area comprises nearly four hundred thousand people. It has a healthy job market, great schools, an active arts community, superior health-care facilities, beautiful neighborhoods, plenty of recreation, and friendly people.

But Springfield's leaders don't plan to stop there. The city currently is working on the second five years of a twenty-year visioning plan, which focuses on areas such as transportation, economic development, quality of life, Center City, and growth issues.

> Springfield has a healthy job market, great schools, an active arts community, superior health-care facilities, beautiful neighborhoods, plenty of recreation, and friendly people.

"This vision is the community's vision, and these priorities are the community's priorities," Mayor Thomas J. Carlson said. Here is a sampling of accomplishments so far.

Increased air service and passenger growth necessitated a name change from Springfield-Branson Regional to Springfield-Branson National Airport. The Springfield Cardinals—after two years of play—attracted more than a million fans, the second-highest attendance in Double A Minor League baseball. Revitalization of a former industrial area, now known as Jordan Valley, has transformed the Center City. Developments in arts and entertainment include opening the Creamery Arts Center as a shared facility for arts groups.

Two successful referenda for parks mean more recreation opportunities at new aquatic centers, a living farm, new metropolitan parks, more Dickerson Park Zoo features, and more miles of popular greenway trails, including the Frisco Highline, Missouri's second-longest Rails-to-Trails project.

Many of these goals have come about through collaboration with partners such as Greene County and the Springfield Area Chamber of Commerce. The City of Springfield's mission statement of "working with the community" embraces a philosophy that more can be accomplished by working in concert with citizens and the public, private, and nonprofit fields.

Signs of Springfield's continued growth include a new airport terminal, creation of new jobs, a major study of the Jordan Creek watershed, and the opening of the Jordan Valley Innovation Center (JVIC), which will attract highly skilled scientists and engineers working in the nanotechnology field through Missouri State University.

The Innovation Center is part of the downtown renaissance launched by Vision 20/20 and anchored by the historic Park Central Square and the new Jordan Valley redevelopment area. Since 1997, more than $250 million in public and private funds have been invested in downtown Springfield. The redevelopment effort continues to expand, moving north to a new live entertainment district at Springfield's original center of commerce on Commercial Street, and west into Jordan Valley's West Meadows.

"We are proud to be both witnesses and participants in this period of historic transformation for Springfield," Mayor Carlson said. ❖

Photo by Scott Indermaur

◄ *Mayor Tom Carlson is the longest-serving elected official in Springfield's history. He entered his twentieth year as either mayor or city council member in 2007. Springfield's historic city hall was built in 1894 and is still used for city council meetings. Next door is the Busch Municipal Building. Constructed in 1937 as the Jewell Station Post Office and Federal Building, it was sold to the City of Springfield, renovated, and renamed for Donald G. Busch, former city manager. Upon completion of the renovations in 1992, the city administrative offices were relocated there.*

Photo by Lisa Means

Summer, kids, and water are the perfect combination. Springfield youngsters cool off in Jordan Valley Park's water feature, one of the park's most popular attractions. ❖

A blur of flying acrobatics, skaters leap at top speeds over and onto obstacles, executing complex maneuvers, each harder than the last. Springfield's Skatepark offers thirty-nine thousand square feet of indoor and outdoor ramps, a rippin' bowl, and a street plaza. The Skatepark provides great fun for skaters and spectators alike. ❖

Photo by Scott Indermaur

Photo by Lisa Means

Visitors looking for peace and serenity need go no further than the Mizumoto Japanese Stroll Garden, located in Nathanael Greene Park. The garden is designed and tended with traditional Japanese techniques and features a teahouse, moon bridge, pagoda, and three lakes. ❖

Photo by Lisa Means

It's fall, which surely means it's pumpkin pickin' time in the Ozarks at the Jones Farm Pumpkin Patch. Youngsters—and their parents—wait all year to select just the right pumpkin for a perfect jack-o'-lantern or pumpkin pie. There are ten acres of pumpkins to choose from, but Ted and Ginny Jones, who own the farm, offer a lot more than just pumpkins to entertain their visitors. Depending on when you visit, you might see a stilt walker, balloon artist, or face painter, or get to take a pony ride, hop on a hay wagon, or even walk through a corn maze. ✣

Photo by Lisa Means

In autumn, happiness comes in many forms and in many colors.

"Which way to turn?" Every fall families find their way through the corn maze at the Campbell produce farm, just outside of Springfield. The maze in the maize is a much-anticipated activity of the harvest season—right up there with picking out the perfect pumpkin at the farm's pumpkin patch.❖

Photo by Lisa Means

KRAFT FOODS, INC.: HELPING PEOPLE AROUND THE WORLD EAT AND LIVE BETTER

Kraft Foods (NYSE: KFT) is the world's second-largest food and beverage company. For more than one hundred years, Kraft has been dedicated to helping people around the world eat and live better. Hundreds of millions of times a day, in more than 150 countries, consumers reach for their favorite Kraft brands, including Kraft cheeses and dinners; Jacobs, Gevalia, and Maxwell House coffees; Oscar Mayer meats; DiGiorno pizzas; Oreo cookies; Ritz and Wheat

Kraft has a long history of providing humanitarian aid in times of natural disasters and other crises locally and around the world.

Thins crackers and chips; Philadelphia cream cheese; Milka and Côte d'Or chocolates; Honey Bunches of Oats cereals; Good Seasons salad dressings; and Tang refreshment beverage. Kraft has also started adding to its shopping baskets the Tassimo hot beverage system, South Beach Diet line, and a growing range of better-for-you Sensible Solution products, continually expanding the list of Kraft favorites.

◄ *Each year, associates at Kraft Foods participate in the United Way Day of Caring. Kraft associates (left to right) Kelly Handley and Randy Sell congratulate a resident of Boys & Girls Town at the annual Day of Caring event.*

The history of Kraft in Springfield began in 1939, in a building on West Mill Street where Kraft produced process cheese. Today Kraft-Springfield operates a facility that produces Philadelphia cream cheese, Kraft natural cheese, shredded cheeses and processed cheeses like Velveeta, Lunchables lunch combinations, Kraft macaroni and cheese dinners, and Easy Cheese pasteurized process cheese spread.

Kraft is committed to the safety, health, and security of each employee. Kraft-Springfield is one of five Kraft plants in the United States that have been designated Voluntary Protection Program Star worksites. This is the highest safety designation of the U.S. Occupational Safety & Health Administration (OSHA).

Kraft-Springfield has an economic impact of more than $88 million annually in Southwest Missouri, through wages and purchases of raw materials, utilities, taxes, goods, and services.

Through the Kraft Cares grant-making program, the plant donates to an extensive list of local nonprofit organizations, with the major focus on hunger, nutrition, and healthy lifestyles. Kraft employees also give generously of their time as volunteers in their communities. Additionally, the company encourages personal charitable donations with a Matching Gift Program.

As the company states, "Community involvement is part of our responsibility, but we also believe it makes us a better company, respected by our employees, consumers, and customers." Kraft has a long history of providing humanitarian aid in times of natural disasters and other crises locally and around the world.

Considering the list of products cooked up by Kraft, it is safe to say that when folks in Springfield and the southwestern part of Missouri sit down to eat, they sit down with Kraft (K.R.A.F.T.). ❖

Photo by Eric Francis

Kraft Foods, Inc., has been part of ▶ the Springfield landscape since 1939 when it was housed in a building on West Mill Street. Currently Kraft-Springfield has an economic impact of more than $88 million annually in Southwest Missouri.

Photo by Rod Reilly

Photo by Rod Reilly

The sign may say Incredible Pizza Company, but what is really incredible are all the things kids—and sometimes even grownups—can find to do here. There is an indoor go-cart track, bumper cars, a Route 66 mini golf course, and a drive-in theatre, which are all great for either working up an appetite or working off a gigantic meal. When it comes time to settle down and eat, patrons have their choice of ingredients at the two pizza bars, or they can visit the potato bar, the pasta bar, or the eighty-item salad bar. For those who clean their plates, there is also a dessert bar with more items than most folks care to count. No one leaves the Incredible Pizza Company without having their fill of both food and fun. ✤

steinertalentin

STEINER TALENT: THE PERFECT ENTERTAINER FOR YOUR NEXT EVENT

Looking for a headliner, a juggler, a jazz singer, a puppeteer, a plate spinner, an actor, a model, a wedding band, a comedian, or a motivational speaker? If it is talent you seek, then Steiner Talent can fill the bill.

"I admire talented people who are the best at what they do, and I love matching them up with people looking to hire top-notch entertainment," said Mark Steiner, owner. Steiner has been in the entertainment business since 1984, working first in New York as an actor and in production in film and television, and later as a booking agent. He met his wife, Allison Wampler Steiner, when they were

> "When people need talent, they make one phone call and we do the rest. They are the best at what they do."

both in New York pursuing their careers in the arts. When they returned to Springfield—her hometown—he knew with a phone, a computer, and the Internet he could offer the same level of professionalism required in a major metropolitan market.

"Steiner Talent is the oldest of my three companies. I broker well-known entertainers and supply clients with the most talented performer in that area," said Steiner.

"Because I began getting calls from talented local and regional acts who wanted me to represent them, I started Gig Salad. I find gigs for these talented

◄ *Kelly Smith and her band, b.i.g., and Allie Hutsell and her band, the Allie Catz, are both exclusively represented by Steiner Talent. They got their starts performing in Southwest Missouri at several well-known Branson theatres. As a way of showcasing their talent, they occasionally perform at business expos.*

newcomers, help their careers along, and provide excellent entertainment for clients with more limited budgets."

Finally there is Steiner People—a speakers bureau. "I find performers for universities and corporations looking for motivational speakers, humorists, or comedians," Steiner explained.

"When I book talent, I can guarantee the client that they are getting a professional, not only in terms of talent, but in attitude, punctuality, deportment, and character."

Clients coming to Steiner are invited to go online to look at the talent roster. Beginning with Steiner Talent, there are links to Gig Salad and Steiner People, so browsing is easy. "When people need talent, they make one phone call and we do the rest. I've screened the talent, I know them by reputation, and if they are on our roster, they are the best at what they do."

Not only is a large part of Steiner's business involved in keeping local and regional entertainers employed, the agency also helps the community. "We've always worked with nonprofits to provide entertainment for fund-raising events. The American Cancer Society, American Diabetes Association, Boys & Girls Town, Children's Organ Transplant Association, Developmental Center of the Ozarks, Habitat for Humanity, and Project Hope are a few examples. In addition, we are thrilled about our board membership with the newly restored Gillioz Theatre."

When the need arises, if you can imagine it, the chances are very good that Steiner Talent, Steiner People, or Gig Salad can find the perfect entertainer for your next event. ✧

Photo by Scott Indermaur

Photo by Crystal Stewart

Just some of the future ▶ *talent from Springfield. Allison Wampler Steiner, wife of Steiner Talent owner Mark Steiner, is an accomplished classical violinist who maintains a large private studio and teaches at their children's private Christian school. Here she works with son Luke, a cellist, and daughter Olivia, a violinist and pianist.*

The Dawson family enjoys visiting the Springfield Conservation Nature Center with its interactive museum and surrounding natural habitat. This particular day seemed perfect for a hike on one of the center's six trails, and Dad's strong shoulders were perfect for a bird's-eye view. The Nature Center is a little piece of the Ozarks right in the city limits. Eighty acres of forests, fields, creeks, and lake frontage offer refuge for white-tailed deer, foxes, mink, muskrats, raccoons, birds, turtles, and frogs—nearly all the creatures that make their homes in the Ozarks. ❖

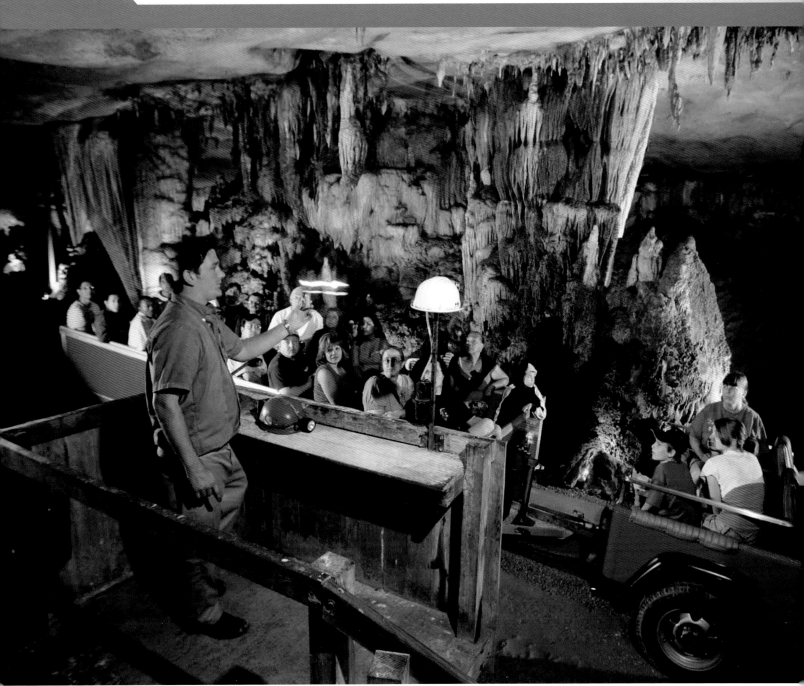

Photo by Eric Francis

Who needs to go spelunking when you can explore one of America's most magnificent caves from the comfort of a jeep-drawn tram? Discovered in 1862 by a farmer when his dog wriggled through an entrance of the winding underground passageway, which had been carved over time by the flow of an ancient river, Fantastic Caverns offers visitors a journey unlike any other. Fifty-minute tours of the country's only ride-through cave provide a glimpse of spectacular subterranean rock formations in a cool and comfortable environment that remains at sixty degrees year-round, thanks to its location beneath the Earth's surface. And the transport tram not only makes a trip through the caverns ideal for people of all ages, but it also helps protect the natural features that have dazzled visitors since Fantastic Caverns opened to the public. ✤

Springfield's Jordan Valley Park comes alive throughout the summer with free concerts sponsored by the City of Springfield and the Springfield–Greene County Park Board. The popular Springfield band Big Smith drew thousands of fans with its genuine Ozarks roots-infused music. ❖

Photo by Alan S. Weiner

If Missouri is the Show-Me State, then Springfield might just be the Show-Me City. With a whole host of performing arts events year-round, Springfield shows its residents and visitors a good time, all the time. The city also offers venues from the traditional, like the Juanita K. Hammons Hall for the Performing Arts and the Vandivort Theatre, to the unusual Tent Theatre, a staple of Springfield and the Southwest Missouri area. People who follow theatrical entertainment know that if it's summer, it must be time for Tent Theatre. Located on the campus of Missouri State University, Tent Theatre is a unique outdoor venue for summer stock. Born in the summer of 1963 out of a need for an airy and well-lighted venue (the theatre in the administration building at that time had steadily had its windows bricked over for heating purposes), Tent Theatre featured its first show in a fifty-five-foot-round tangerine-and-green structure that seated about two hundred. Actors John Goodman, Kathleen Turner and Tess Harper performed in MSU theatre when they were students here. Today Tent Theatre is not only thriving as the oldest of its kind in the country, but also continues to provide a preprofessional experience for theatre students to act alongside veterans. Springfield's performing arts culture is fertile ground for aspiring actors, musicians, and dancers, many of whom go on to Hollywood, Broadway, and beyond. ❖

hoto by Alan S. Weiner

UNIVERSITY PLAZA HOTEL AND CONVENTION CENTER: A BETTER PLACE TO MEET

With 39,000 square feet of versatile meeting space, not to mention a staff that embodies the word "versatile," it is no surprise that year after year the University Plaza Hotel and Convention Center is the go-to facility in Springfield for corporate groups and professional organizations.

"As the region's largest full-service hotel and convention center, and as a John Q. Hammons property, we follow a standard of unsurpassed customer service for businesses and for individuals. It is evidenced in the quality of our facility. It is evidenced in our amenities. And it is evidenced in the longevity of our staff.

"It is evidenced in the quality of our facility. It is evidenced in our amenities. And it is evidenced in the longevity of our staff."

That's why we think of University Plaza Hotel and Convention Center as a better place to meet in Springfield," says Bob Pottberg, general manager.

In addition to the function space on site, which includes twenty-one meeting rooms and banquet facilities for up to two thousand guests, the hotel manages the adjacent Springfield Expo Center, adding another 112,000 square feet, and another location for events demanding exceptional proportions. From serving as a venue for the gymnastics competition of the Missouri Winter Games, to the state meetings for groups like the

◀ University Plaza Hotel and Convention Center's Terrace Grille lounge welcomes visitors and local guests for breakfast, lunch, and dinner with trademark superior service and excellent cuisine.

Missouri Lions Clubs or the Missouri Local Government Employees Retirement System, University Plaza is adept at handling functions of all sizes. "They have the best design and flow of any hotel we've used so far for our annual state meeting," says Bob Wilson, manager of member services for the Missouri Local Government Employees Retirement System. "Most importantly, everyone at the hotel really values our meeting. They take it seriously. There's a young man in the AV department that I think gets more excited than I do about making certain our equipment is working."

One of the outstanding attributes of the University Plaza Hotel and Convention Center is indeed the strength of the sales and catering staff. Armed with a wealth of experience and knowledge, the staff knows how to ask the right questions to help the clientele. American National Property and Casualty (ANPAC) has been holding bimonthly education and training meetings for its agents at University Plaza since 2001. "It helps to know the people you work with," says Jerry Neville, director of agency development and administration for ANPAC. "When you need something, you know it'll get done," he says.

Jeff Collins, executive director for the Missouri Winter Games, agrees. "Not only was the hotel a sponsor of the inaugural year of this event, they went above and beyond what a hotel should do," he says. For example, Collins cites something as simple as the staff assisting in hanging a banner and setting up for a press conference. "They didn't have to do that.

Continued on page 80

Photo by Lisa Means

Photo by Lisa Means

Not only can executive ▶ chef John Luchtel cook, he can carve. This ice carving will soon be the centerpiece for a fourteen-hundred-person banquet.

From weddings to business functions, University Plaza Hotel and Convention Center hosts all types of special events, accommodating from ten to two thousand people.

Continued from page 79

They just did it because they saw we could use the help." That is music to the ears of Christine Huffington, University Plaza's director of sales. "There's nothing more satisfying than helping our customers look good to their organizations," she says.

While the hotel's meeting space is second to none, the 271 guest rooms are equally outstanding. Whether standard guest rooms, executive suites, oversized king rooms, or a presidential suite, all are well appointed and a real example of how style and hospitality blend to make guests feel welcomed. Guests also enjoy casual dining at the Terrace Grille restaurant, which serves breakfast, lunch, and

Photo by Lisa Means

◀ Warm greetings and
friendly faces make
certain that guests
become part of the family.

Photo by Lisa Means

dinner. A fully equipped fitness facility, indoor/outdoor pool, sauna and whirlpool, and convenient business center are among the most popular amenities.

Another plus is the hotel's location in the heart of Springfield's historical and cultural district. Just blocks from Hammons Field, home of the Double-A Springfield Cardinals, and close to an array of entertainment venues and restaurants, hotel guests can always find something to do. "People are not going to work twenty-four hours a day," says Neville. "They like to get out of the hotel and need something within walking distance." If time and transportation permit, guests can also visit the Battlefield Mall, Bass Pro Shops, and Wilson's Creek National Civil War Battlefield and Museum—all within twenty minutes of the hotel. From convenient location to quality services, it's easy to see why University Plaza Hotel and Convention Center is a better place to meet in Springfield. ❖

American cuisine and ▶
superior service combine
to make breakfast, lunch,
and dinner delicious
and enjoyable.

Photo by Scott Indermaur

Photo by Scott Indermaur

Boaters like Gary and Janet Ellison, cruising the day away on their pontoon, are a common sight at Table Rock Lake. The lake's depth, clarity, and underwater interests make Table Rock a perfect place for year-round diving. Anglers also flock to the water for its renowned fishing, with bass, crappie, walleye, and catfish making for some great catches and eating. In addition to campgrounds, trails, and parks, the shoreline is dotted with marinas and a host of accommodations that make any stay at the lake an enjoyable one. ❖

In their lifetime, the Boller Brothers of Kansas City, Missouri were responsible for over one hundred of this country's most opulently designed theaters and movie palaces. One of them, the Orpheum, was built in Springfield in 1908. Known today as the Landers Theater, the Baroque Renaissance masterpiece is Missouri's oldest and largest civic theater. Placed on the National Register of Historic Places in 1977, it has undergone numerous renovations, the most recent honored with awards from the American Institute of Architects. In continuous use as either a theatrical or film venue since opening, it has served as the home theater for the Springfield Little Theatre since 1970. Here, Ashley Smith, a member of Springfield Little Theatre's Y.E.S. Troupe, performs at the Frannie Awards, held each year at the Landers to honor SLT volunteers. The Y.E.S. Troupe is one of SLT's three pre-professional training troupes. ❖

Photo by Scott Indermaur

There are nearly as many stories about the origin of coffee as there are coffee beans. Supposedly the world's first coffee shop opened in Constantinople in 1475, and at one time, Turkish law made it legal for a woman to divorce her husband if he failed to provide her with her daily quota of coffee. The first coffeehouses in England were called "penny universities" because a penny was charged for admission and a cup of coffee. The prices and the menu may have changed, but the Mudhouse Coffee and Tea Co. is still a favorite place for businesspeople and students to hang out. The Mudhouse moved into downtown before it was cool to be there. One of the owners, Brian King, used to have his pottery shop in the back of the building. Although he has moved to new quarters, he is still frequently behind the counter making and serving coffee in mugs he created. His partner, Rob Weislocher, is kept busy with their other businesses. We Americans owe a debt of gratitude to Captain John Smith, the founder of Jamestown, Virginia, for introducing the brew to North America. ✤

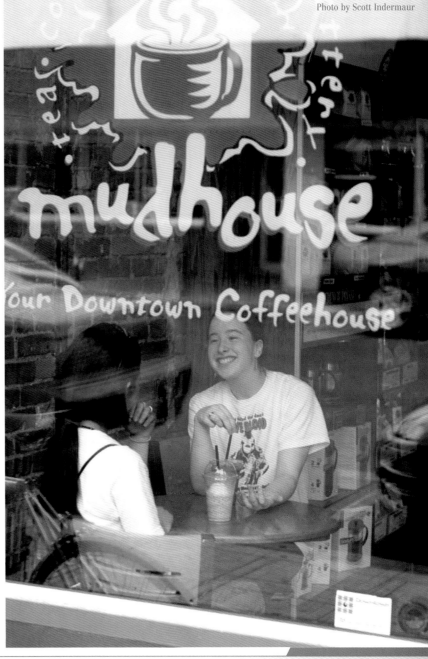

Photo by Scott Indermaur

Photo by Scott Indermaur

POSTEL MAPS & ATLAS: STAYING THE COURSE

By forming a vision and staying the course, Postel Maps & Atlas is fast becoming a prominent name in the mapping industry.

No small feat considering the global scope of the competition. But Kevin Postel, founder and owner of the company, had three years of industry insight when he started his own mapping business. That background, combined with innovative thinking and a sheer determination to succeed, led to the pursuit and acquisition of some key accounts in the region.

"I overcame the largest obstacle of convincing retailers that even an unknown in the mapping industry could slay the giant if given the chance to perform," says

The Postel sales team makes regular calls on clients in order to coordinate proper inventory levels while collaborating on future needs.

Postel. "As a result, I've been able to obtain over two thousand accounts in convenience stores, truck plazas, and department stores in six midwestern states, all in less than six years."

Today, the company counts among its clients such prominent names as Quik-Trip, Rapid Roberts, Jump Stop, Bullseye, Coral/Sentis Group Shells, Shell Super-Stops, and even select Wal-Mart stores.

Performing for these clients, in part, means providing direct delivery to stores. The Postel sales team makes regular calls on clients in order to coordinate proper inventory levels while collaborating on future needs. These face-to-face visits give Postel Maps & Atlas an edge when it comes to customer service. "When we enter a customer's store, we greet them

▲ *Sales representative Brenda Waller talks with QuikTrip store manager Tim Weber about his store's product display and the newest Springfield City Map and Springfield Quick View Map. A key to Postel's growth has been a sales team making regular calls on clients to ensure that their current and future needs are met.*

by name," Postel says. "And when we leave, we let them know how much we appreciate their business."

Founded in 2001, Postel Maps & Atlas has built a company on a mainstay of Postel-branded city, state, and county road maps. Its lineup includes a Deluxe Folded® map series, retailing between four and five dollars; a Quick View® Series, sold for about two dollars each; and a Fast Finder® Series of laminated maps that sell in the range of seven dollars.

While based out of Marshfield, Postel Maps & Atlas knows the ins and outs of Springfield, offering more specific map products of the larger city than any other location. In addition to deluxe detailed, quick-view, and fast-finder laminated maps of the Springfield market, Postel also markets a city street guide atlas, a Greene County map, and more.

Postel Maps & Atlas has partnered with the paper division of the online map giant MapQuest, Inc. (AOL Time-Warner), for its supply of atlases in a variety of sizes, and now, as the new and exclusive provider for the local-based KTTS FM (94.7) Storm Alert Map project, Postel provides information that assists the region with its weather preparedness needs.

Already giving back to its Marshfield/Webster County community, Postel joins its neighbors in avid support of the Lady Jays basketball team. The company donates back to the team 10 percent of sales of the area's map, sporting a mascot on the cover.

There are many roads to consider on the path of life. For Postel Maps & Atlas, every road leads to success. ❖

Photo by Scott Indermaur

▲ *Postel Maps is a homegrown company producing a full complement of road maps for highways and byways nationwide. Here, owner Kevin Postel, with a variety of his wares splayed across his dashboard, heads off on a trip to wherever his maps take him.*

Photo by Scott Indermaur

◀ *Postel Maps warehouse manager Mark Mikkelsen loads one of the company's delivery trucks in preparation for its departure. In only a half-dozen years, Postel has grown its client base to include more than two thousand accounts in a six-state area.*

Photo by Scott Indermaur

The Fourth of July parade in downtown Springfield is a summer tradition for Tony and Lori Shank and their children, Andrew, Ainsely, and Alex. Originally from Springfield, Tony brings the family back to visit Grandma and also to take in the sights and sounds of the parade. The more noise the better for Andrew, who favors the bands and the fire trucks. But Mom says the big hit for him is the candy that parade participants throw to the crowd. ❖

Photo by Scott Indermaur

Don the red, white, and blue, and start the hand waving as the annual Fourth of July parade rolls through town.

Photo by Scott Indermaur

MEMORIES ARE MADE AT BATTLEFIELD MALL

Whether it is a mother and daughter finding that perfect prom dress, a father buying his son's first tools, a young couple looking for a fine engagement ring, or schoolmates working side by side at their first jobs, Battlefield Mall is a place where families and friends create memories of a lifetime.

Opened as an indoor shopping center in 1970, Battlefield Mall has become the area's premier shopping destination by listening to what shoppers want. By being attuned to shoppers, the mall has continued to change with the market. The first renovation doubled the mall's size by adding the west wing, including

> Battlefield Mall has become the area's premier shopping destination by listening to what shoppers want.

the food court, while the next renovation a decade later gave shoppers a newly rejuvenated destination to shop.

A 2003 makeover added fifteen thousand square feet of space, gave existing storefronts exterior entrances, and made Battlefield the first mall to marry the concept of a traditional mall with a lifestyle center. New stores joining the Battlefield Mall experience at that time were Chico's, Ann Taylor Loft, Coldwater Creek, and Jos. A. Bank Clothiers.

The success of the lifestyle concept paved the way for a multimillion-dollar renovation in 2006, which included

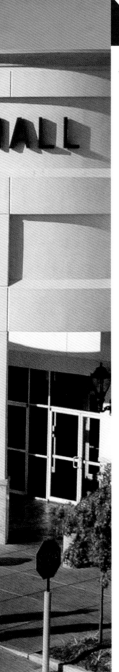

◄ *Battlefield Mall is the first shopping center to marry the concept of a traditional mall with a lifestyle center. In addition to indoor shopping, some storefronts offer exterior entrances as well.*

interior changes in flooring, interior lighting, carpeting, and seating areas as well as the addition of new, expanded restrooms and family restrooms.

Today, Battlefield Mall encompasses 1.1 million square feet of lease space. In addition to five department stores, the mall houses over 150 specialty retailers, including ALDO shoes, Banana Republic, American Eagle Outfitters, Sephora, White House Black Market, Build-A-Bear Workshop, Aeropostle, and Hollister. Battlefield Mall also offers a full selection of snack stops and eateries, with choices ranging from Godiva Chocolatier and Auntie Anne's Pretzels to Nakato's Japanese Steakhouse and J.Buck's Restaurant.

Located at Battlefield Road and Glenstone Avenue, the mall draws from a ninety-mile trade-area radius and is the only enclosed super-regional shopping center in Southwest Missouri. Battlefield Mall is host to a variety of events, including health events with area hospitals, lifestyle shows, and a fun kids club known as the Simon Kidgits Club.

The mall also gives back to the community from which it draws business. Through its Simon Evening of Giving, an annual charitable shopping night, the mall has generated more than eighty-five thousand dollars for area charities and for the Simon Youth Foundation, which since 1999 has awarded over nine thousand dollars in scholarships to outstanding Springfield-area high school seniors.

Battlefield Mall is a vital part of the Simon Property Group portfolio. Headquartered in Indianapolis, Indiana, Simon is a real estate investment trust engaged in the ownership and management of income-producing properties such as regional malls, community shopping centers, and specialty centers. For up-to-date information on Simon Property Group and Battlefield Mall, visit www.simon.com. ❖

When shoppers talk, ► *Battlefield Mall listens. That's how it came to be the area's premier shopping destination, with 1.1 million square feet of lease space encompassing five department stores and over 150 specialty retailers.*

With newly completed indoor courts, the Cooper Tennis Complex received the 2006 Facility of the Year award from the USTA/Missouri Valley. This complex hosts the professional World Team Tennis Springfield Lasers and championship collegiate and regional matches, along with other spectator events. ❖

Photo by Thomas S. England

The 2006 Springfield Lasers, Springfield's professional tennis team, warm up with Coach Trevor Kronemann. The Lasers play in the World Team Tennis League, founded by tennis legend Billie Jean King. July is Lasers month, and they play to enthusiastic fans at Cooper Tennis Complex. ❖

Photo by Thomas S. England

Photo by Scott Indermaur

If you want to know what's really going on in Springfield, head over to Mille's Turn of the Century Café. Located at 313 South Jefferson, this café is where the locals gather for dining, networking, and get-togethers of every sort. Classy, yet casual, Mille's offers American cuisine ranging from steaks, chicken, and seafood to pasta, sandwiches, and wraps. If salad is your pleasure, Mille's has an array of specialties made with a selection of homemade dressings. Drinks, including a full wine list, are also on the menu. ❖

JOHN Q. HAMMONS HOTEL
A LEGACY OF ACHIEVEMENT

In 1958 Springfield-based real estate developer John Q. Hammons partnered with a local contractor to develop ten Holiday Inn Hotels located throughout the Midwest. Over the next half-century, Hammons grew those initial ventures into what has become a hotel dynasty, making John Q. Hammons Hotels one of the top innovators in the hospitality industry today.

John Q. Hammons has not only spent his life building, he's spent it sharing. Deeply grateful to the city of Springfield for affording him the

> Starting in the
> early 1980s,
> Hammons embarked
> on a venture to
> revitalize a neglected
> section of
> Springfield's downtown.

opportunity to grow his business, he has returned the favor many times over. More than anything, he is one of Springfield's greatest champions, believing from the beginning in the city's potential for growth and prosperity.

Starting in the early 1980s, Hammons embarked on a venture to revitalize a neglected section of Springfield's downtown. By the end of the decade he had built in the area the 270-room University Plaza Hotel, the twenty-two-story Hammons Tower office building, a new U.S. courthouse, and the Hammons Enterprise Center

▲ *Longtime and enthusiastic supporters of the arts, John Q. Hammons and his wife, Juanita, made a generous gift to Missouri State University toward the construction of their premier performing arts venue. Today, the Juanita K. Hammons Hall for the Performing Arts hosts a wide variety of drama, dance, and musical performances and is the home venue of the Springfield Symphony.*

which houses the Springfield Area Chamber of Commerce. Today, University Plaza is a bustling center not only for commerce and tourism, but also for recreation. With great fanfare, Hammons Field baseball stadium opened, and through personal negotiations with the St. Louis Cardinals, their Double A Minor League team now calls Springfield home.

That same generous spirit also prevails in numerous civic, educational, cultural, and health-care initiatives, both in Springfield and in the communities in which Hammons has built hotels. As a former teacher, education has always been important to Hammons. Over the years he has contributed substantially to his alma mater, Missouri State University, as well as to Ozarks Technical Community College and Drury University. Springfield Public Schools also benefits on a regular basis from his challenge grants. Most recently, Hammons generously announced a $30 million commitment to Missouri State University for the construction of JQH Arena, which will be home to the MSU Bears and Lady Bears basketball teams in 2008.

Health care has been another longtime concern. When Hammons suffered a heart attack in 1960, he never forgot the quality of care he received at St. John's Regional Health Center. As a result, his support led to the establishment in 1972 of the center's Hammons Heart Institute.

Along with his wife, Juanita, Hammons is also a great supporter of the arts in Springfield, a devotion that goes back to 1972. That year, Springfield's public television broadcasting facility was seeking matching funds for a federal grant. John Q. Hammons stepped up to the plate with a capital founder's gift of one hundred thousand dollars. Twenty years later, he more than doubled that gift in another pledge drive. He and Juanita have also helped raise over $1 million to benefit the Springfield Ballet, Little Theater, Regional Opera, and Symphony.

When John Q. Hammons builds a hotel, the entire community benefits, because with construction come increased jobs, visitors, and economic development. In these ways and more, John Q. Hammons has established a legacy of generosity that makes Springfield, and dozens of other American cities, great places to call home. ❖

Photo by Scott Indermaur

Equally impassioned about all things sports-related, Mr. Hammons brought to Springfield its first high-end country club. Developed in 1989, the resulting Highland Springs Country Club is distinguished by its challenging and scenic obert Trent Jones II–designed golf course and spectacular clubhouse overlooking the 18th green.

Photo by Thomas S. England

a hub for Springfield's live music scene, the Outland Ballroom has become both a premier live music venue and the crucible in which raw talent is encouraged to hone their craft. There's live music every night of the week, featuring cutting-edge local, regional, and national acts of all genres. Local bands are also encouraged to bring in their demos for a chance to test their sound on a live audience. ❖

*t*he music scene in Springfield is going strong. In pubs and clubs throughout the city, you will find a host of local musicians playing every kind of music you can name: hard rock, heavy metal, country, classic rock, punk, bluegrass, acoustic, jazz, and blues. Sometimes the music comes to you, courtesy of musicians like Scott Criswell, who liven up the downtown area. Visitors and citizens alike are making downtown the place to be when it comes to outdoor cafés, fine dining, shopping, strolling, the arts, and entertainment—both formal and informal. ❖

Photo by Rod Reilly

Springfield Brewing Company, located at the corner of Market Avenue and McDaniel Street, occupies a building originally built in the early 1900s for the Newton Grain Company. When the Paul Mueller Company bought the property in 1996 it was used as a storage facility for flea market wares and, like so many buildings in old downtown Springfield, was in dire need of restoration. The building was completely restored to an appearance very similar to the original, with the help of the design team at Butler, Rosenbury & Partners and work by Hoke Brothers Construction. New windows and a traditional storefront were given to the old structure, the brick mortar was cleaned and tuck-pointed, and new brewing equipment, restaurant furniture, and kitchen equipment were installed in this completely remodeled building. Today, the interior decor includes a large collection of brewery memorabilia from the mid-1900s and historical black-and-white photographs of Springfield, reproduced with permission of the History Museum for Springfield–Greene County. ✤

HAWTHORN PARK HOTEL: SIMPLE ELEGANCE . . . SUPERIOR SERVICE

A great hotel is more than just a beautiful building with stylish guest rooms. To be truly great, a hotel must offer superior service and be dedicated to providing an exceptional experience for every guest who walks through the door. A great hotel must continually strive to improve and recognize the guests' needs. And a great hotel does the same thing most smart businesses do: it reinvents, reinvigorates, makes itself over, renovates. Call it what you will, a well-planned and well-timed metamorphosis often brings out the best. That is certainly the case at the Hawthorn Park Hotel.

"Our hotel is so flexible that our corporate guests feel that they are in business environment during the week, and our families feel like they are in a resort setting," Ray says.

One of the first things people notice is the hotel's excellent location, as well as its ten-story high-rise prominence. Conveniently located off I-44 and U.S. Highway 65, and fifteen minutes from the airport, the Hawthorn Park Hotel rises above the rest in more ways than one. "We have the location, we have the product, and we have the service. . . . It's all here," says Director of Sales Mary Wise. Then why renovate? "To ensure that we are the premier place to stay in Springfield," Wise adds. The complete transformation of the hotel was done to bring the property not just into the twenty-first century, but well beyond.

◄ *When first stepping in the hotel, guests often comment about the spacious and breathtaking atrium setting. With glass elevators, tiered seating, and exquisite furnishings, this first impression is just a hint of what's to come.*

"The Hawthorn Park Hotel creates a memorable impression on our guests," explains General Manager Donald Ray. "We're known for our service, a high level of hospitality. For example, we begin building rapport with our guests right at check-in, learning their names and letting them know ours. Then, twenty minutes later, we follow up with a courtesy phone call just to ensure that they have everything they need for a comfortable stay."

During the week, the Hawthorn Park Hotel is filled with business travelers, many of whom return frequently. Low staff turnover, coupled with the hotel's signature level of service, keeps them coming back. Many choose to bring their families on the weekends, yet the hotel's environment is well suited to both business and leisure travelers. "Our hotel is so flexible that our corporate guests feel that they are in business environment during the week, and our families feel like they are in a resort setting," Ray says.

Even though the hotel already had the "wow factor" in the lobby with stately marble floors, lighted elevators, and a ten-story atrium, the "wow" just became "WOW!"

New and somewhat unexpected landscaping graces the hotel's exterior. Inside, the lush atrium now has a waterfall that draws the eye and sets the mood for a relaxing, restful experience. To accommodate the growing demand for functions, the hotel doubled its existing banquet and meeting room space, and upgraded its audiovisual capabilities. The hotel can accommodate everything from intimate board meetings to large banquets and conferences. The

Continued on page 100

Photo by Scott Indermaur

Photo by Scott Indermaur

The Hawthorn Ballroom is a ► *spacious forty-one hundred square feet, which offers additional flexibility when divided into three sections. Its high ceilings, drop chandeliers, and lighted perimeter columns provide an elegant setting for any occasion.*

◀ The goal of Hawthorn Park's courteous and experienced staff is always founded on exceeding customer expectations.

Continued from page 99

latest audiovisual equipment is available to produce efficient and effective presentations. All meeting space is conveniently located on the first floor, including the atrium, which can double as a unique venue for receptions. T. Tymes, the hotel's bar and grill, is also located in the atrium, and offers a full dinner menu and cocktail service when guests are ready to switch gears.

Other improvements include expansion of the fitness center, open twenty-four hours a day, featuring the latest cardio and weight equipment, a sauna, and whirlpool. The Hawthorn Park Hotel boasts the area's only indoor/outdoor pool. A glass partition, which guests swim under, separates the outside from the inside. And because the pool is heated, the outside is appealing even in the dead of winter. The Gift Shop has been expanded. Guests will find the must-have necessities they might have left behind, as well as nice-to-have items to take home.

A full-service restaurant serves ▶ an array of delectable and tantalizing selections for even the most sophisticated palate. Room service is also available for those who prefer to dine in.

*◄ As part of the Springfield-
Branson Chef's Association,
the culinary team of the
Hawthorn Park Hotel brings
talent and experience to the
kitchen and to the table.*

Photo by Scott Indermaur

Amenities and features of the two hundred guest rooms at the Hawthorn Park Hotel include the expected, as well as the unexpected: complimentary high-speed Internet access, plasma televisions, fine linens, and ultra-comfortable beds. "People feel so comfortable in the rooms, they might just order room service because they don't want to leave," says Ray. "An experience that leaves a lasting impression—that's been our focus since we opened in 1985, and it remains our focus today." ❖

Photo by Scott Indermaur

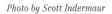

*Ultra-comfortable sleeping ▶
rooms offer guests an array
of conveniences. From
luxuriant bedding, including
a premium mattress, down
comforter, and feather-
stuffed pillows, to the
oversized oak desk with
computer data ports,
twenty-seven-inch TV, coffee
maker, and hair dryer, the
room is almost like home.*

Photo by Alan S. Weiner

All Photos by Alan S. Weiner

Established in 1992, the Xeriscape Demonstration Garden in Springfield offers more than meets the eye. Made possible by the cooperation of the Master Gardeners of Southwest Missouri, the Park Board, and City Utilities, this sumptuous wonderland of plants and flowers is also fertile ground for learning and making decisions about which grasses, groundcovers, shrubs, and trees will flourish in one's own backyard. These colorful and varied plants are selected for the three sections of the garden according to their irrigation and sunlight needs, demonstrating the most efficient use of water in landscaping. Citizens who qualify as master gardeners can maintain the gardens and promote horticulture awareness, or, like Mike and Heather Jones and their son Garner, they can simply stroll through and enjoy the sights and scents of nature. ❖

OZARKS COCA-COLA/DR PEPPER BOTTLING COMPANY: REFRESHING THE OZARKS

What is the "Real Thing" in the Ozarks when it comes to refreshment, community involvement, and job creation? Since 1920 it's the people of Ozarks Coca-Cola/Dr Pepper Bottling Company. That's when Edwin Cook Rice Sr., his wife Clara, and family invested in a Coca-Cola Company franchise and moved to Springfield from Kentucky.

For nearly two decades, Rice and his brothers, Earl and Richard, worked to grow the Coca-Cola brand in the bottling company's territory by focusing on the production and sales of Coca-Cola, then sold in six-and-one-half-ounce glass bottles packed in wooden cases. In 1939,

> For nearly two decades, Rice and his brothers, Earl and Richard, worked to grow the Coca-Cola brand in the bottling company's territory.

Rice's son-in-law Ed Heer joined the business as the company met the challenges of World War II and the Great Depression. Sugar rationing meant decreased production, and parts of the territory were sold only to be repurchased in later years. The plant's location changed from Commercial Street, to 454 South Campbell, then to 545 West Phelps, before locating at 930 North Clay near Central High School and Drury University in 1928.

Edwin Cook Rice Jr., "Cookie," started in the business as a young man in 1950 just as the production of carbonated soft drinks began to change dramatically. New

◀ *Everywhere youth gather, Coca-Cola and Dr Pepper products add fun and refreshment. A strong commitment to education, athletics, and facilities define the investment Ozarks Coca-Cola/Dr Pepper Bottling Company has made in the Ozarks.*

Coca-Cola Company brands Sprite, Tab, and Fresca, using low-calorie sweeteners, were introduced, and packages moved from glass to the aluminum can. During construction of Springfield's Central High School football stadium, crushed glass from old soda bottles were used as "fill," and the corner of Clay and Central streets was converted to a practice green for Springfield Coca-Cola employees who sharpened their golf game while on work breaks.

Baseball was a passion for the Rice-Heer family business, which often sponsored teams of young adults and youth. The Springfield Cardinals of the 1940s were cheered on by fans banging their glass Coke bottles against the wooden bleachers. "Coca-Cola" sponsored cars were favorites during the growth of stock car racing at the Ozark Empire Fairgrounds and other local racetracks. Many Springfield children have memories of field trips to the "Coke plant" to observe the manufacture of the world's most recognized brand. Rice Sr. enjoyed rewarding young students who received "grade A reports" with a Coca-Cola tablet, ruler, and pencil.

In 1976, a new 50,000-square-foot plant opened two miles west at the headwaters of Jordan Creek on Packer Road. Rice and his sister, Virginia "Tookie" Heer, acquired the Dr Pepper franchise in 1986 from the Garland Reynolds family, and began production for both franchise companies. The plant now occupies 128,000 square feet and employs 334 people. In true family tradition, annual service awards recognize those who have devoted their entire careers to one business, and hiring family members is common.

For decades, supporting activities that foster growth and education of youth has been a priority, strengthening the bonds that tie Ozarks Coca-Cola/Dr Pepper Bottling Company to Springfield and the Ozarks. A year of celebration in 2005 was dubbed "One Hundred Years of Refreshing the Ozarks" as customers, consumers, employees, and family ownership marked eighty-five years in business, and the Coca-Cola Centennial. ❖

Photo by Rod Reilly

Photo by Lisa Means

Mother and daughter ▶ *Sandra and Sydney Long enjoy a refreshing Ozarks Coca-Cola product during a ride on the carousel at the Ozark Empire Fair. The fair is a long-standing tradition among Ozarks families.*

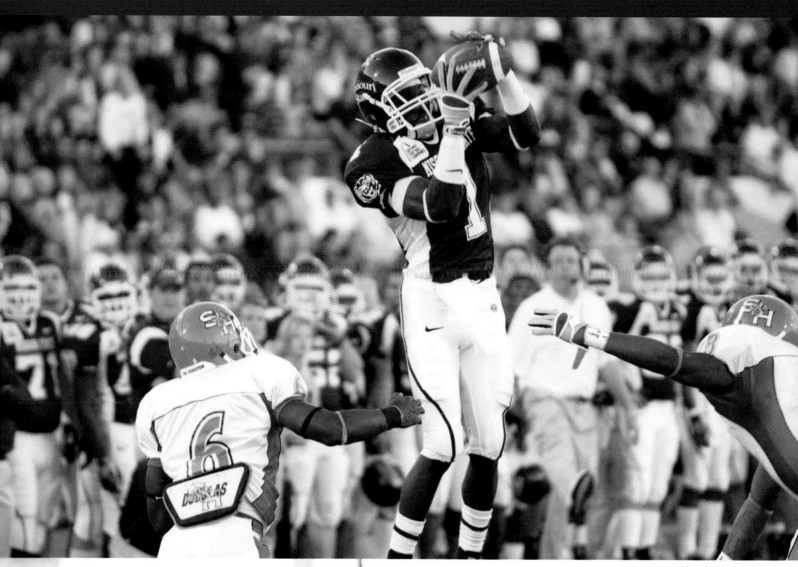

Photo by Thomas S. England

For nearly a century, the people of Southwest Missouri have thronged to Missouri State University athletic competitions. Playing all but three years since 1909, the football Bears have posted forty-five winning seasons, including three five-year runs over the course of the team's history. Missouri State's Division I basketball teams are also the pride of Springfield. The men's team won the Missouri Valley Conference title in 1992 and reached the NCAA Sweet 16 in 1999. The Lady Bears basketball team is a perennial powerhouse, putting Springfield in the national spotlight with NCAA Final Four appearances in 1991 and 2001. The NCAA's all-time leading scorer is former Lady Bear Jackie Stile, who went on to be Rookie of the Year in the WNBA. For many years, the teams played at Hammons Student Center, regularly drawing over one hundred thousand fans in a single season. But thanks to $30 million in gifts from alumni and friends, including hotel developer John Q. Hammons, the teams' new home, JQH Arena, is sure to break those records. The Missouri State cheerleaders, who consistently take home top-ten awards in the UCA College Nationals, also serve as ambassadors for the school. ❖

Photo by Thomas S. England

Photo by Scott Indermaur

Photo by Scott Indermaur

Division I
sports play big
in Springfield

▲ *The meat shop at Price Cutter offers Creekstone Farms Natural Black Angus Beef. USDA-certified from 100 percent hand-selected Black Angus cattle, with no antibiotics or added hormones, Creekstone Farms is unlike other Angus programs. Most are based simply on the hide of the animal being a minimum of 51 percent black. Creekstone Farms chooses cattle with known Black Angus genetics.*

Photo by Rod Reilly

RPCS, INC.: INNOVATIVE AND CUSTOMER-DRIVEN

From neighborhood grocer to regional supermarket chain, RPCS Inc. is one of Southwest Missouri's most enduring retail success stories. The company's beginnings date back to 1919 when John Ramey opened his first store in Springfield. Within twenty years the enterprising young man was running eight stores plus the area's first modern supermarket. Although located just outside of town, the store flourished, and the area where it once stood is now Springfield's busy intersection of Glenstone and Sunshine.

Today RPCS has evolved into an innovative, modern grocery store chain that still retains its old-fashioned customer service values.

In 1946, Ramey sold his venture and the business continued to grow. Starting in 1967 under the management of Richard Taylor and eventually his son Erick, the company evolved into a highly successful regional grocery store chain with locations throughout Springfield and Southwest Missouri. Today Erick Taylor serves as president and CEO of RPCS Inc., the Springfield-based parent company of thirty-four full-service retail grocery stores and twenty pharmacies, all under the Ramey, Price Cutter, Price Cutter Plus, and Smitty's banners, with many stores featuring Starbucks kiosks.

RPCS Inc. is a business with a legacy of providing personalized customer service. That legacy continues, only with a high-tech twist. Recognizing that today's family is busier than ever, in June 2006 Price Cutter became the only grocery store chain in Southwest Missouri to offer its customers the convenience of online shopping and delivery. Orders may be placed twenty-four hours a day, seven days a week, with delivery available twice daily Monday through Friday to homes and businesses throughout Springfield, Ozark, Nixa, Rogersville, Republic, Battlefield, Brookline, and Willard. Pickup is available at Price Cutter Plus, 4228 South National Avenue, in Springfield.

In August 2006, Price Cutter launched another innovative program, this one designed to meet the demand for locally produced products, while expanding the distribution options for growers and manufacturers of those products. In partnership with the Missouri Grocers Association and Agri-Missouri, Price Cutter's Missouri-Made program sets aside select shelf space in each store for high-quality, locally produced products.

Established as a neighborhood grocer, RPCS naturally retains close ties with the communities it serves. As one of the area's largest employers, the company not only provides an excellent living for approximately eighteen hundred employees, it also empowers them as owners. On January 1, 2005, RPCS launched its Employee Stock Ownership Plan (ESOP), which gives its employees an important stake in the company's growth and success.

Extending their commitment beyond store walls, RPCS also regularly donates time and money to a variety of local and regional initiatives. And as the title sponsor of the Price Cutter Charity Championship golf tournament, a PGA Tour stop, each year RPCS raises hundreds of thousands of dollars for local children's charities.

Today RPCS has evolved into an innovative, modern grocery store chain that still retains its old-fashioned customer service values. That approach has earned the company a loyal customer following, one that sees the value in shopping not only with a company, but also with a neighbor and a caring member of the community. ❖

Photo by Rod Reilly

Price Cutter's produce department is the next best thing to a summertime stroll through a farmers market. You'll find a wide selection of deeply colored, fiber-rich produce with more than five hundred different fresh fruits and vegetables in stock daily. When available, Price Cutter is proud to carry fruits and vegetables from local farmers, such as Missouri homegrown cantaloupe and peaches and Arkansas tomatoes.

Kimberly Varhalla practices her serve in one of Phelps Grove Park's eight courts. Several times each year, runners throng to the Park for the many charitable running events that are held here. The park is just one amenity of this neighborhood, which boasts of an eclectic mix of long-term residents and university students. Together, these groups make Phelps Grove a place where vitality is appreciated but calm reigns. ❖

Photo by Thomas S. England

The quaint beauty of Phelps Grove Park makes it a popular choice for outdoor enjoyment in Springfield. Encompassing forty-four acres, the park offers picnic areas, a walking and fitness trail, a rose garden, tennis courts, and a wading pool for pre-schoolers and parents.❖

SPRINGFIELD-GREENE COUNTY PARKS DEPARTMENT: A BLOSSOMING FUTURE

Growing seasons are normally determined by climate and location, but the growing season for the Springfield–Greene County Parks Department seems to stretch in an unbroken line into a blossoming future.

The department has a long and interesting past. Springfield's first two parks—Washington and Lafayette—were platted in 1869. The Park Board was established in 1913 and purchased its first property, Grant Beach Park, in 1914. Currently the department oversees ninety facilities with a total area of over 3,000 acres. However, it is the future that will be amazing.

Seven major projects are in various

Springfield–Greene County Parks Department is committed to the goal of building a safe, accessible, comprehensive system of parks.

stages of planning and completion. Perhaps the most ambitious is the proposed Botanical Center located at Nathanael Greene/Close Memorial Park and Gardens on South Scenic. "The nineteen-thousand-square-foot center will be built on top of the vista overlooking Drummond Lake, the arboretum, and the flower gardens that grace the south side of the park," said Jodie Adams, director of parks. "Its main role will be educational, and it will be home to the University of Missouri Extension Center as well as housing some Park Board offices."

Friends of the Garden, a local nonprofit group, has been working with the

◄ *For an hour or an afternoon, "Wednesdays at Noon" in Founders Park provide a welcome respite from the office or simply a great way to enjoy the outdoors. Local groups provide live music and performances during the summer months.*

Extension Office and the Parks Department to make this dream a reality. The facility will be a "green building" with construction due to begin within the next five years.

"Rutledge-Wilson Park is destined to be one of our park system's jewels," said Adams. "It's a very ambitious project for us, but when finished, it will encompass more than 207 acres in west Springfield and will be a live demonstration farm with outdoor classrooms and a renovated early 1900s farmhouse. The Ozarks Greenways trail system will run through the park, connecting with Jordan Valley Park and the Wilson's Creek National Battlefield."

North of Springfield another metropolitan park is being developed on property formerly owned by the Jack Owen family. "The 143-acre Lost Hill Park will be a nature reserve area," Adams explained. "The purchase of this property came about through the direct citizen input into our Vision 20/20 plan. The property, with its unique archaeological features, will serve as a trailhead for the South Dry Sac Trail that will wind from Ritter Springs to Valley Water Mill Park." Lost Hill is projected to open in 2007.

Valley Water Mill Park, through a partnership with City Utilities and the Watershed Committee of the Ozarks, will be managed by the parks department. The focal point will be a watershed center for water-quality study, research, and public education. Within this unique park, nature trails, streams, and lake-side learning centers, will be developed. An additional highlight will be the Valley Water Mill Equestrian Center, located on the former Wilkie Farm adjacent to the park.

Continued on page 114

Photo by Scott Indermaur

It starts in parks! Galloway ► Trail, which is part of Springfield's Linear Park Trail System, winds through Sequiota Park. It is a great way to spend a day enjoying good weather. The trails provide opportunities for people of all ages and abilities to walk, bike, run, or skate. The trails are also accessible to wheelchairs.

Photo by Scott Indermaur

Continued from page 113

Canine pet parents will soon have a place to call their own. The Cruse Family Dog Park will be developed at the Old Loren Street Landfill on West Catalpa. Several years ago a citizens' group started working with the Park Board to develop the canine park. A donation from the Cruse Family Foundation added significantly to the group's annual fund-raising efforts, which include the Bark in the Park, Dog Swim, and Dog Festival. Construction is anticipated to begin in 2007.

Renovations are currently under way on the north shore of Lake Springfield Park, for which the Park Board assumed management in 2006. New playground equipment has already been installed, with plans for a boat-house marina with kayaks and canoes for rent. Visitors can fish from the shoreline for bass, crappie, and bluegill.

Due to the public support for a countywide parks referendum in 2006, renovations derived from a citizens' master plan are scheduled for area pools and lakes, including Sequiota Park. In the plan is a new aquatic center at the Doling Family Center as well as ten new school-parks. With the addition of the ten school-parks, there will be a total of twenty completed. The public schools use the parks during the day, and the Park Board provides after-school programs at each of the school-parks.

▲ Ranked four and a half stars out of five and a Top 5 Missouri Public Course by Golf Digest magazine, Rivercut is the crown jewel of the Springfield–Greene County Park Board's public courses. Golfers of all skill levels can enjoy this 7,066-yard par-72 track.

Remember the wonders of ▶ summer camp? Each summer the Springfield–Greene County Park Board offers memory-making days at Ritter Springs Day Camp. Sessions offer numerous daily activities to engage young minds and promote lasting friendships.

hoto by Scott Indermaur

*◄ Senior water aerobics
programs are just one of
the many fitness and
activity classes to be found
at Chesterfield and
Doling Family Centers.
Chesterfield's Aquatic Center
offers zero-depth entry,
a one-hundred-foot water
slide, resistance walk,
whirlpool, and child's area.
Members of all ages will
find many ways to exercise
and enjoy the process of
staying healthy.*

Photo by Scott Indermaur

With unique park system elements—
including the Mizumoto Japanese Stroll Garden
in Nathanael Greene/Close Memorial Park, the
Dickerson Park Zoo, the Jordan Valley Ice Park,
the state-of-the-art indoor/outdoor Cooper
Tennis Complex, the Connie Morris Golf
Learning Center at Rivercut Golf Course, the
Railroad History Museum in Grant Beach Park,
and an indoor-outdoor skate park—it is clear
that the National Gold Medal Award–winning
Springfield–Greene County Parks Department is
committed to the goal of building a safe, accessible, comprehensive system of parks, trails,
and open space that enhance the quality of life,
preserve land, and connect the people and
communities of the area now and for the
not-so-distant future. ❖

*Splish-splash! It's better than ▶
taking a bath. An area youth
enjoys a great day for a swim
at Fassnight Park Pool, one
of Springfield's historic
public pools.*

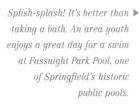

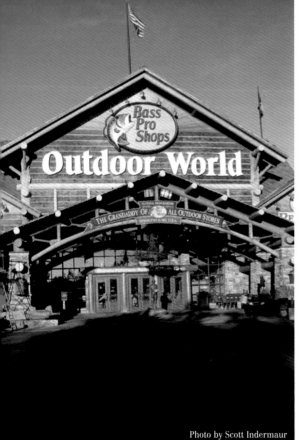

Who would have dreamed that when John L. Morris began making homemade bait and worms in the back of the Brown Derby liquor store, Bass Pro Shops would someday become the world's largest mail-order sporting goods store and the leading supplier of premium outdoor gear—not to mention the most popular tourist destination in Missouri? Construction on the Outdoor World Showroom in Springfield started in 1984 and quickly emerged as such an attraction that the State of Missouri opened the Wonders of Wildlife museum next door. However, even with all its success, Bass Pro Shops maintains its sense of humor. Over the main entrance to the original shop is a sign that proudly proclaims, "Welcome Fishermen, Hunters and Other Liars." ❖

Photo by Thomas S. England

Golfers of all handicaps appreciate the public courses of Springfield–Greene County. A par-3 course offers a fun and quick round, while three 18-hole courses provide more traditional play. From May through October, the fairways and greens in and around Springfield are popular, although some courses are open year-round, weather permitting. ❖

Photo by Thomas S. England

A musical mélange brings out the crowds to the Commercial Street Historic District, the eclectic six-block northern neighborhood of Center City, also known as "C-Street." The Ozark native band Big Smith offers its flavor of tunes—hillbilly rock. During the annual C-Street Jam, music ranging from jazz to indie rock fills the air. Other events throughout the year include a loftwalk and a summer silent film festival. ❖

What better way to celebrate the season than a horse-drawn carriage ride in Park Central Square? The rides, one of many holiday activities in Springfield, are offered weekend evenings throughout December. From caroling and ice skating to concerts and parades, there's a seemingly endless list of happenings in downtown and around the city. ✤

Photo by Scott Indermaur

Building
SPRINGFIELD

Nicknamed "The Birthplace of Route 66," Springfield is the third-largest city in Missouri. Bustling with activity, the downtown area offers live music, theaters, museums, galleries, and a variety of shops and eateries. This city's government respects the past and looks to the future by revitalizing streetscapes with historical lighting and landscaping, and rehabilitating its older buildings and lofts into restaurants, commercial retail, and residential space. Over six thousand parking spaces are available within walking distances of downtown Springfield's many attractions.

Springfield's title as "Missouri's economic engine" is fitting. The city that the Frisco Railroad put on the map is also the city that gave birth to Route 66. From the early years through today, engines of all types have moved people and goods through Springfield and provided the catalyst for a robust economy—one of the fastest growing in the country.

An affordable and stable area in which to do business, Springfield attracts companies in the manufacturing, high-tech, hospitality, financial, health-care, and construction sectors, some with a worldwide presence. Springfield's family-friendly culture also lends itself to family-owned businesses. Entrepreneurs and artists thrive in this city devoid of big-city challenges, and full of opportunity.

The people of Springfield are noted for their work ethic, midwestern sensibility, and fortitude. They understand that economic growth is inextricably linked to a city's appeal, yet they also work as hard to maintain the area's quality of life as they do to make Missouri's economic engine purr. Their spirit creates a near-perfect blend of prosperity and preservation, and it is one of the reasons that Springfield often makes headlines as a top city in which to do business. As often overheard by city leaders, "Everywhere should be like this." ❖

In recent years, businesses, government, organizations, and local artists have come together to build a community that openly expresses its artistic talents. The result, in part, can be seen in the murals found here and there on walls in Springfield's downtown arts district. Located on the east side of Jefferson Street, between McDaniel and Park Central East, is *Friday Morning, 10 AM*, a mural by artist Ellen Schaeffer Baird. More than a dozen murals can be found in the downtown area, complementing the retail shops, restaurants, galleries, coffeehouses, and a host of nightlife amenities. ❖

Throughout Springfield's downtown arts district are vibrant examples of the city's cultural talents, murals that enhance the ambience of the area's galleries and gift shops, cafés and coffee shops, theaters and taverns.

Photo by Scott Indermaur

Photo by Thomas S. England

COMMERCE BANK DELIVERS ON PROMISE TO ASK, LISTEN, AND SOLVE

The Springfield banking landscape has seen much change over the past several years, with mergers, start-up banks, and acquisitions. But the one bank that hasn't changed its strength of position throughout the upheaval is Commerce Bank. Local, Missouri-based Commerce has been the community's solid, steady leader among financial institutions for more than one hundred years.

"Commerce operates a 'super community' bank model," says John Himmel, chairman, Commerce Bank, Springfield Region. "We truly distinguish ourselves with customers in the Ozarks because we're large enough to offer the technology and sophisticated products of a large bank, but small enough to provide highly personalized service." According to Himmel, the bank has an unwavering focus on customer service. In fact, Commerce formally developed a customer promise, simply stated: *ask listen solve*. "Rather than having the mind-set of providing services, Commerce bankers are committed to providing solutions to customers," he says. "We know that any decision involving money—your money—is important. When we truly deliver on our promise to *ask listen solve*, we're doing what's best for our customers, and serving customers best is how we're going to continue to grow in Springfield."

> "Rather than having the mind-set of providing services, Commerce bankers are committed to providing solutions to customers."

◄ *Commerce Bank's Battlefield Banking Center is more than a beautiful building; it serves as the financial institution's regional headquarters, and symbolizes one of Springfield's "best places to work."*

Convenience is also important to customers. Commerce Bank boasts fifteen full-service banking centers in the region, including metro Springfield and neighboring communities Ozark, Nixa, Republic, Willard, Branson, Bolivar, and Lebanon. Additionally, customers enjoy banking statewide and beyond with more than 360 Commerce locations in Missouri, Kansas, Illinois, and Oklahoma.

Aside from a network of convenient branches and ATMs, Commerce works to ensure that banking is simple, quick, and easy for customers. For individuals, that means truly personal banking—making all the financial tools available, such as online banking and bill pay, home loans, home equity loans, checking and savings accounts, credit cards, and investment, trust, and money management services. Each knowledgeable, experienced banker is committed to helping customers make informed choices.

Photo by Eric Francis

Photo by Eric Francis

Students appreciate the ► *convenience of Commerce Bank's MSU campus branch.*

"When we provide convenience, plus the products and services in a highly personalized environment, that's what drives our success," says Robert A. Hammerschmidt Jr., president. "Altogether, we refer to it as providing a positive customer experience. It's all about the customer."

For example, Commerce Bank serves as the official bank on campus at Missouri State University with a full-service banking center and four ATMs. Addressing the university population means helping students and parents alike with responsible banking, borrowing, and money management. Commerce is actively involved with the Plaster Student Union and campus organizations. Plus, the bank has a segment of its Web site dedicated as a learning center, offering information and tools designed for the specialized needs of students and their families. Commerce doesn't just offer its student customers accounts and services, it offers tips and resources on important topics such as how to pay for college,

Continued on page 126

Building Relationships

Commerce Bank

Member FDIC

EQUAL OPPORTUNITY LENDER

Continued from page 125

▲ *Springfield businesses of all sizes rely on Commerce's lending solutions to grow and expand.*

how to budget and manage money, and how to establish and maintain good credit.

For business customers, offering top-notch customer service means developing relationships. That translates to Commerce taking business banking personally. "We believe that a business banker should be a trusted advisor and partner— someone who takes the time to look ahead," Hammerschmidt says. "Our goal is to give customers an advantage with tailored, proactive solutions, to help their business be as successful as it can. By combining technology, expertise, and financial strength, we can provide the right solutions for all of our customers, serve our community, and deliver on our promise of *ask listen solve*." ❖

Young people at the YMCA can ▶ *enjoy the challenge of the climbing wall, thanks in part to Commerce Bank. The YMCA is one of many community organizations that benefits from the bank's philanthropic and volunteer support.*

Photo by Thomas S. England

Chamber staff members Brad Bodenhausen, left, and Sandy Howard, along with Governmental Relations Committee chairman Cliff Davis, meet with Speaker Pro Tem of the Missouri House of Representatives Carl Bearden. The Governmental Relations Committee is a vital and active arm of the Springfield Area Chamber of Commerce. Staff members monitor legislation that will affect businesses, and communicate regularly with legislators to keep them informed of key issues. The chamber also hosts a series of legislative breakfasts, allowing members to network with governmental officials. ❖

Benjamin Franklin Plumbing: If There's Any Delay, It's You We Pay

Kid gloves are not what one would normally associate with plumbing, but then Benjamin Franklin Plumbing is no ordinary company. First, all their plumbers are certified. They arrive on the job site at the appointed time, or Ben Franklin pays the customer five dollars per minute up to a three-hundred-dollar maximum. Ben Franklin customers get pricing up front, and all work comes with a two-year—not a thirty- or sixty-day—guarantee. And that's just the beginning.

Ben Franklin does background checks and drug testing on all employees. "That's out of the ordinary," says owner John Nicholson, "but we're going into peo-

> "People expect a higher standard from us, and we make a point to live up to that," said Nicholson.

ple's homes, and we treat them with respect." Other signs of respect are that all Ben Franklin plumbers are bonded, neat, and well-groomed nonsmokers. They all wear shoe covers while in customers' homes. When the job is complete, they clean up before leaving.

"People expect a higher standard from us, and we make a point to live up to that," said Nicholson. "We know it's working because our top revenue source is return clients and referrals.

"Our second-best source are our five trucks. Each one carries 93 percent of everything we have in stock. It's like a warehouse on wheels, as well as being a moving billboard."

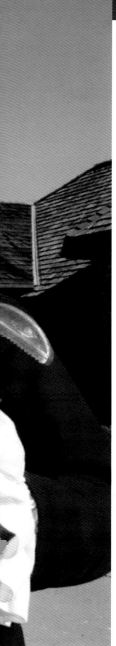

Photo by Alan S. Weiner

◄ *Ben Franklin said, "Do not squander time, for that is the stuff life is made of." John Nicholson, owner of Benjamin Franklin Plumbing, would no doubt agree, since his company is the nation's first plumbing service to promise customers punctuality. The company hires, trains, and cultivates the most talented people and pledges, "If there's any delay, it's you we pay."*

Nicholson ran his own plumbing company in Springfield for seven years before becoming part of the Ben Franklin franchise. "Ellen Rohr, who was president of Ben Franklin at that time, was a friend and a mentor. I always dreamed of working with her, but not every company that wants to buy a franchise is accepted. Only about 1 percent make it. The company has to be established, have a good reputation with the Better Business Bureau, and be financially sound. Employees also have to pass a number of tests before the company gets the OK."

There are approximately 130 dealerships nationwide, and Nicholson's company was number 25. He has been associated with Ben Franklin since 2003.

Becoming a master certified plumber or pipe fitter—as several of the staff are—is no small accomplishment either. It requires passing a six-hour written test, which includes math, drawings, schematics, and mechanical knowledge.

"The staff deserves a lot of credit for our success," said Nicholson. Presently that includes Jeanene Volmert, sales and service director; Marsha Ellingson, customer service representative; Gail Ritter, bookkeeping; Duke Daniel, senior certified plumber; Charles Jeffcoat II, senior certified plumber; Raymond Main, senior licensed plumber; and Richard Delgado, apprentice plumber.

Ben Franklin works hard on the job and in the community. Each year Nicholson participates in the Muscular Dystrophy Lockup, during which he goes to jail and has to raise money for Muscular Dystrophy to be released. The company also takes part in the American Cancer Society Relay for Life, and recently donated all the parts and labor to help build a house for Habitat for Humanity.

Clearly Ben Franklin Plumbing is a top-drawer company all the way. ❖

Photo by Thomas S. England

Skilled, certified plumbers ▶ like Charles Jeffcoat, Richard Delgado, Duke Daniel, Raymond Mann, and John Nicholson, owner of Benjamin Franklin Plumbing, are ready to jump into action, delivering time-critical customer service. Each truck is GPS equipped and fully stocked, which facilitates doing the job efficiently and correctly the first time.

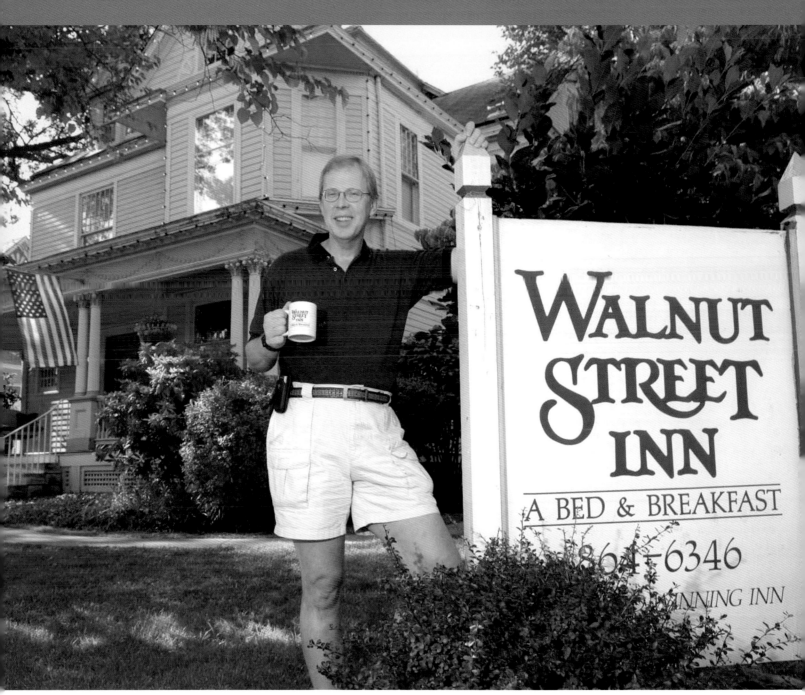

Photo by Thomas S. England

Many guests of the Blankenships' Walnut Street Inn are interested in the story of how Gary and wife Paula went from corporate America to innkeeping. "A lot of people see this as the ideal second job, or as a retirement job, and I encourage that. But I also tell them they must understand what it takes to be successful in the hospitality business. We came into this with our eyes open, having first studied the industry and attended classes and seminars for innkeeping," says Gary. The couple had always been fascinated by historic homes, antiques, and B&Bs, and pounced on the opportunity to blend those interests with a desire to return to Springfield and raise their daughter, Catherine. "We wanted her to know there are other folks in addition to her mom and dad who love her, and we wanted her to get to know her grandparents, aunts, uncles, and cousins." The Walnut Street Inn features twelve guestrooms in three buildings—the main house and carriage house, built in 1894, and one Sears Catalog home built in 1906. Being ideally located in the center of town, just blocks from Park Central Square and from the Springfield Cardinals baseball field, is an added attraction. "There's a lot to do close by, which makes it a great place for our guests, but also a great place for us to live, too." ❖

The candy business must be fun, because who could frown while buying sweets, especially confections such as nut clusters from the Candy House, being sold here by Anna Fisher. The original shop in Joplin, Missouri, opened for business in 1970, and today (with two locations in Joplin and two in Springfield) it enjoys nationwide fame for its hand-dipped chocolates. In 2004, owners Terry and Pat Hicklin opened the Candy House Chocolate Factory—a production facility that allows visitors to watch the creation of candies that are almost too beautiful to eat. Offering goodies from a mouthwatering assortment of chocolate kids' molds to chocolate-covered Oreos to English Toffee, it's no wonder that the Candy House's bite-sized truffles come with a warning: "Beware—taste buds will never forget the experience of fresh, heavy cream." ❖

Photo by Lisa Means

Photo by Lisa Means

HUSCH & EPPENBERGER: CONFIDENCE CLIENTS EXPECT

Clients come to law firms for many reasons, all of which require the utmost trust between attorney and client — the kind of trust built by serving a community for years. Husch & Eppenberger delivers this promise of trust to its clients. The firm is the successor to the esteemed Springfield law firms of Farrington & Curtis, founded in 1926, and Greene & Curtis, founded in 1975.

In 1997 the partners of Farrington & Curtis joined Husch & Eppenberger. In 2002 the partners of Greene & Curtis followed. "Being affiliated with a major regional law firm means we can offer a higher level of sophistication and expertise," said Gary Powell, who serves as the Springfield representative to Husch's Management Committee.

> "Being affiliated with a major regional law firm means we can offer a higher level of sophistication and expertise."

For more than eighty years, the firm has served the legal needs of businesses and individuals in Springfield, Branson, Joplin, and other Southwest Missouri communities.

Husch employs more than three hundred attorneys in St. Louis, Kansas City, Jefferson City, and of course, Springfield. Husch also has offices in Peoria, Illinois, and Chattanooga, Memphis, and Nashville, Tennessee.

"A good example of ways we are able to serve clients occurred when one of our major retailers was opening a store in Tennessee. We were able to handle that transaction smoothly through our Springfield and Memphis offices," Powell explained.

That same kind of efficiency also works on an international basis. "We are a

◄ *(Left to right) Attorneys Chuck Greene (sitting), Chris Greene, Joe Greene (sitting), Gary Powell, and Bill Hart from Husch & Eppenberger review plans for a major developer in Springfield.*

member—in fact, the only member in Missouri—of TerraLex, a worldwide network of lawyers. One of our Springfield clients was opening up markets in China and asked us to recommend a law firm there. A quick check of the directory, and I was able to put him in touch with a member firm in China," explained Powell.

The list of services Husch provides is impressive, including the formation of corporations, partnerships, and limited liability companies; mergers and reorganizations; acquisitions and sales of businesses; real estate transactions and development; executive compensation planning; retirement plans; lease transactions; joint ventures; buy-sell agreements; loan transactions; representation in commercial litigation; real estate disputes; planning and zoning disputes; employment matters; personal injury and product liability claims against its clients; shareholder disputes; will and trust disputes; bankruptcy and insolvency matters; estate planning; probate and trust services; and business succession planning.

"Husch has always been a vital part of Springfield, and many partners serve on community boards. At one time in the past, we simultaneously had one partner serving as the chairman of the Greene County Republican Party and another serving as chairman of the Democratic Party," said Powell.

Another indication of Husch's commitment to the community is the firm's inclusion among the Top 200 law firms dedicated to providing pro bono legal services for people who could not otherwise afford them.

With Husch in their backyard, clients in the Springfield area have a large, full-service law firm that can handle all of their legal needs. ❖

Photo by Rod Reilly

Photo by Rod Reilly

(Left to right) Link Knauer, ▶ ...ger Gooch, and Bryan Wade, all attorneys from Husch & Eppenberger, strategize to accomplish the goals of the client.

Photo by Rod Reilly

Since 1979, the Greater Springfield Farmers Market has brought fresh produce, locally grown meats, homemade foods and crafts, homegrown plants and flowers, and a variety of goods to the people of Springfield. Located in a parking lot at Battlefield Mall, the market is open Tuesday, Thursday, and Saturday throughout the growing season. Above, Pam M. Coticchio from Jensen Gardens in Ozark, Missouri, freshens some of the bouquets she sells in addition to chemical- and pesticide-free fruits and vegetables. Left, Suzanne Miller of Springfield looks over the produce at one of the more than ninety vendor booths that regularly participate in the farmers market. ❖

TelComm Credit Union: People Helping People

With five locations and a strong presence in southern Missouri, TelComm Credit Union is committed to using leading technology to stay ahead of members' needs; offer progressive, competitive, and convenient products; and prove that caring, personal service is not just a trend. It's a tradition!

Jacques Sachs, a fifty-three-year volunteer on the Board of Directors, elaborates, "TelComm offers you, as a member-owner, the opportunity to pay yourself first and become financially sound through your own efforts, using our methods."

Simply put, TelComm is an organization committed to its members' best interests. One example is Excess Share Insurance, through which TelComm provides additional deposit insurance up to $350,000 on savings accounts (up to $500,000 for IRA accounts). TelComm is the only area financial institution awarded the privilege of providing this benefit after having submitted to an extensive voluntary financial audit.

TelComm firmly believes financial education starts at home, so they sponsor the Kirby Kangaroo Club to assist families in teaching children from birth to twelve how to develop prudent savings and spending habits.

> "TelComm offers you, as a member-owner, the opportunity to pay yourself first and become financially sound through your own efforts, using our methods."

◄ Carolyn and Charles Bauer are all smiles as they accept the keys to their new home from Tara New, one of the mortgage specialists at TelComm Credit Union. The Bauers are now member/homeowners with all the advantages that membership offers. Because credit unions are not-for-profit, they exist only to serve their membership, which means higher dividends on savings and lower rates on loans. No wonder the Bauers are smiling.

TelComm member-owners have the opportunity to share in the many benefits it extends to its membership, such as lower loan rates, higher return on savings, convenient services, and financial education. In addition, Benefits Plus is a worldwide program that offers benefits such as discounted air travel, vacations, cruises, car rentals, hotels, long-distance phone service, grocery coupons, and much more.

A not-for-profit, member-owned financial institution, TelComm was founded in 1940 to serve the financial needs of Southwestern Bell employees. Over the years, TelComm's membership base has expanded to include anyone who lives or works within the 417 area code. Today, TelComm has grown into an organization of more than fourteen thousand members, with assets approaching $70 million. A full range of products and services including checking, savings, loans, mortgages, home equity loans, direct deposit, nationwide ATM network, and online banking and bill pay are available. Numerous local businesses (and new businesses opening within the Southwest Missouri area) already offer TelComm's services to their employees as a valuable, no-cost benefit.

Perhaps TelComm's greatest asset is its crew of friendly, helpful professionals who treat members like extended family. Members expect an old-fashioned level of service and a sense of familiarity at TelComm. From a cheery greeting to a perfectly suited product, members know their financial matters will be handled with courtesy, confidentiality, and efficiency.

"We strive to be good stewards in the community," said president Don Ackerman. "Every year we donate staff time, money, and resources for the Credit Union for Kids golf tournament benefiting Children's Miracle Network, and our family of volunteers also works cooperatively with United Way and Consumer Credit Counseling. We believe those actions set our credit union apart from other local financial institutions. TelComm is about people helping people." ❖

Photo by Lisa Means

Photo by Thomas S. England

Throughout the year, ► TelComm Credit Union employees volunteer with a number of different charities in the 417 area code. Sometimes their efforts are directed to fund-raising activities; at other times, the contribution is more hands-on, such as sorting donations at the Family Violence Center. TelComm's goal at all times is to serve the underserved.

First formed in 1959 with three officers and an equal number of dogs, the Springfield Police Department's K9 unit operated for twenty years before coming to an end. In 1994, the unit was formed for a second time, recording over ninety thousand service calls in the first year it was brought back. Today, the unit is part of the Operations Division, which is the largest and most visible division in the department. Typically five dogs, paired with five officers, make up the K9 unit. The teams undergo extensive training before entering field service, which includes training in both patrol and narcotics policies and procedures. The department's dogs are trained to track and apprehend criminals, search for evidence in buildings and high-risk situations, and tolerate gun battle and felony stop incidences. As part of their rigorous training, the department's police dogs are trained to grab and hold suspects until the officer gives a release command. ❖

Photo by Eric Francis

Officers Chris Kahmke (left) and Rick Noble (right) are "Bike Cops," members of a unit of the Springfield Police Department that serves Missouri State University and a large portion of the Phelps Grove neighborhood. Based out of a substation on the university campus, these bike riding officers have earned a reputation as problem solvers for their implementation of a community-based approach to policing. By working as a team with residents and government, the bicycle patrol has helped the neighborhood rid itself of many of its chronic issues and concerns. ✤

LATHROP & GAGE L.C.: STEEPED IN LOCAL HISTORY

Lathrop & Gage L.C. is a national firm steeped in the rich history of Missouri and the Midwest. While it offers the depth and strength of a national firm, it is well-known for its regional midwestern values. Founded in 1873, it is the oldest law firm west of the Mississippi River; the firm is honored that it still represents its very first client, now known as BNSF Railway Co., more than 125 years later.

Lathrop & Gage is committed to providing the highest level of client service and to giving back to the Springfield community.

"We have had the unique opportunity to work with many of our city's leading

> "We have had the unique opportunity to work with many of our city's leading companies," said Frank Evans, partner in charge.

companies," said Frank Evans, partner in charge.

The Springfield office opened in March 1998 and later merged with Miller & Sanford and Cunningham, Harpool & Cordonnier. It now has twenty lawyers providing legal expertise in corporate and general business, intellectual property, wealth strategies, litigation, health care, and labor and employment. Attorneys include Gary Cunningham, a Fellow in the American College of Trial Lawyers, and four other lawyers listed in the latest edition of *The Best Lawyers in America*: Michael Cordonnier, Evans, Dan Nelson, and Randell Wallace.

A partial list of the firm's clients

◄ Neil Guion (right) installs floor joists at a Habitat for Humanity construction site with the help of volunteer Dave Whitson. Guion, an attorney at Lathrop & Gage, is president of Habitat for Humanity of Springfield, Missouri, Inc.

includes Daimler-Chrysler, the City of Springfield, the City of Branson, St. John's Health System, Willow Brook Foods, Great Southern Bank, Ramey Price Cutter Supermarkets, BKD, LLP, City Utilities, O'Reilly Auto Parts, Paul Mueller Company, and Springfield Underground.

Along with its reputation for hard work and high achievement, a hallmark of Lathrop & Gage is a deep desire to give back to the community and help those less fortunate. Pro bono legal service is a major part of the firm's efforts, as is charitable giving.

Throughout the years, members of the firm have taught classes at local universities and served in a variety of city, state, and federal governmental positions. Lathrop & Gage attorneys participate in numerous local and regional charitable and civic organizations, and the firm boasts two former chairmen of the Springfield Area Chamber of Commerce, Evans and Wallace.

Lathrop & Gage attorneys have ties to the following service organizations in Springfield: Community Blood Center, Habitat for Humanity, the Chamber of Commerce, Legal Aid, Regional Girls' Shelter, Rotary Clubs, Boys & Girls Town, Ronald McDonald House Charities, Hospice Foundation of the Ozarks, Court Appointed Special Advocates, the Optimist Club, the Council of Churches, and the Kitchen, Inc.

"We're very proud of our commitment to Springfield," Evans said, "and to projects and organizations that make our city an even better place to live and work. We actively seek out projects that allow all of our personnel to contribute directly to the community. We strive to put our work and our words into action." ❖

Photo by Rod Reilly

Lathrop & Gage's Randell ▶ Wallace poses with a statue in Beijing's Forbidden City. As the 2005 chairman of the Springfield Area Chamber of Commerce, Wallace led the city's first official trade mission to China.

Photo by Eric Francis

Over on Walnut Street is a place that immerses visitors in the works of local and national artists: Hawthorn Gallery, a showcase of art in a variety of media ranging from photos and fibers to jewelry and glass to paintings and pots. In addition to being open year-round for art enthusiasts looking for that special piece, the gallery's exhibits provide the perfect backdrop for private gatherings. Hawthorn Galleries also provides consultation services for both home and office. Carol Adams, who oversees the business, keeps the gallery in tip-top shape for visitors. ❖

Wedding bells, wedding rings, the Wedding March from Lohengrin; what would weddings be without tradition? Little girls dream of walking down the aisle in a beautiful white dress, but in this case the dream wasn't just wearing a wedding dress, it was owning a wedding boutique and offering an exclusive collection of designer gowns. Stephanie Weiss owns Ella Weiss Wedding Design, which is named for her grandmother. "She was the epitome of feminine style. She was never seen without her heels, but she was undeniably strong. Feminine, strong, and timeless, that's what Ella Weiss is all about." Apparently bride Emma Hopkins agrees, as she tries to choose from the many beautiful creations. ❖

Photo by Eric Francis

GUARANTY BANK: SPRINGFIELD'S HOMETOWN BANK

It is unusual to think of a company coming of age when it is already ninety-four years old. However, that is exactly the transition Guaranty Bank has been going through since 2003.

"We started in 1913 as Guaranty Savings & Loan Association, and for over ninety years we've been Springfield's hometown bank catering mainly to residential customers," said Shaun Burke, Guaranty CEO. "With our progressive, forward-thinking staff, our recent growth, and our name change, we've broadened our vision. We are a full-service bank that offers corporate small businesses the same one-on-one service our retail customers rely on. Ninety-four years of experience and an unparalleled product mix combined with our relationship-driven approach ensure a consistency our customers demand."

Guaranty Federal Bancshares, Inc., the parent company of Guaranty Bank, is publicly traded and listed on NASDAQ. "As a publicly traded entity we have access to liquidity and capital for growth over the next ninety-four years. Headquartered in Springfield, all our decisions are made locally. We have a history here. We know our customers and our community, and we can act quickly."

A prime example of Guaranty's new vision and focus is its involvement in the revitalization of downtown Springfield. Guaranty has provided over $30 million in financing for downtown renovation. Projects include the one-hundred-thousand-square-foot Wilhoit Building, built in 1920, and the Gillioz Theatre, built in 1926. Originally the largest office space in Springfield, the new Wilhoit Plaza now includes commercial space for restaurants and shops and thirty-two loft apartments. It is Springfield's first multi-use lifestyle center, which exemplifies the exciting changes in the Springfield community.

After extensive restoration, the Gillioz Theatre reopened in 2006, with a new addition housing an arts center. "We're excited about our involvement in providing the downtown area with a new lease on life," said Burke.

Photo by Eric Francis

▲ *Guaranty Bank has been part of the development of Springfield since 1913. Bank personnel Shelley Evans and Dana Elwell are proud to be part of the bank's growth and vision, which continue through its strong emphasis on the construction and commercial real estate industry.*

"With our progressive, forward-thinking staff, our recent growth, and our name change, we've broadened our vision."

As a community bank Guaranty's commitment to the future is not just providing banking services. Looking to the Future—Investing in Our Community is prominently displayed in the corporate headquarters. This philosophy signifies the bank's renewed focus on community involvement. Guaranty staff members passionately serve a number of nonprofit groups and donate thousands of volunteer hours each year. Guaranty Bank has been the lead corporate sponsor and one of the top fund-raisers for the American Cancer Society's local Relay for Life event for the past several years. Staff members proudly serve organizations such as Ozarks Literacy Council, Big Brothers/Big Sisters of the Ozarks, Families for Children, March of Dimes, and United Way of the Ozarks, just to name a few.

For nearly a century Guaranty has served the Springfield community. Guaranty Bank's commitment to its motto "Strength, Growth, Vision" will be instrumental in the growth of the Springfield area for at least the next ninety-four years. Member FDIC. ❖

Photo by Eric Francis

When the Gillioz Theatre, ▶ which originally opened in 1926, reopened in 2006, Guaranty Bank saw its name displayed in recognition of financing the bank provided for the extensive restoration. Bank personnel Shaun Burke and Becky Scorse proudly [sta]nd under the new marquee with a group that was [in]volved in the project. When the theatre first opened, it [w]as the largest and finest in Southwest Missouri. [T]oday the Gillioz is again the community asset it once [w]as—bringing theatre, music, [a]nd arts back to Springfield's downtown.

Photo by Scott Indermaur

"The Frisco put Springfield on the map," says Al Weaver, a volunteer at the Railroad Historical Museum. Weaver should know. He's a retired railroader who began his career working on the St. Louis–San Francisco Railroad, aka "The Frisco," as a young man still in his teens. "When I was young, I lived right by the track, and I knew I wanted to be a locomotive engineer. At seventeen, I was big enough to get in the fire boxes, so they hired me for that job," he says. From there, Weaver was promoted to engineer, where he stayed until the late 1950s when the diesel engine eclipsed the old steam engine. Today, Weaver, who is one of only six of the original steam engineers in the Springfield area still living, enjoys keeping the steam engine "alive" by sharing his knowledge at the museum. Dedicated to the preservation of railroad history, the museum is located in Grant Beach Park in an actual locomotive—the St. Louis–San Francisco 4524. Children and adults can explore the Frisco 4524, the Burlington baggage car, the Chicago and Northwestern commuter car, and the Northern caboose. Free to the public and open on Saturday afternoons from May through October, the museum is a Springfield treasure. ❖

Photo by Scott Indermaur

Megan Hensley, an MSU photography student, readies her photos for display at Well Fed Head Books—one of the area merchants that regularly participates in the First Friday Art Walk, a monthly art event sponsored by the Springfield Regional Arts Council. Megan, whose love for her creative medium emerged when she took photography classes in high school, specializes in still life. "I love being able to create a separate reality—of making stories with objects and giving a little bit more attention to ordinary objects that most people don't pay attention to," she says. Works from emerging artists like Megan, as well as established area artists, are featured in the galleries, studios, and shops in Springfield's Center City district. It's one of the elements of a successful downtown revival, according to Beth Buczynski, owner of Well Fed Head Books. "When we opened our store in 2002, we didn't want to be just a great place to buy books, but also a part of the cultural community. Supporting the creative goes hand in hand with the literary arts." ❖

Photo by Scott Indermaur

BNSF Railway: Moving the Goods That Connect the World

America's expansion into the Midwest and West would not have been possible without the development of the railroad. As various transcontinental lines wove across the heart of the country to the Pacific Coast, they moved the people, raw goods, and finished products that not only built a nation, but eventually a world power.

Many of those lines remain in operation today, including the BNSF Railway Company, the product of the merger or acquisition of some 390 different railroad lines during the last 150 years.

One of those lines was established in Springfield in 1870, an extension of a rail route intended to run from St. Louis to San Francisco. Known as the St. Louis–San Francisco Railway Company, or "Frisco," the line never reached its West Coast destination, but it did become an important part of the mid-South economy, eventually reaching Florida's Gulf Coast, western Oklahoma, and Texas. Thanks to the Frisco, Springfield developed into a busy and important rail hub.

It remains so today. In 1980, the Frisco merged with the Burlington Northern Railroad, which in turn merged with the Santa Fe Railway in 1995 to become BNSF Railway. BNSF is a major contributor to Springfield's economy. With the same pioneering spirit and innovative

Just as BNSF's predecessors were building a nation, today the railway is investing and working to expand Springfield's connections to the global marketplace.

◄ Springfield is an important rail hub for BNSF, with an average of fifty trains per day passing through the city en route to Kansas City, Memphis, St. Louis, and Tulsa.

thinking that established the railroad, BNSF continues to safely and efficiently transport the products and materials that enrich our lives: consumer goods, new automobiles, grain and other food products, the coal used to generate our electricity, even the materials used to build new homes and to print newspapers and magazines.

Just as BNSF's predecessors were building a nation, today the railway is investing and working to expand Springfield's connections to the global marketplace. Serving all major ports on the West Coast and Gulf of Mexico, the railway's land-bridge container trains allow the easy transfer of products between the United States, Asia, and Europe. A state-of-the-art, football-field-sized, data-driven Network Operations Center keeps track of all cars and their goods.

And behind the machines and the technology are a team of highly skilled, progressive, and enthusiastic people charged with the mission to keep it all running smoothly and efficiently.

In Springfield, BNSF serves more than 180 customers, with principal routes running from Kansas City through Springfield on to Memphis and various points throughout the Southeast, and from St. Louis through Springfield on to Tulsa, and various points throughout Texas and the Southwest. Not counting the coal trains that serve City Utilities, in 2005 local customers shipped or received nearly eighty-four hundred railcars of goods. That's the equivalent of more than twenty thousand truckloads of freight, only at a lower cost and with a greatly reduced impact on the environment. And as a major regional employer, BNSF provides over nine hundred of the best-paying jobs in Southwest Missouri, with an average annual wage of sixty-five thousand dollars.

No doubt BNSF has evolved into one of the country's most technologically advanced and efficient transportation companies. But one thing hasn't changed from those early days: the railway's unwavering commitment to its core values to celebrate its rich heritage and build on its success as it shapes a promising future. ❖

Photo by Lisa Means

Photo by Lisa Means

BNSF employs nearly one thousand ► people in the Springfield area and is the economic source of many additional Springfield jobs provided by BNSF contractors, such as the rail welding complex.

Gay Ross, above, knows she'll always find treasures at Galloway Village, where she is a co-owner of one of the Village's businesses. Once a quaint town in the 1800s, the area bounded by Republic and Battlefield roads now is hopping with shoppers who wander along South Lone Pine Avenue through the eclectic collection of renovated shops. Poke your head in the Rabbit Patch, a gift shop that delights the senses with everything from fragrant candles to soft, fuzzy stuffed animals. For your four-legged friends, stop by the Gourmet Paw Bakery and Flea Market, where you can pick up presents for Pooch, including fresh-baked treats and pet accessories. When the craving for the creative inspires you, make your way to Firehouse Pottery. At right, Kimberly Nicole and Martha Andrews paint their own ceramics. ✤

Photo by Alan S. Weiner

There's shopping, and then there's bargain shopping, best done sans list and sans watch, because you just never know what you'll find when you have an open mind and plenty of time.

Photo by Alan S. Weiner

Photo by Alan S. Weiner

"I think if you're very proud of the company you work for, that pride extends out. Everyone here wants to do quality work," says Karen Scherar, one of the company's long-standing employees. Baymont Inn and Suites, Springfield, Missouri, is one example of the type of work of which the company can be proud.

LARRY SNYDER & COMPANY: EXPERIENCE, QUALITY, AND SERVICE

If it's true that a commercial general contractor is only as good as the last project, then Larry Snyder & Company is that good. Nearly 80 percent of the company's projects are a result of repeat business with existing customers. And that's exactly how founder and CEO Larry Snyder likes it.

"We've not only been building major projects since 1978, we've been building relationships," says Snyder. "Our design/build process is based on trust between the company and the owner of the property. Our experience in the industry, our qualified employees, and the subcontractors we work with all combine to increase efficiencies, keep within budget, and keep quality high." Today the company Snyder founded is a leader in commercial and industrial construction with clients throughout the Midwest and southern states. Areas of expertise include commercial and retail, industrial, multifamily housing, vacation resorts, hotels, and site development work. In the Springfield area, for example, Larry Snyder & Company built Baymont Inn and Suites, and Ozark West Elementary School. In Branson, projects range from Meeks Lumber Yard to the Palace View Resorts. In Oklahoma, LS & C Development

> "We've not only been building major projects since 1978, we've been building relationships," says Snyder.

Services, the company's site excavation division, handled the site excavation, and Larry Snyder & Company handled the building of Avondale Estates, a multifamily housing facility in Claremore. The versatile company also completed a historic renovation for the Frisco Senior Apartments in Joplin and constructed the upscale Seaside Resort in Galveston, Texas.

While building in Branson, the company discovered a need to travel with its clients. "We began working for national companies there who wanted us to go into other areas and build for them." Traveling and building where the clients are is one of the elements that distinguishes Larry Snyder & Company from other commercial contractors. While the original reason to travel is rooted in the relationship Larry Snyder & Company develops with its clients, the ultimate outcome is the ability to maintain quality. "We make a commitment to investing in and taking care of our customers so that we always deliver quality projects on time and on budget," says president Bob Keller.

Another distinction of Larry Snyder & Company is the quality and experience of the employees. Karen Scherar,

corporate secretary/treasurer, joined the company within a year of its inception. "Larry's always had a tendency to draw good people," she says. "He's put the management in place." Scherar points out that along with being raised in a construction family, Snyder obtained a degree in marketing/management from Missouri Southern State College, which has helped him assemble a thriving design/build construction organization. In addition, every employee has experience in the industry, most with a specialized degree in construction.

Since the beginning, professionalism has driven Larry Snyder & Company's steady growth. When customers are a priority, and a team approach is employed from the beginning, cost savings are maximized and quality is enhanced. "We handle each and every project with uncompromising attention to detail," says Keller. "We also believe we're the area's most efficient builder, and as such, our capabilities are unlimited." ❖

Photo by Alan S. Weiner

The executive team at one ▶ of the company's projects— Plantation Resort in Branson, Missouri.

Photo by Eric Francis

Donna and Kevin O'Connell and their family own and operate one of the best-kept secrets in Springfield, O'Connell's Center City Grocery. And the best-kept secret about this small, downtown grocery is the deli in the back serving gigantic sandwiches and a "meat and two." Donna, who is from Tennessee, had to explain to customers that meant meat and two vegetables. "They just call it home cooking here," she said. In addition, the grocery sells all locally raised organic beef, organic chicken and eggs, bulk spices, bulk pasta, beer, wine, and alcohol, as well as staples such as milk, bread, and health and beauty aids. "We cater mostly to the folks living or working downtown," said Kevin. Along with separate tables, there is also a communal table where someone like Matt Edwards can usually find a daily newspaper and sometimes someone to share dinner conversation as well. ✤

During the week, Bill Bowler works as branch sales manager for Univar, one of the world's largest chemical distribution companies. On weekends, he tends the lawn and garden of his University Heights home. One of the oldest neighborhoods in Springfield, University Heights appealed to Bill and his wife because of its well-kept homes and convenient location. "Essentially, we're about ten minutes from anywhere in the city." Bill's parents moved to Springfield when he was eleven, and while he's visited many places, he's never considered moving. "This is a great place to visit and an even better place to live," he continues. "I think the values that Springfield and Southwest Missouri people have are what makes it so attractive. And since we're essentially a college town, we've evolved into a service community. That keeps things diverse and interesting." ✤

Photo by Eric Francis

Clients like Springfield Underground appreciate BKD's personalized and personable advisement services. (Left to right) BKD partner Charles Rodgers, Springfield Underground president Louis Griesemer, Springfield Underground CFO Sam Cox, Springfield Underground vice president John Griesemer, and BKD Wealth Advisors office director Randy Saul are shown in the company's underground facility.

THE BKD EXPERIENCE: UNMATCHED CLIENT SERVICE

As the CPA and financial advisory firm of choice for growing companies and high-net-worth individuals, BKD, LLP knows what it takes to invest wisely, enhance value, and grow a bottom line. BKD knows the bottom line is about more than just numbers. It's about consulting with an independent, principled, and savvy advisor personally committed to helping clients reach their financial goals.

Established in 1923 in Joplin, Missouri, BKD has grown into one of the country's top-ten-largest CPA and advisory firms. With headquarters in Springfield's Hammons Tower, the firm supports more

> "Our firm's highly specialized professionals dedicate themselves not only to specific industries, but also to strategic areas within those industries."

than 1,600 personnel, including approximately 220 partners and principals, located in twenty-seven offices in Arkansas, Colorado, Illinois, Indiana, Kansas, Kentucky, Missouri, Nebraska, Ohio, Oklahoma, and Texas.

BKD delivers its expertise to thousands of clients in a wide spectrum of industries, including health care, manufacturing and distribution, financial services, construction, real estate, not-for-profits, and government entities, to name a few. A member of the Public Company Accounting Oversight Board, BKD audits Securities and Exchange Commission (SEC) registrants and performs

Continued on page 158

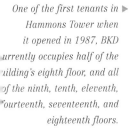

One of the first tenants in ▶
Hammons Tower when
it opened in 1987, BKD
currently occupies half of the
building's eighth floor, and all
of the ninth, tenth, eleventh,
fourteenth, seventeenth, and
eighteenth floors.

Photo by Thomas S. England

Photo by Lisa Means

Continued from page 156

consulting services for a diverse range of SEC-registered companies. BKD's foundation values of passion, respect, integrity, discipline, and excellence have evolved into a client-service philosophy based on five core principles: Integrity First, True Expertise, Professional Demeanor, Responsive Reliability, and Principled Innovation. Together these principles make up what the firm calls the BKD Experience, the goals and standards that govern every client relationship.

"We all believe firmly in these principles," says Springfield partner-in-charge John E. Wanamaker. "As a hands-on, service-oriented firm, we have to be responsive when a client calls. That call usually means the client has a significant, immediate need, and it's our job to provide a timely solution."

BKD's industry niche expertise is another hallmark of the firm's unmatched client service. "When we work with a hospital client, we know they need more than just auditing services," Wanamaker continues. "They need someone who can also provide reimbursement advice and strategic consulting services. Our firm's highly specialized professionals dedicate themselves not only to specific industries, but also to strategic areas within those industries."

Several firmwide service niches whose central administrative operations are based in Springfield are an integral part of BKD's advisory practice:

BKD Risk Management Group

Clients who require independent, objective evaluations of their risk management, internal control, and corporate

▲ Representatives from BKD's Risk Management and Technology division visit Convoy of Hope to discuss the disaster relief organization's Mobile Command Center. Business continuity and disaster recovery planning is one of several information technology consulting services the firm provides to its clients. (left to right) BKD Risk Management and Technology operations manager Tod Eastlake, Convoy of Hope U.S. Disaster Response director Kary Kingsland, and BKD Risk Management and Technology partner-in-charge Mike Burlew.

governance processes rely on the expertise of BKD Risk Management Group. This dedicated group helps public and privately held companies gain stakeholder trust and confidence with internal audits, Sarbanes-Oxley compliance consulting, loan reviews, and SAS 70 examinations, as well as information security services to help mitigate risk such as information technology reviews, business continuity and disaster recovery planning, network penetration testing, and social engineering.

BKD Technologies

The outgrowth of years of information technology support that BKD's accounting advisors gave to hundreds of clients, this division is now an authorized reseller of market-leading business application software. BKD Technologies also assists clients with software selection, implementation, training, and ongoing support.

Forensics and Dispute Consulting

Another firmwide initiative with a presence in Springfield, BKD's Forensics and Dispute Consulting division provides litigation support services to law firms throughout the country. Areas of expertise include financial fraud investigations, expert testimony and consultation, strategic insolvency and bankruptcy, business valuations, and computer forensics. This division supports dozens of

industry and service resource people, consulting attorneys, forensic accountants, certified fraud examiners, certified valuations professionals, and other litigation services consultants familiar with courtroom testimony and the forensics needs of attorneys. The division even offers professional mediation and arbitration services to settle disputes out of court.

Continued on page 160

◀ *Jeff Roberts, senior managing consultant, and Angela Morelock, partner with BKD's Forensics and Dispute Consulting division, provide expert testimony and litigation support services for law firms throughout the country. They specialize in fraud, economic damages, and computer forensics.*

Photo by Lisa Means

Continued from page 159

BKD Corporate Finance, LLC

A wholly owned subsidiary of BKD, LLP, BKD Corporate Finance, LLC helps clients in diverse industries navigate the complex world of mergers and acquisitions. When the time is right to transition their businesses to new owners, these companies rely on BKD Corporate Finance to thoroughly analyze market value and capital market conditions. Corporate finance professionals have managed the sale process of hundreds of companies to national and international buyers to achieve higher values for their clients.

BKD Wealth Advisors, LLC

BKD Wealth Advisors, LLC is another wholly owned BKD subsidiary, and assists high-net-worth families in managing their wealth. BKD Wealth Advisors, LLC is an investment advisory firm registered with the SEC to provide investment management, and financial and estate planning through the firm's WealthPlan services. WealthPlan is an integrated suite of services that combines tax, estate, retirement, financial, and investment planning backed by the insight, vision, and experience of BKD's professional advisors.

Photo by Alan S. Weiner

Photo by Thomas S. England

▲ *Vice president of BKD Corporate Finance Patrick Hayes and senior financial analyst Jason Corson confer on a merger while riding on the company plane. With BKD encompassing twenty-seven offices in eleven different states, the plane allows partners to quickly respond to any client need.*

◄ *BKD Wealth Advisors are active participants in a variety of Springfield's cultural events, including the Springfield Symphony. (Left to right) Senior managing advisor Shari Hoffman, director of investment services and senior managing advisor Jeff Layman, Springfield Symphony music director Ron Spigelman, senior managing advisor Jill Reynolds, staff advisor Chad Tillery, portfolio manager Jeffrey Gann, and office director Randy Saul.*

The BKD Experience

Uniting each of BKD's specialized services is an unwavering commitment to a key BKD Experience principle: Integrity First. Offering solutions that are innovative, practical, timely, affordable, and above all ethical has been a hallmark of BKD since its inception. The firm's pioneering Public Interest Council is a voluntary group that adds yet another layer of ethics oversight to the firm.

Bottom line: trust builds success. In a recent comparative study by an independent research firm, BKD clients report they are significantly more satisfied with their service than clients of other top U.S. accounting and advisory firms. Furthermore, BKD's overall results are higher than those of any other CPA firm the researcher has surveyed in the past twenty-five years. "For us, it's about being more than just good accountants and auditors," says Wanamaker. "It's about knowing our clients and their businesses, and dedicating ourselves to helping them do better at what they are in business to accomplish." ❖

Photo by Thomas S. England

Each fall, BKD invites its employees, their families, and their friends to celebrate with a day of food and fun at the annual company picnic. In 2006, folks gathered together at Celebration City, a popular theme park located in Branson, Missouri.

Photo by Alan S. Weiner

Paul Mueller Company is a major manufacturer in Springfield known for producing equipment used in the processing of consumer goods in many industries. Mueller established the Springfield Brewing Company for brewery equipment research and development. Not just a pub to enjoy a bite and a brew, the Springfield Brewing Company now serves as a state-of-the-art brewery to showcase Mueller products to domestic and international customers. Master brewer Ashton Lewis oversees brewing operations at the brewery. ✤

Photo by Alan S. Weiner

Photo by Alan S. Weiner

Fueled by growth in population and jobs, Springfield is Missouri's economic engine. Springfield's labor force is equally strong, representing a midwestern work ethic that values productivity. Between the need for new facilities by companies moving into the area and redevelopment of existing areas, the construction industry is one of the booming sectors. ❖

EMPIRE BANK: YOUR FINANCIAL FRIEND

Empire Bank has been a financial friend to its neighbors in the Ozarks since 1956. Empire Bank has grown from a single branch to fifteen banking facilities throughout the Ozarks. As it has increased its scope as a local financial institution, Empire Bank has maintained its reputation as a place to turn for one-on-one attention and quick answers to both personal and business financial needs.

In addition to its physical expansion, Empire Bank has also added to its service offerings, bringing clients a range of progressive options like personal and business online banking, investments and trust services, insurance, and a comprehensive choice of loans.

As a local bank, Empire knows the importance of helping to build a strong community. Through its charitable giving and volunteer support, Empire has helped many organizations grow in their ability to serve their communities.

Empire Bank has also played a significant role in economic development throughout the Ozarks. In addition to services that help consumers gain financial security, the bank assists businesses large and small with loans for construction and development, business operations, and real estate.

Stability is a trademark of Empire Bank. Just ask any of the thirty-two employees who are members of the bank's "25 Year Club." They know, as do people of the region, that working with Empire is like being with friends. ❖

> As it has increased its scope as a local financial institution, Empire Bank has maintained its reputation as a place to turn for one-on-one attention and quick answers.

▲ *Empire Bank celebrated its fiftieth anniversary with employees and customers at a Springfield Cardinals game on July 29, 2006. The bank opened its doors fifty years before to the day on July 29, 1956. Empire Bank was the lead financial institution for the $32 million Hammons Field project when it was built in 2004.*

Photo by Lisa Means

Kinetic Man, fondly known as K-Man to Springfield residents, is a twenty-four-foot towering but friendly robotic sculpture created by artist Russ RuBert. Children clamor to crank the handle that makes K-Man move his legs, each weighing one hundred pounds. "Born" in 1994 to debut at the Walt Disney Children's Arts Festival held at the Missouri Capitol grounds, K-Man made encore appearances at the capitol for two more years, and then just disappeared. In 2002 a grassroots effort began to "Free K-Man." Not until 2004—when the Springfield Southeast Rotary Club purchased K-Man for $17,500, as a centennial commemoration project and donation for Jordan Valley Park—did the interactive giant find his permanent home. ❖

Photo by Lisa Means

Tumbler, a twelve-by-thirteen-by-ten-foot sculpture of no-maintenance steel, has stood in Park Central Square since 1971. Created by California sculptor Aris Demetrios, *Tumbler* was originally designed to be tumbled. The idea behind it was that the sculpture could be moved twelve different ways, changing it for each season, thus giving people another reason to come to the downtown area. ❖

UMB Bank: Growing the Springfield Community

Building on nearly one hundred years of experience and tradition, there's something special about UMB Bank. Based on the company's rich history, it's no surprise that UMB has the momentum to reach an even greater level of success in the Springfield community. The bank's tightly knit team of associates is committed to the company's long-term growth, as evidenced by their engagement not only with customers, but also across the community.

Established in Kansas City in 1913 as a storefront bank with first-day deposits of around one thousand dollars, UMB has grown to become one of the country's strongest financial holding companies, with multibillion-dollar assets. Today, UMB offers complete banking and related financial services to individual and business customers at over 141 banking centers throughout Missouri, Illinois, Colorado, Kansas, Oklahoma, Nebraska, and Arizona.

UMB Bank's vision is to be recognized for the unparalleled customer experience. With that in mind, UMB's brand promise is "Count on more," because its associates expect more from each other and deliver more to their customers.

"We love to surprise our customers by approaching things from a creative perspective," says president Ann Marie Baker. "We enjoy innovating and advocating for them by truly listening to their needs."

Whether crafting effective financial solutions or impacting the community through volunteer leadership, bank asso-

> "We love to surprise our customers by approaching things from a creative perspective," says president Ann Marie Baker.

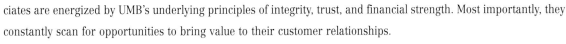

◀ Could this be a future leader of tomorrow? UMB Bank believes in the promise of today's young people and supports organizations committed to their success. Furthermore, UMB has created a workplace environment where volunteerism and community involvement are valued.

ciates are energized by UMB's underlying principles of integrity, trust, and financial strength. Most importantly, they constantly scan for opportunities to bring value to their customer relationships.

"At the end of the day, it's the quality of those relationships that makes UMB such a success," says Baker. "Our team believes we offer the best of both worlds: sophisticated financial services and attention to detail built through personal relationships."

Not only does UMB strive to deliver the finest products and services to its customers, it works to provide an exceptional place for its associates to develop. Sharing the core values of honesty and respect with each other as well as with clients is central to the culture at UMB. Reliance on the underlying strengths of the institution and its people defines the bank's profile. The local management team has over eighty-five years of experience with the company, and that commitment provides clear direction for the bank's future.

UMB Bank associates are attuned to the needs of the Springfield community. The bank is known for hosting Springfield's Salvation Army Christmas Tree of Lights for over two decades, developing award-winning center-city redevelopment programs, and bringing creativity and new energy to local nonprofit endeavors. Taking a special interest in area organizations like Leadership Springfield, Good Samaritan Boys Ranch, and Junior Achievement connects UMB staff with Springfield's future leaders.

Proud to remain independent, UMB Bank is unquestionably here to stay. Dedicated to the community, to its customers, and to its associates, UMB Bank is ready for the future. ✦

Photo by Thomas S. England

Photo by Thomas S. England

Friends and family enjoy ▶ Springfield on Board, a Monopoly-style game celebrating Springfield. The board game was a record-breaking fund-raiser for Leadership Springfield. UMB Bank proudly supported the project through volunteer and financial commitments.

Since opening in 1987, Waverly House Gifts & Gallery has become a regional destination for fine art and contemporary American arts and crafts. A treasure trove of gorgeous glass, wood, ceramic, and fiber objets d'art, the gallery is also known for watercolor and oil paintings by some of the Midwest's most well-known painters. Customers also enjoy Waverly House for its year-round Christmas room, a cheery assemblage of collectible holiday ornaments, figurines, and handcrafted German nutcrackers. ✤

One of the joys of antique shopping is discovering how something old can be new again. Home to dozens of flea markets, antique dealers, and shops like the South Peer Antique Mall, Springfield is a delight for those seeking not only antiques, but also collectibles of all kinds. You can bet that somewhere out there, someone is looking for this exact Orange Crush koozie! ❖

Photo by Eric Francis

BLACKWELL SANDERS PEPER MARTIN: COMMITMENT TO CLIENT AND COMMUNITY

When Blackwell Sanders Peper Martin LLP established a law office in Springfield in 1996, it was a perfect match. Business was booming in Southwest Missouri, and Blackwell Sanders, renowned nationwide for its innovative transaction and litigation practices, was firmly established as one of the leading commercial law firms in the Midwest.

The relationship remains just as productive today. "Many law firms came into the area during the mid-1990s by taking over an established firm," explains office managing partner Virginia Fry. "Blackwell Sanders did not come in and take over an existing office. We built an entirely new office from the ground up."

Guiding their clients through a host of business and regulatory needs both in and out of the courtroom are 22 attorneys and five paralegals. These professionals, coupled with an extended Blackwell Sanders network of over forty practice groups and 320 attorneys, allow the Springfield office to provide specialized services in a host of practice areas, including corporate, real estate, labor and employment, health care, aviation, estate planning, creditors' rights, education, and commercial litigation.

> Commitment to both client and community is what distinguishes Blackwell Sanders Peper Martin as one of the best law firms in the Midwest.

◀ *(Left to right) Blackwell Sanders Estate Planning partner Robert Penninger, College of the Ozarks president Dr. Jerry C. Davis, and Blackwell Sanders office managing partner Virginia Fry in front of Williams Memorial Chapel. At College of the Ozarks, students learn that a good work ethic shapes character and helps build relationships. The credo also forms the basis for the school's relationship with Blackwell Sanders, which has served as its legal counsel since 1998.*

Blackwell Sanders is the firm of choice for many Fortune 500, multinational, middle-market, public and privately held companies. Commitment to both client and community is what distinguishes Blackwell Sanders as one of the best law firms in the Midwest.

That same depth and breadth of service distinguishes its Springfield operations as well. "We are a full-service firm capable of meeting many different business and regulatory needs," says Fry. "If we don't have the knowledge locally, we can go to any one of our other offices to get it."

In addition to Springfield, the firm has offices in Kansas City and St. Louis, Missouri, as well as Omaha and Lincoln, Nebraska; Washington, D.C.; Overland Park, Kansas; Belleville, Illinois; and London, England.

Following a long-standing practice of hiring lawyers not only for their legal knowledge and academic excellence, but also for their distinctive leadership and experiences, Blackwell Sanders' Springfield attorneys are consistently recognized for their passionate commitment to the community. Attorneys and staff regularly commit their resources to local charitable organizations, including the Breast Cancer Foundation of the Ozarks, Springfield Business Development Corporation, Big Brothers Big Sisters, the Discovery Center, Ronald McDonald House Charities, and Make-A-Wish Foundation, to name a few.

Continued on page 173

Photo by Lisa Means

resident and CEO of Federal ▶ Protection Inc. Kim Hancock (left) confers with Blackwell Sanders estate planning artner Evelyn Gwin Mangan nd corporate partner David gee. Federal Protection Inc., family owned and operated ince opening in 1969, has a long-standing relationship ith Blackwell Sanders. The firm has advised Federal Protection throughout its development into one of the gest security services firms n the central United States.

Continued from page 171

Virginia Fry currently serves as the chairman of the board of City Utilities. She has been named one of "The Best Lawyers in America" and one of "The 20 Most Influential Women in Business in Springfield." Corporate department leader David Agee, also named one of "The Best Lawyers in America," represented John Q. Hammons in the restructuring of Hammons Hotels and is a past chairman of the Springfield Area Chamber of Commerce. Litigation department leader Randy Scheer has successfully tried over one hundred cases in state and federal court and was named one of "Missouri & Kansas' Super Lawyers." In 2003, the Springfield office was awarded the *Springfield Business Journal*'s Economic Impact Award and in 2006 was recognized as one of Springfield's "Best Places to Work."

Photo by Scott Indermaur

▲ *(Left to right) Blackwell Sanders Real Estate partners Richard Walters and Shawn Whitney with office managing partner Virginia Fry at the firm Springfield offices. Blackwell Sanders values strong client relationships and holds a long-term view of those alliances, working to ensure that ea client, large or small, receives nothing but the most expert service.*

Photo by Lisa Means

◀ *(Left to right) Blackwell Sanders Labor and Employment partner Bob Lawson, Herrman Lumber president and CEO Ed Powell, and Blackwell Sanders Business and Commercial Litigation partner J. Michael Bridges at Herrman Lumber's lumberyard. Firmly rooted in each of the communities it serves, Blackwell Sanders excels at guiding locally owned and operated companies in their growth.*

Photo by Rod Reilly

Come in with an appetite if you're ordering the "Hungry Student Special" at Anton's Coffee Shop. "It's one of our most popular menu items," says Anton Tasich, who has owned the coffee shop with wife Roberta since 1973. The special features three homemade buttermilk biscuits, topped with sausage gravy, hash browns or grits, and a choice of ham, bacon or sausage. Specializing in satisfying the taste buds of the eclectic clientele is what motivates Anton and staff. "I don't think anybody in town serves thirty-some kinds of omelets. We also serve daily specials for breakfast and lunch, because it keeps people coming back," he says. "We like to think of ourselves as an oasis in the restaurant business. We do so many things that people just don't do anymore."

ACR Nally Marketing Group: Building Partnerships, Building Business

As the saying goes, "It takes a village to raise a child"; it also needs to be said that "It takes a team to keep a business on a solid foundation." ACR Nally Marketing Group has been that team for twenty years. With ongoing passion for their clients' success and a strong desire for business growth, the group has never looked back—only forward.

This is not your typical ad agency. "Since our business backgrounds are made up of professionals from the non-profit sector, the hospitality industry, and from manufacturing/distribution, we look at the strategic planning for a company truly from our client's viewpoint. Because at one time, we were the clients," says Mike Nally. "That experience is our point of difference, and we use it to build strong, result-oriented marketing plans

> "We find that by being involved with community efforts and initiatives, we are able to enhance our company philosophy."

and partnerships with clients that range from locally owned businesses to an international software company." Cindy Howell adds, "It's essential that we not lose touch with our past experiences. They form the foundation for our unique positioning and enhance our ability to focus on our clients' strengths."

ACR Nally also builds strong partnerships within the community. As Lisa Nally explains, "It's very important to us that we give back to the community. In fact, it's one of our core values. We find that by being involved with community efforts and initiatives, we are able to enhance our company philosophy, thus making us better strategic partners with our clients to help them achieve their business goals." ❖

The depth and diversity of the business backgrounds of the executive team—Cindy Howell, Mike Nally, and Lisa Nally (left to right)—is a key point of differentiation for the agency.

Louie, the Springfield Cardinals' mascot, points to the Cardinal players' locker room doors, made by another Springfield all-star: The Maiman Company team. One of the nation's top manufacturers of beautiful and durable architectural-quality wood stile and rail doors is also an innovator in the wood flush door market. In 2002 the company introduced the first new commercial wood flush door product in thirty years, utilizing thermal-fused technology to produce a high-quality, economical, and ecologically sound flush door for a variety of applications. While complementing the interior of this beautiful new Springfield landmark, The Maiman Company's doors fulfill a very important function: protecting the occupants in the unthinkable occurrence of a fire. The Maiman Company ensures continued life safety and security requirements for building occupants by volunteering in the code development process. Successfully combining beauty and functionality has made The Maiman Company the premier manufacturer in the architectural door industry. ✤

Photo by Scott Indermaur

Established in 1940 Paul Mueller Company has grown to occupy nearly 1 million square feet of state-of-the-art manufacturing space under roof. ✤

▲ *CUCCU employees gather to pick up litter along Republic Road, an adopted street site located near one of the credit union's branches. Keeping Springfield clean and beautiful is just one way CUCCU people contribute to their community's quality of life.*

CREDIT UNION OFFERS SOLUTIONS FOR TODAY AND TOMORROW

At CU Community Credit Union (CUCCU), members are more than just keystrokes on a calculator; they are people with lives to build.

Started in 1931 as City Utilities Employees Credit Union, CUCCU changed its name when it expanded its service territory to Greene and Christian counties. Today, this not-for-profit financial institution serves some fifty-two hundred members and has reached over $47 million in assets. While a majority of members are still CU employees, whose loyalty has formed the foundation of the credit union's rich heritage, anyone who lives or works in CUCCU's two counties, is related to a member, or is offered association through an employer can become a member of the credit union.

> CUCCU's size and personable staff are its true assets, allowing the credit union to stay in touch with its members and their needs.

From two full-service locations in Springfield, CUCCU offers a full range of checking, savings, and loan products. CUCCU also offers credit cards and online banking as well as access via over twenty-five thousand automated teller machines worldwide.

CUCCU's size and personable staff are its true assets, allowing the credit union to stay in touch with its members and their needs. "Our desire to work closely with individual members reinforces their desire to utilize our services," says Judy Hadsall, president and chief executive officer. "Members take comfort in knowing they can call someone directly when an issue arises."

This close community association, combined with a progressive business outlook, also allows CUCCU to retain a rare nimbleness in the financial services industry. "One reason for our success is our ability to easily identify needs, brainstorm for solutions, implement changes, gauge each new program's success, and then alter it if needed," explains Hadsall.

In evidence are some of CUCCU's tailored solutions. While the CUCCU loan lineup includes selections for home buyers and owners, automobile and sport vehicle shoppers, and students heading off to college, its savings choices range from holiday and health accounts to certificates of deposits and individual retirement accounts. For area employers, CUCCU offers payroll services and free finance seminars for personnel. And, in an effort to instill financial sense at an early age, CUCCU provides savings programs for kids and older youth.

As an organization so closely connected to its neighbors, CUCCU understands that corporate philanthropy makes for a strong community and, in turn, a stronger financial institution. "We realize the importance of being connected with our employees, members, and communities' needs," says Hadsall. "It's evident that the success of a business is directly related to the health of those who support it."

That's why CUCCU promotes wellness at work, stays active in the Springfield Area Chamber of Commerce, and supports at least one charity each month through monetary donations or hands-on involvement. From collecting food for the hungry to celebrating the holidays with students to golfing each year in support of kids, CUCCU and its people give back to the community that helped make it what it is today—a place that people rely on to help them grow. ❖

Photo by Lisa Means

As part of the annual fall ▶ celebration party at Campbell's Farm, young members of CUCCU Kids Club get to pick out a pumpkin and spend time with "Cuccu," the club's mascot. Membership in the club is intended to plant the seed of fiscal awareness at a very early age.

Photo by Rod Reilly

For great Italian food, head to Bruno's Restaurant. Located on South Avenue in a historic 1905 building, the restaurant offers diners a comfortable atmosphere and authentic cuisine. From pasta to seafood and savory meats, the specialties at Bruno's are prepared with the freshest ingredients. Add a glass of wine and a special dessert, and you'll see what it means to truly get a taste of Italy. ✣

Here is a bit of trivia guaranteed to get a conversation—and maybe a meal—going. Did you know that cashew chicken, a staple of any good Chinese restaurant, was created in Leong's Tea House in Springfield? David Leong, who came to the United States in 1940, was looking for a way to combine the foods of his homeland in a way that appealed to American tastes. His solution was cashew chicken. He passed his recipes and his skills along to his son, chef Wing Yee Leong, pictured right, who still follows the original recipe and proudly serves his father's recipe at Fire & Ice Restaurant in the Oasis Inn and Convention Center. Drop in any Wednesday and enjoy this house specialty. ✣

Photo by Thomas S. England

The warm ambience of WineStyles welcomes visitors to a world reminiscent of wine country in traditional Europe. From their first steps through the doorway, customers are captivated by the rich Tuscan colors, antiqued wood, and a visual seduction of wine encased in a boundless array of old stone alcoves. Oak barrels surrounding the wine cooling units mask the present-day commodities, transporting clients back to the days when wine was the drink of choice for discriminating gourmands. WineStyles offers consumers a unique shopping experience in an engaging in-store world. Wines are conveniently organized by taste "styles" and accompanied by informational cards that assist with wine choices. Here, wine server Jeff Sale explains beverage characteristics to Laura Hendricks (left) and Christy Pennell. ❖

photo by Thomas S. England

GREAT SOUTHERN BANK: A PART OF SPRINGFIELD SINCE 1923

There is something comforting about doing business with a longtime, trusted friend.

Springfield residents have a good reason to view Great Southern with that familiarity. The company has been a part of the fabric of the community since 1923, when it was chartered as a building and loan association with a five-thousand-dollar investment.

Over the years, Great Southern has developed into a full-service financial institution with assets exceeding $2.2 billion and serving ninety-one thousand households. The company has enjoyed tremendous growth in the past decade. "It took us over seventy-five years to hit

> "We've been able to achieve that growth because of the strength of the markets we serve, and products and services we provide to make our customers' lives better and easier."

our first billion dollars in assets, and then just another five and a half years to top $2 billion," said Joe Turner, president and CEO. "We've been able to achieve that growth because of the strength of the markets we serve, and products and services we provide to make our customers' lives better and easier."

Customer convenience has been a focus for the company for many years. "One of our company mainstays has always been serving our customers when and where they need us. We are open longer hours, and have more ATMs and more banking centers than any other financial institution in the Ozarks.

◀ *For more than twenty years, Great Southern Bank has offered membership in the Summit Club for its customers fifty and older. As southern Missouri's largest bank club package, it includes exclusive banking, travel, insurance, and investment benefits. There are more than fourteen thousand active members, and approximately seventeen hundred attend the club's annual birthday party held at the Juanita K. Hammons Hall for the Performing Arts.*

With our telephone and online banking services, we are available twenty-four hours a day, seven days a week," adds Turner.

Great Southern not only has traditional commercial banking services, but it has also ventured into other related financial services over the past several decades. Great Southern Insurance was started in the 1950s, Great Southern Travel in the '70s, and Great Southern Investments in the early '80s. In addition, the company now has loan production offices in northwest Arkansas, Kansas City, Columbia, and St. Louis.

With headquarters in Springfield, the company presently has thirty-seven banking centers serving communities throughout the Ozarks. Great Southern has been actively committed to helping Springfield and the Ozarks continue to grow and prosper. "We are very proud of our involvement in the communities we serve. We are the only financial institution with a locally based community development corporation. That allows us to respond to community needs that aren't traditionally a part of commercial banking. From developing a new headquarters for a local nonprofit to transforming a boarded-up residence in an underserved neighborhood into a new family residence, Great Southern CDC provides the capital and expertise to help revitalize our neighbors and neighborhoods in need," states Turner.

Other innovative community financial services include an extensive seniors' banking program, which includes on-premise services at residential care facilities; a Latino customer initiative; a dedicated, comprehensive corporate services department; and a deposit service that allows commercial customers to make deposits into their checking accounts without ever leaving the office.

From providing the widest range of services and convenience for customers to working with neighbors to rebuild communities, Great Southern remains a trusted friend to the Springfield area. ✣

Photo by Jim Lersch

Photo by Scott Indermaur

Customer Appreciation Days ▶ *at any of Great Southern's thirty-seven banking centers have all the elements of a family reunion and a neighborhood cookout. Each location chooses a date, hangs up its banner, and issues one-to-one invitations to customers to stop by, say hello, and enjoy refreshments. Bank associates do the cooking and serving while customers—as well as family, friends, and neighbors—get to relax and enjoy the day.*

Photo by Lisa Means

*h*ead west on Missouri Highway 14 and witness a beautiful sunset. Head east and catch a sunrise. This two-lane ribbon of a road winds across Southwest Missouri, offering a peek at the countryside and towns that line the journey from West Plains, its east terminus, to Marionville at the west end. ❖

SPRINGFIELD AREA CHAMBER OF COMMERCE: ADVOCATING FOR COMMUNITY

Nearly every day is a "chamber-of-commerce kind of day" in Springfield—a day when all the elements align to bring about a near-perfect environment in which to live, work, and play. It happens this way because the Springfield Area Chamber of Commerce is constantly working behind the scenes for the greater good of the community.

While there are certain things the chamber cannot control, this dynamic organization makes every effort to have a positive impact on economic prosperity and quality of life. "We do what many people think just happens," says Jim

> "The chamber has firmly established itself as a leader, not only in Springfield, but in the entire state of Missouri."

Anderson, president. "If that's the impression we leave, then we've been successful. We have a dynamic community, and I believe our chamber is a reflection of that. We're an activist organization, a change agent, that's all about the greater good."

The clichéd idea that the only function of a chamber of commerce is to sponsor festivals and the like is far from what defines the Springfield chamber. Often cited by other communities as a model for collaboration, economic development, and business advocacy, the Springfield chamber commits significant resources—time, capital, and staff—to

◀ *The staff of the Springfield Area Chamber of Commerce gather outside the chamber office in the John Q. Hammons Enterprise Center.*

such endeavors. "Under Jim's leadership, the chamber has firmly established itself as a leader, not only in Springfield, but in the entire state of Missouri," says Jim Jura, president of Associated Electric Cooperative. "Consequently, the chamber is involved in all critical aspects of the region's economy."

The organization understands that a region's economic prosperity and quality of life are inextricably connected, or, as Anderson puts it, "What's good for business is good for the community." As such, the chamber partners with the City of Springfield, City Utilities, and Greene County to make it easy for businesses to connect with Springfield. When a company sends a site selector to evaluate the area, the chamber and these partners gather around the table with the key players to discuss their needs. Whether it's the expansion of a local business or the relocation of a company from another area, such cooperation streamlines the process.

"The chamber understands that we want economic growth, but not at the expense of quality of life," says Robin Melton, president and owner of Environmental Works, a past recipient of the chamber's Small Business of the Year award. Melton echoes the sentiments of other chamber members when she notes that the organization has been successful because it attracts and retains a broad mix of top-rated companies and organizations, while preserving the quality of life that is the hallmark of the area. ❖

Photo by Thomas S. England

Photo by Lisa Means

The chamber's economic development team works to attract new business and industry to the Springfield region and assists existing business with needs such as workforce development. Pictured at Springfield's Expo Center are (left to right) Ryan Mooney, Allen Kunkel, Kristen Westerman, and Greg Williams. ▶

The fire and rescue personnel of the Springfield Fire Department are well-trained and ready to respond to any emergency situation that arises within the department's 79.8-mile territory, which, by the way, is physically larger than the area the St. Louis fire department covers. That's one reason that every member of the department receives a minimum of twenty hours per month of training. "Every day, there is something to train on, whether that's going out and learning the district, or full-blown auto extrication training," says Nigel Holderby, one of three training captains in the department's training division. With eleven stations, just over two hundred personnel, and twenty-six fire apparatus per shift, the Springfield Fire Department is well-equipped to be the first to respond. ✣

Photo by Scott Indermaur

Springfield, the state's third-largest city and Greene County seat, has it all: a strong job market, great schools, superior health care, abundant outdoor recreation, a temperate climate, and top-quality services. Springfield citizens are protected by more than three hundred police officers and firefighters who use specialized tools, equipment, and transportation to do their jobs. The two departments share space at the combined South District Station and Fire Station Number Six. ✤

RICK'S AUTOMOTIVE, INC.: 400 YEARS OF ACCUMULATED EXPERIENCE

Since the first Model T rolled off the assembly line in 1908, Americans have had a love affair with their automobiles. "My plan, when my wife Karen and I opened the business in 1980," said Rick Hughlett, owner of Rick's Automotive, Inc., "was to fill the gap between quick-service shops and the dealerships."

Back then, Rick's was a five-bay, three-employee operation. Today there are eighteen service bays and twenty-six employees. "We make car repair as convenient as possible by offering free shuttles; efficient service with fourteen technicians and five service advisors, who are the liaison between the customer and the technicians; and loaner cars when necessary. We also honor all extended warranties."

Another convenience is that Rick's is still in its original location on South Campbell. "We considered opening another branch, but I didn't want to split our management team, so we expanded here," Hughlett explained.

Maintaining continuity is important to Rick's philosophy. "My local ties go back to my grandparents, who owned dough-nut shops in Springfield in the '40s. I want my employees to feel this is a place where they can learn, grow, and retire, so we offer a complete benefits package, and

> "Springfield has been good to us, and we believe it's important to give back to the community. We will continue to do that in trust, service, and support."

The friendly technicians at Rick's Automotive are highly trained experts dedicated to keeping their customers' vehicles in top-notch working order. That kind of focus on customer service caught the attention of the Springfield Area Chamber of Commerce and resulted in Rick's being honored as a Small Business of the Year finalist. Since its founding in 1980, Rick's has filled the gap between dealerships and chain stores with quality, affordable auto repairs.

that has paid off. Several employees have been with us more than twenty years, like Tim Cummings, our general manager. We have more than four hundred years of accumulated technical experience, and you just can't beat that."

As cars become more technically advanced, continued training becomes essential. Rick's is a founding member of the Automotive Service Association (ASA) in Springfield, which offers ongoing technical training. A number of his technicians hold the highest level of American Service Excellence certification. Rick and four of his managers have received an accredited degree from the prestigious Automotive Management Institute.

To further emphasize his belief in training, Hughlett sits on the advisory board of Ozarks Technical Community College and provides a mentoring program for students to get hands-on training. "Three technicians who have gone through this program are now on our staff."

Official recognition has come to Rick's in the form of the Facility of the Year Award—out of 468 shops considered—presented by the Missouri/Kansas ASA. The business was also honored as an ASA Green Star Service Facility for its environmental excellence. To acknowledge its outstanding philanthropy, Rick's was named the Outstanding Small Business of the Year by the Association of Fundraising Professionals. Finally, Rick's is one of only three shops in Springfield approved by the American Automobile Association (AAA). "This is an extremely difficult certification to get and to maintain, and we're very proud to have it," Hughlett said.

"Springfield has been good to us, and we believe it's important to give back to the community. We will continue to do that in trust, service, and support, and we have plans in place for the business to continue for a long, long time." ❖

Photo by Alan S. Weiner

For more than ten years, Rick Hughlett, owner of Rick's Automotive, has had an interest in ballooning. Hughlett's roots in Springfield go back several generations, and as a way of giving back to the community, he often donates balloon rides and/or gift certificates to local charitable organizations. "Springfield's been good to us, and this is just one way we can have a small part in repaying that trust," Hughlett said.

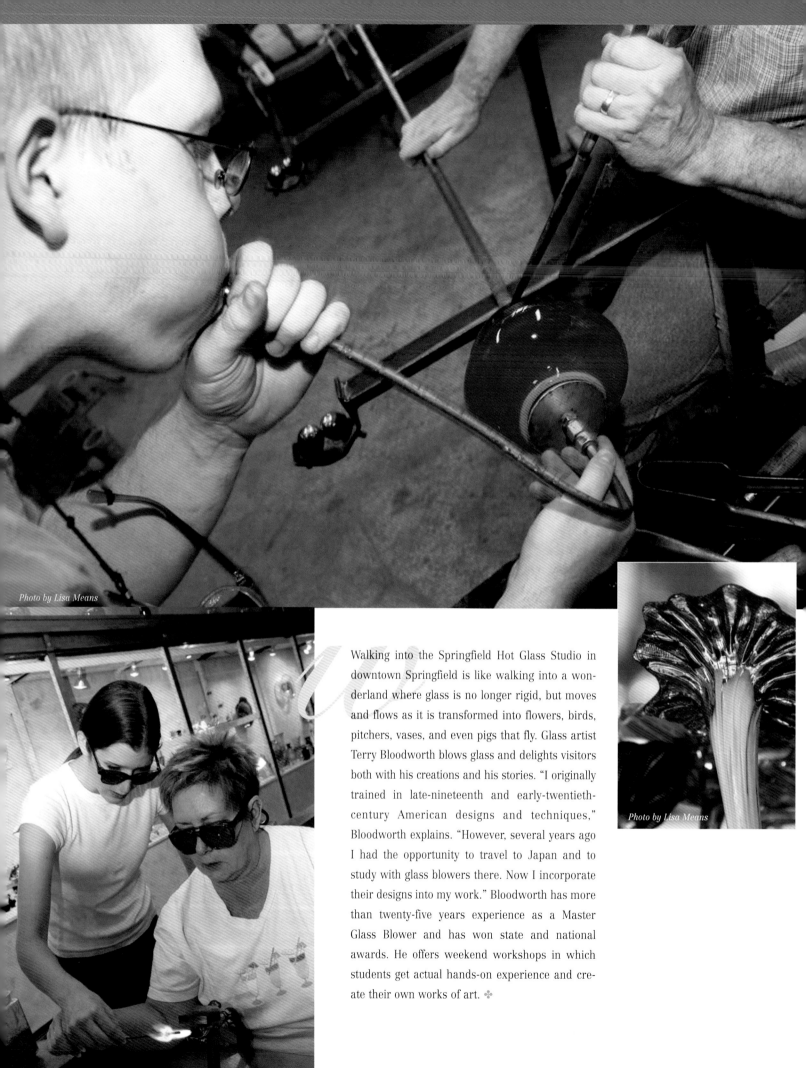

Walking into the Springfield Hot Glass Studio in downtown Springfield is like walking into a wonderland where glass is no longer rigid, but moves and flows as it is transformed into flowers, birds, pitchers, vases, and even pigs that fly. Glass artist Terry Bloodworth blows glass and delights visitors both with his creations and his stories. "I originally trained in late-nineteenth and early-twentieth-century American designs and techniques," Bloodworth explains. "However, several years ago I had the opportunity to travel to Japan and to study with glass blowers there. Now I incorporate their designs into my work." Bloodworth has more than twenty-five years experience as a Master Glass Blower and has won state and national awards. He offers weekend workshops in which students get actual hands-on experience and create their own works of art. ❖

The Walnut Street National Register Historic District in downtown Springfield is more than a mile long and has 150 homes built between 1870 and 1940. They represent a variety of styles including Queen Anne, Periodic Revival, and Bungalow, but one thing they all have in common is the need for constant maintenance. Bob Foster, whose house is on Walnut Street—which, by the way, runs along Route 66—takes advantage of a dry, sunny day to do some work on his roof. Stately manors and gingerbread landmarks anchor the east end of Walnut Street while the west end features shops, restaurants, lodging, and apartments. In addition to being an interesting place to live, Walnut Street is also the location for Springfield's Artsfest and Cider Days celebrations. ✤

Photo by Thomas S. England

Photo by Thomas S. England

Robert Nava takes a break to enjoy time in the backyard with his dog Winston. Nava's beautiful century-old Queen Anne house on Walnut Street is full of history. "Sometimes you forget what time you're living in, because some of these homes date back to the Civil War," Nava says. "There's lots of intriguing history here, and that's just part of the ambience of living on Walnut and in downtown Springfield as a whole." ✤

THE MAIMAN COMPANY: MAKERS OF FINE ARCHITECTURAL AND SPECIALTY WOOD DOORS

The next time you walk through the threshold of a hotel, hospital, museum, office building, or university, there's a good chance the door you just opened was manufactured right here in Springfield at The Maiman Company.

A manufacturer of fine architectural doors since 1971, and the 2001 recipient of the Springfield Area Chamber of Commerce's Manufacturer of the Year Award, The Maiman Company provides the highest-quality commercial openings products available today. A short list of some of its most prestigious clients include Yale, Harvard, Princeton, the City of Los Angeles Cathedral, Torrey Pines, Augusta National Clubhouse, the White House, the Old Executive Office Building, Trump Towers, AOL–Time Warner, and John Q. Hammons Properties.

Owners Jane and Tim Bennett believe their company's mix of high tech and high touch makes them an industry standout. "We make every effort to have the most technologically advanced manufacturing equipment in the industry, with our own IT department to develop and maintain our systems," says Tim Bennett.

In lieu of adding a large number of employees, the company secures the employment of its current workforce of fifty-five by continually analyzing and improving operations, products, and procedures.

> "Every day they are challenged to produce a high-quality product at a competitive price with excellent customer service. And they live up to that challenge."

◀ Over thirty-five years doing business in Springfield, The Maiman Company team proudly stands in front of its headquarters, taking great pride in crafting beautiful architectural wood doors sold throughout the country. Maiman employees average over ten years with the company.

"We believe in the growth of our employees, not necessarily in the number of our employees," says Jane Bennett. "Every day they are challenged to produce a high-quality product at a competitive price with excellent customer service. And they live up to that challenge."

Trusting and listening to their employees is an integral part of how the Bennetts do business. In fact, the company's first expansion into a forty-five-thousand-square-foot manufacturing plant, which opened in 1996 in the Partnership Industrial Center, was entirely employee-designed. Here, The Maiman Company primarily manufactures wood stile and rail doors for architectural use. It also excels in fire-rated, acoustic, lead-lined, and bullet-resistant doors. The company even has a historical replication division, for effortless matching.

The company's open book management policy also ensures that everyone involved knows exactly where the company stands and where it is going.

"The company is an innovator and a problem solver," says The Maiman Company's national sales manager, Steve Hubert. "Those qualities gain us access to new and exciting challenges. And that allows us to feed our imagination and to not only respond to improvements in the marketplace, but to initiate them."

For instance, in 2002, the company's product development team brought to market the first change in commercial wood doors in thirty years. The company decided to expand its product line by researching and producing a better flush door at a better price. The result revolutionized the industry. The Maiman Company's Thermal Fused solid-core flush door is made from nearly 100 percent recycled and recovered materials—not endangered rainforest

Continued on page 194

Photo by Scott Indermaur

Photo by Scott Indermaur

Tim and Jane Bennett, ▶ co-owners, visit with ten-year Maiman veteran Chad Lugar as he prepares a door for Bear Mountain Inn and Resort in Georgia. This type of interaction is part of the Bennetts' staying in touch with the process and the people at The Maiman Company. Tim and Jane make it a daily ritual to be among their employees.

Continued from page 193

...woods and finished with a patented Noor Veneer® that is fused to the door using heat and pressure, eliminating the delamination problems that plague traditional glued-veneer doors. A $10 million, one-hundred-thousand-square-foot plant located across the street from their current location was built to manufacture the innovative new product. This new plant not only ensures growth of the company itself, but also augments Springfield's economic development.

This beautiful, solid, high-quality door is also offered at the same price as traditional five-ply flush doors. And like their stile and rail doors, all Thermal Fused doors are available as either nonrated or fire-rated at 20, 45, 60, and 90 minutes.

"The pursuit for continuous improvement is the driving force of our employees and our products," says technical director David San Paolo. "We can never rest on our laurels. We can be happy, but never satisfied. The word 'can't' is not in our vocabulary." In recognition of this attitude The Maiman Company is the recipient of two other national awards, the 1997 Southern Governor's Cup and the WMIA 1997 Innovator of the Year. ❖

Operating the most fully automated wood flush door production line in the United States is a matter of pushing computer buttons for Kevin Pratt (back) and Jim Anderson (front). With only a handful of people, this line can produce four hundred wood flush doors in a day.

Photo by Scott Indermaur

Photo by Scott Indermaur

One of The Maiman Company's special doors—a wooden twenty-minute fire-rated walnut, two-panel door, for the San Antonio Drury Plaza Hotel Riverwalk—is assembled by Maiman employees Kevin Broz (left) and Stephen Muller (right).

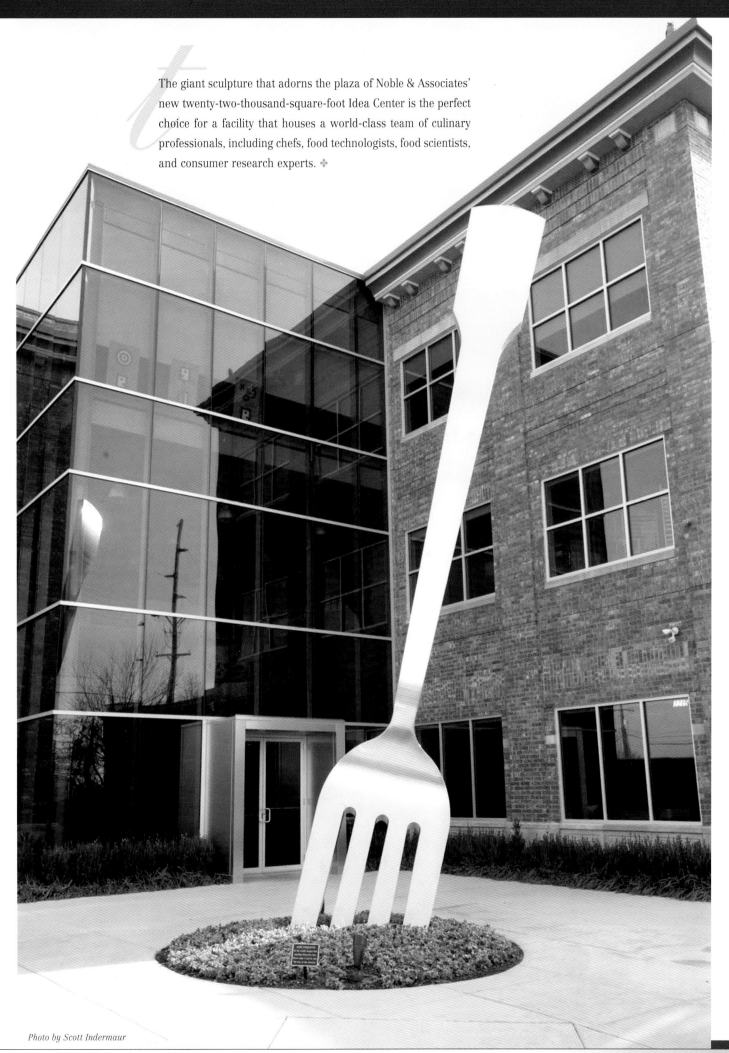

The giant sculpture that adorns the plaza of Noble & Associates' new twenty-two-thousand-square-foot Idea Center is the perfect choice for a facility that houses a world-class team of culinary professionals, including chefs, food technologists, food scientists, and consumer research experts. ✤

Photo by Scott Indermaur

TCSI/TRANSLAND REALLY KNOWS HOW TO DELIVER

Back in the late 1970s, Glen Walker was a less than truckload (LTL) freight sales man who was considering an opportunity become an entrepreneur. At the time, Glen was also involved in securing the truckload freight that was landed onto rail vans for transport to the East and West coasts by the railroads. It was that concept combined with Glen's knowledge of over-the-road trucking that inspired him to start up a transportation business in Springfield.

> Whether in person, by phone, through e-mail, or via Internet Web sites, the TCSI team has a talent for developing relationships with clients.

With no assurances in this new area the industry, Walker began his own freight hauling business with one tractor, two employees, and ten thousand dollars borrowed funds. So began Terminal Consolidation Company.

Today, that small freight operation has become TCSI/Transland, a $50 million-a year company that provides trucking for long- and short-haul loads, flatbed transport intermodal transport, less than truckload and special equipment services. With nearly two hundred drivers, an equal number of trucks, and over five hundred trailers, TCSI hauls freight in and out of its thirty-three acre Strafford, Missouri, complex to all corners of the continental United States.

Photo by Eric Francis

▲ *President Mike Walker (left) and CEO Glen Walker, who together—through a strong work ethic and a belief in going the extra mile for clients—have built TCSI/Transland into a multimillion-dollar trucking company.*

For TCSI, success can largely be attributed to a strong work ethic, shared by management and staff, which stems from an inherent belief in going the extra mile for clients. Whether in person, by phone, through e-mail, or via Internet Web sites, the TCSI team has a talent for developing relationships with clients, some that have lasted twenty years or more.

The motivation to excel can in many ways be traced to Mike Walker, who joined his father in the business at its inception in 1982. In his role as president, Mike has helped to create a corporate-family type of culture by practicing an open-door style of management, taking a personal interest in each associate's success and providing avenues for drivers to speak directly to him regarding business and quality-of-life issues.

As a result, members of the TCSI team have demonstrated an exceptional loyalty to the company and, in turn, have experienced personal and financial growth. Having never implemented a layoff, TCSI is known as a company of security and growth. Its above-average pay and significant benefits have helped many staffers and drivers become first-time homeowners.

Staff development is also pivotal to TCSI's success. From daily mentoring by management, to ongoing software training for increased efficiency, to an eight-week driver training program pairing seasoned professionals with new hires, TCSI knows that its quality lies in having well-trained people who feel good about the work they do.

TCSI also believes in supporting the community that helped make it successful and contributes to both trade and civic activities in the area. In addition to involvement with multiple trade associations, the founder and his son have each chaired the Missouri Motor Carriers Association. The company also works to be a good steward by investing time and resources in organizations that benefit children, seniors, sports teams, and others in need of assistance.

From one individual taking a chance on the future, TCSI/Transland has become a company of dedicated professionals who know how to deliver. ❖

Photo by Eric Francis

With a fleet of over five ▶ hundred trailers, TCSI/Transland delivers long- and short-haul, flatbed, intermodal, less than truckload, and special equipment loads to all corners of the nation.

Photo by Thomas S. England

Photo by Thomas S. England

Beekeeping is one of the world's oldest forms of food production and can be seen in rock paintings dating to around 13,000 B.C. Although today crop pollination services can often provide a major part of a commercial beekeeper's income, the harvesting of honey is still a strong tradition, employing techniques passed down for generations. Luckily for Lena Meyer, the owner of Honey Heaven and the Vineyard Tearoom, her husband Michael is a beekeeper and the supplier of all the honey she sells. "Our raw honey is extracted by centrifugal force and bottled without filtering. That means our Really Raw Honey is real food, and none of the natural properties have been altered or destroyed by having been heated," said Meyer. Visitors to the Vineyard Tearoom can not only buy various types of honey and sample wonderful delicacies, they may well find Meyer or her assistant Julie Franklin watching the bees, who are hard at work making more honey. ❖

Josh Mitchell is a unique photographer always looking for an angle . . . even if that means jumping up on a table to catch a different perspective. He's a "collected" visual artist who blends his passion for fine arts with commercial photography. In shooting fine-art images, Mitchell says he can create images that last. "If you're going to bring something to the people, you need to understand what they want to buy, and I think what they want is an image that stands the test of time," he says. His timeless images may be a great American scenic, or a "mentalscape"—something Mitchell hopes will evoke a sense of wonder or escape. In Springfield, Mitchell opened the Art Station in Pickwick—featuring the Josh Mitchell Gallery and Pickwick Framing. "We brought photography to Springfield because we believe it has a place right alongside the other arts in the city." As such, Josh Mitchell enjoys participating in the First Friday Art Walk, as it gives him the opportunity to entice others to look for a different angle. ❖

Photo by Alan S. Weiner

PAUL MUELLER COMPANY: PART OF OUR DAILY LIVES

Paul Mueller Company's products and services are a routine part of the daily lives of people in over one hundred countries. Mueller equipment is utilized in the processing of consumer goods for the food, dairy, beverage, cosmetics, pharmaceutical, power, and fuel industries. The homegrown Springfield business designs, manufactures, and installs stainless steel processing systems and equipment for a wide variety of applications.

In 1940, Paul Mueller and Gordon Mann started Mann and Mueller Heating and Sheet Metal Works in an old building at Olive Street and Campbell Avenue in

> When customers want to heat, cool, transfer, ferment, pasteurize, evaporate, condense, liquefy, solidify, mix, or simply store, Mueller's systems help them do so with efficiency.

Springfield. Paul Mueller became the sole proprietor of the company in 1943 due to Gordon Mann's failing health; the company was officially renamed Paul Mueller Company in 1945. In 1950, the company moved to a twenty-seven-thousand-square-foot building on three acres at the corner of Kansas Expressway and Phelps Street. Mueller currently has plants in Osceola, Iowa; Torreón, Mexico; and Springfield. The headquarters and the main manufacturing facilities are located on approximately fifty acres at the corner of Chestnut Expressway and Kansas Expressway in Springfield. Today,

◄ *Mueller manufacturing supervisor Steve Norris reviews progress with Jesse Wasson as final assembly work on a pharmaceutical fermentation system nears completion.*

Mueller's manufacturing facilities encompass more than 1 million square feet of the best fabrication and machining capabilities available.

You don't have to work for Paul Mueller Company to experience the impact of their equipment. If you consume dairy products such as ice cream, whole milk, cheese, or yogurt; if you drink juice, beer, wine, or spirits; if you eat vegetables, bread, beef, chicken, or any number of snack foods; if you use paper, pens, glues, or adhesives; if you use cosmetics, shampoo, toothpaste, or mouthwash; if you take anti-inflammatory medicine, cholesterol medicine, or cancer drugs; or if you've ever taken a ride on the space shuttle, Mueller has been part of your life.

Mueller is much more than tanks. They have the technical, manufacturing, specialty hauling, and field construction resources to be a one-stop supplier. When customers want to heat, cool, transfer, ferment, pasteurize, evaporate, condense, liquefy, solidify, mix, or simply store, Mueller's systems help them do so with efficiency. "We have a sincere commitment to provide quality solutions that satisfy the unmet needs of our customers," says Matt Detelich, CEO and president. "We achieve this by carefully examining each opportunity through the eyes of our customer, developing a genuine understanding of the issue, and then applying our know-how and creativity to implement effective solutions that positively improve our customer's bottom line."

Continued on page 202

Photo by Rod Reilly

While the name of the ▶ company is Paul Mueller, other individuals stood alongside Paul Mueller, the businessman, and were instrumental in making the manufacturer what it is today. The 1960 board of directors (left to right): James E. Davis, Paul G. Gille, Paul Mueller, Edwin V. Cox, Paul J. White, and Joe W. White.

Milk coolers played an important role in the company's growth and success. Mueller built its first dairy farm milk coolers in 1955 and is now recognized worldwide as the producer of the highest-quality farm milk cooling and storage systems.

Continued from page 201

The success of the company has its origins in the fundamental principles established by the founder, Paul Mueller (fondly known by employees and friends as "PM"). PM had the ability to choose talented people such as Paul and Joe White, Paul Gille, Jim Davis, and many others, who over the years established a standard for personal dedication and commitment to excellence that provides the foundation for continued success. Through the adherence to PM's fundamental principles of quality and innovation, the company has grown to international status. Paul Mueller Company continues to provide a good living for over one thousand dedicated employees by creating products and services that positively impact the daily lives of people throughout the world. ❖

Customer representatives review final details in preparation to carry out factory acceptance testing of a buffer hold super-skid in one of Mueller's large manufacturing bays.

Guaranty Bank has been the lead corporate sponsor for the American Cancer Society's Relay for Life for several years. This fund-raiser, which is the signature event of the ACS, promotes survivorship and increases cancer awareness in Springfield and across the nation. Guaranty Bank joins with other companies, families, schools, hospitals, and community groups to create teams that take turns walking around a track through the night to raise money for ACS. ❖

Photo by Eric Francis

Photo by Lisa Means

What do you get when you put a group of third-graders in a room with a kangaroo? If the kangaroo's name is Kirby, and he's the children's account mascot for TelComm Credit Union, the answer is: a lesson in finance. These students at Pittman Elementary School are learning about earning, saving, spending, and donating money. The children may not be old enough for payroll deduction, but they can open a special club account that teaches them the importance of saving for something special. ❖

LAW OFFICES OF DEE WAMPLER: SPRINGFIELD'S BEST DEFENSE

Innocent until proven guilty. It's a founding principle of the American judicial system and one that sets us apart from nearly every other nation. With a practice limited to the defense of felony criminal cases in both state and federal courts, the Law Offices of Dee Wampler specializes in upholding that founding tenet.

You could say that law is in the blood of senior partner, Dee Wampler. His father, Homer D. Wampler Jr., established the firm in Springfield in 1938. After young Wampler earned his Juris Doctor from the University of Missouri School of Law in 1965, he served in the army for four years,

> "We believe that people make mistakes, and it's our duty to defend them. We listen to our clients, we don't lecture."

then as assistant Greene County prosecutor and eventually prosecuting attorney. In 1973 he joined his father in private practice, specializing in criminal trial work.

Wampler later teamed with Joseph S. Passanise, an undergraduate at Missouri State University. Impressed with the young man's savvy, Wampler hired him first as a runner, then as a paralegal. When Passanise attained his Juris Doctor from Washburn University School of Law in 1997, Wampler took him on as an associate. Passanise made partner in 2004.

The firm is distinguished by its close client/attorney relationships. "We never

◀ *Nationally recognized as one of the country's top criminal defense teams, Dee Wampler (right) and Joseph Passanise also lend their expertise to numerous civic and charitable initiatives. Wampler has served on the Springfield Area Chamber of Commerce and Greene County Bar Association boards, and the* Springfield Business Journal *has recognized Passanise for his leadership, accomplishments, and community involvement.*

forget the fact that we are attorneys and counselors at law," says Wampler. "We believe that people make mistakes, and it's our duty to defend them. We listen to our clients, we don't lecture."

When necessary, the firm requires clients to attend drug and alcohol counseling and anger management classes, attend church, and seek regular counseling. As a result, says Wampler, "Very few of our clients are repeat offenders."

Wampler's work as a criminal trial attorney has earned him a national and international reputation. His cases have been featured on *The O'Reilly Factor*, *Unsolved Mysteries*, the *Today* show, and *Good Morning America*. In addition to victorious trial work, Wampler is widely recognized for his writings, having published over two hundred articles in various professional journals and four books on criminal law. Consistently named a top attorney in Springfield, Wampler is also one of the top ten attorneys in Missouri and is one of two hundred criminal trial attorneys nationwide to be elected as a Fellow to the American Board of Criminal Trial Attorneys.

Joseph Passanise is likewise making his mark. Selected in 2003 by *Missouri Lawyers Weekly* as one of the top five "Up and Coming Lawyers" in Missouri to watch, Passanise was recently elected president of the Missouri Association of Criminal Defense Lawyers. He currently serves on the Springfield Metropolitan Bar Association as director to the board, lectures at Missouri's Judicial College, and is recognized statewide for his traffic law expertise.

The Law Offices of Dee Wampler is among the nation's few law firms specializing in the defense of major felony cases in state and federal court. With over fifty years of combined experience in criminal law between them, Wampler and Passanise exert their expertise in all facets of a client's defense, from interview, investigation, and discovery on to the actual trial. The result is nothing less than the most formidable defense available. ❖

Photo by Scott Indermaur

Photo by Scott Indermaur

In 2003, the firm moved ▶ into its new offices, this striking Frank Lloyd Wright–inspired building located at 2974 East Battlefield Road. In 2007, Springfield's 417 Magazine *named the building one of its top-five best office buildings for its beauty and functionality.*

Come ramble along the streets of

downtown Springfield, past fabulous

restaurants, inviting entertainment

venues, welcoming hotels, and

sensational shops. You won't

be alone—any night of the week

folks of all ages celebrate in

the heart of the city.

Downtown Springfield is easy to enjoy. On any given night, you'll find lots of ways to unwind. For good eats, any one of the many restaurants will fill you up and make you smile. Downtown also offers a number of clubs for an evening of dancing and mingling, and you'll find galleries and theatres representing many forms of artistic talent. All this awaits within minutes of home. Easy parking, little traffic, plenty to do . . . what more can you ask for? ✤

Photo by Scott Indermaur

Photo by Rod Reilly

▲ *In the state-of-the-art drill room, Nancy takes a break to demonstrate the difference in size between one of Northrop Grumman's largest and smallest printed circuit boards. Some of the company's most important work takes place here, as highly specialized, computer-automated machines drill the millions of minuscule holes that prepare the boards for final assembly.*

NORTHROP GRUMMAN: AN INNOVATIVE LEADER IN A COMPLEX TECHNOLOGY

Northrop Grumman Printed Circuit Boards (NGPCB) is a world-leading supplier of high-performance printed circuit boards to major customers in the defense, telecommunications, computing, and medical industries. With a presence in Springfield for over forty years, NGPCB currently employs over 250 manufacturing, engineering, and professional individuals locally, with an average term of service of more than twenty years.

Established in Springfield in 1963 by the United States Engineering Company (USECO), a division of Litton Industries, NGPCB soon became known as the Advanced Circuitry Division of Litton Industries. When Northrop Grumman Corporation purchased the division and later divested the assembly and integration portion of the business to focus on its core technology, the name changed to Northrop Grumman Printed Circuit Boards.

> "What has made this facility one of the best backplane manufacturers in the world are our people. I have never worked with a more dedicated group."

Staying at the forefront of printed circuit board technology over the years has prompted much more than just name changes. The company's longtime focus has ensured continual development of leading-edge data transmission channels to meet the needs of its customers today and into the future.

During the 1970s and 1980s, when the state-of-the-art was in miniaturization and reliability and the largest client was the automotive industry, Northrop Grumman led the way as both an innovator and supplier. During the 1990s, the technology shifted to meet the telecommunications industry's vastly different requirements. The company rose to meet those requirements by building large, complex backplanes—printed circuit boards that sit at the core of major electronics systems. As a result of this shift in focus, the division became a recognized manufacturer of the largest, thickest, and most complex printed circuit boards in the world.

At the same time, NGPCB is also responding to the latest technology imperatives set forth by our military's "digital battlefields." A primary objective of current and future military electronics systems and unmanned vehicles is to reduce the need to put our soldiers in harm's way. To accomplish this, these systems require rapidly increasing printed circuit board complexity. Once again, NGPCB reengineered its technologies by developing new materials, faster signal speeds, and outstanding reliability requirements.

Just as NGPCB works to meet the complex needs of next-generation advanced electronic systems, so too does it devote its resources to problem solving within the Springfield community. Partners in Education (a Springfield Public Schools program), the American Cancer Society, United Way, March of Dimes, and the Christmas gift projects of the Missouri Department of Social Services and Mount Vernon's Veterans Home, to name just a few, all regularly benefit from NGPCB's generosity.

General manager Bill Moore explains that Northrop Grumman's continual innovation—whether in business or in the community—comes down to one important element: people. "We are not great because we have the most technical equipment—which we do—or because of our technical knowledge," he says. "What has made this facility one of the best backplane manufacturers in the world are our people. I have never worked with a more dedicated group. They have a great work ethic and superior can-do attitude, and they are just fun to work with day to day." ❖

Photo by Rod Reilly

◀ *They don't call them "flying probes" for no reason. Machines like the sixteen-head (or probe) Everett Charles A6 Electrical Tester use electrical currents to test up to 150 points per second on each circuit board. While all circuit-board companies test their boards for soundness in this manner, only Northrop Grumman can test so many points so quickly.*

An institution in Springfield for over half a century, Lawson's Barber Shop is known for its great cuts, close shaves, and energetic conversations. Located at 1846 East Division Street, the shop was established in 1957 by Harley Lawson. In 1985, son Terry took over. Shown here doing what he does best, Terry says that despite competition from salons, his family's shop has always done well. "We have customers who have been coming to us since my dad first opened," he says and then laughs. "In fact, one of them came in the other day and said he's going to keep coming in until he gets a decent haircut." Lawson also pays tribute to his vocation with a collection of old and new barber mugs and brushes. In the old days, Lawson says, customers used to bring in their own and store them. Today, they're just for show, but the tradition of great service continues . . . as does the tradition of family service: Terry's son Zachary is about to join the business. ❖

Farrier Jamie Dedmon, owner of Hoofn' It Horseshoeing, takes care of Major Sunrise, one of the entries in the 2006 Missouri Fox Trotting Horse Breed Association's Annual Fall Show and Celebration. Dedmon, who has been working with the area's foxtrotting show horses for years, knows all the shoeing tricks to help riders get the best performance out of their horses. Ava, Missouri, where the foxtrot gait originated, is the epicenter for enthusiasts of the breed, with saddle club shows virtually every weekend throughout the summer months. For farriers like Dedmon, that means shoeing as many as twenty-five head a week from his traveling shop. ✤

Photo by Alan S. Weiner

Photo by Lisa Means

Photo by Lisa Means

From hay to hogs, Missouri is one of the nation's leading agricultural states. Around Springfield, with its pastures more suitable for grazing than raising crops, farms tend toward dairy, ranching, and livestock production.

Photo by Lisa Means

For more than a quarter of a century, the Ozark Fall Farmfest has drawn farmers and ranchers from far and wide to see some of the latest happenings in the agricultural world. Held at the Missouri Entertainment and Event Center, Farmfest offers three days of perusing more than 750 exhibits featuring products for the farm, ranch, and rural home. Over five hundred head of registered livestock are also available for viewing, accompanied by displays of horses and goats, sheep and swine, and a range of exotic species. ❖

THE SIGNATURE BANK: CAPITALIZING ON ITS NONFINANCIAL ASSETS

Eight hundred forty-seven million dollars in assets in nine years! The Signature Bank continues to capitalize on its strengths of agility and flexibility. The exceptional customer service provided daily by the outstanding frontline team, supported by the equally outstanding deposit-and-loan-operations team, give The Signature Bank a clear advantage.

The Signature Bank was founded in 2004 by the merger of Signature Bank and THE BANK, both locally owned. Each bank had approximately $325 million in assets in 2004. After six and one-half years, both banks were named among the fastest-growing banks in the nation, according to the Independent Bankers' Association.

The Signature Bank is the largest locally owned independent bank in the Springfield region. It has six retail locations in Springfield and a loan production office in St. Louis. St. Louis will have two retail locations by the second quarter of 2007.

"Our mission statement says that as The Signature Bank grows, we will never lose our focus of being a strong,

> "Our mission statement says that as The Signature Bank grows, we will never lose our focus of being a strong, community-focused bank."

◄ BancorpSouth and The Signature
Bank announced in October 2006
that they were joining forces.
(Left to right) Jim Kelley and Aubrey
Patterson of BancorpSouth and
Rob Fulp and Dave Kunze of The
Signature Bank make it official.
The Signature Bank is the largest
locally owned independent bank in
the Springfield region.

community-focused bank. On a daily basis we will continue to provide responsive solutions to our customers' needs," said David Kunze, chairman and CEO. "That is the foundation of our success."

Robert Fulp, president, credits the bank's success to strong economies in Springfield and St. Louis along with a capable, ambitious staff. The Signature Bank is the thirteenth-largest bank in Missouri. "The bank's calling officers actively solicit business with a focus on one-on-one business development," said Fulp. "We are fortunate to have a strong group of bankers with a passion to deliver the highest level of service to their customers." They completed over five thousand prospect and customer calls during 2006.

Aaron Jernigan, president, Mortgage Bank, and his team of lenders operate the largest mortgage bank in Springfield. In 2006, The Signature Bank filed 1,451 deeds of trust in Greene County for a total of $307 million—the third year the Mortgage Bank ranked number one.

The Nadia Cavner Group at The Signature Bank Investment Services joined the bank in September 2005. During 2006, Cavner was named one of the nation's top female advisors in *Barron's*. She is among only three women on the list who are not from large metropolitan cities nor who work for a major brokerage house. Cavner has consistently ranked in *Barron's* top one hundred brokers in America; she ranks thirteenth in the nation and has been listed as one of the twenty-five most influential women in banking.

Continued on page 216

Kevin Dull, vice president, ▶
Mortgage Bank, left,
attends The Signature Bank
Academic Spotlight at a
Missouri State University
football game. Pictured with
Kevin are Southwest
Missouri Congressman Roy
Blunt and Missouri State
University president
Michael Nietzel.

Photo by Lisa Means

Continued from page 215

The bank's St. Louis loan production office opened on August 15, 2004. It provided a low-cost lead into a full-service banking facility in that city. St. Louis is an important strategic focus for the future, and the bank is dedicated to expanding its presence in that community.

The Signature Bank is a proud member of the Springfield community. The bank supports the United Way as a Pacesetter in their annual campaign, Partners in Education with Springfield Public Schools, is the Academic Spotlight sponsor for Missouri State University during sporting events, and provides support to many other organizations in the area. ❖

◀ *Aaron Jernigan and his team of mortgage lenders provide personal, caring service, which is one of the reasons The Signature Bank–Mortgage Bank is the top mortgage bank in Greene County.*

Ted Hamilton, president, ▶
South Campbell Bank, meets with customer and developer Rob Montileone at his latest residential real estate development.

Photo by Lisa Means

Photo by Lisa Means

At the Library Center, a "destination library," there are no limits to the ways in which people can learn. Along with thousands of books, daily story times, and reading-related special events, the center's Children's Department provides kids like Caleb Ledgerwood and his sister Paige with access to a number of computerized educational games and software sites. The eighty-two-thousand-square-foot Library Center also includes a 185-seat auditorium, a glass-enclosed recreational reading room, a story hour room, outdoor story garden, meeting rooms of various sizes and capacities, a gift shop, and a café. As the headquarters for the Springfield–Greene County Library District, the center is also home to the city's major collections of print and electronic resources, special collections, genealogical histories, as well as fully equipped computer labs, private study rooms, and state-of-the-art reference technology. ✜

Living
IN SPRINGFIELD

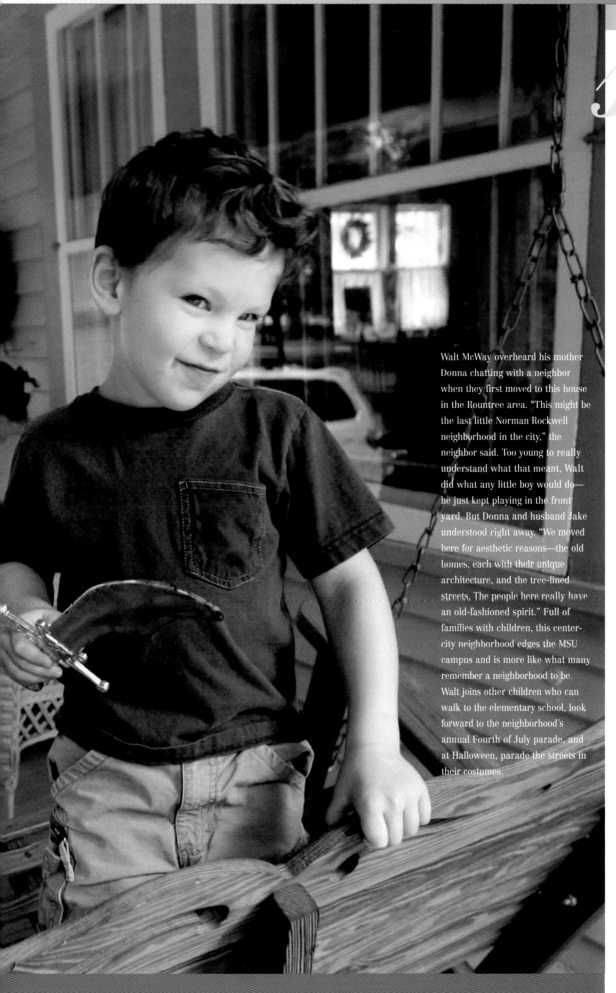

Walt McWay overheard his mother Donna chatting with a neighbor when they first moved to this house in the Rountree area. "This might be the last little Norman Rockwell neighborhood in the city," the neighbor said. Too young to really understand what that meant, Walt did what any little boy would do—he just kept playing in the front yard. But Donna and husband Jake understood right away. "We moved here for aesthetic reasons—the old homes, each with their unique architecture, and the tree-lined streets. The people here really have an old-fashioned spirit." Full of families with children, this center-city neighborhood edges the MSU campus and is more like what many remember a neighborhood to be. Walt joins other children who can walk to the elementary school, look forward to the neighborhood's annual Fourth of July parade, and at Halloween, parade the streets in their costumes.

Start with one of the most affordable housing markets in the country; add a distinguished public school system and forward-thinking higher education institutions, world-class health care, and a robust economic engine; and you've got a city with all the attributes for the highest quality of life. You've got Springfield.

The third-largest city in Missouri, Springfield is an urban oasis that not only functions effectively, but also preserves its relationship with the surrounding Ozarks. Springfield is the kind of community that easily draws people to experience its riches, whether as visitors for a few days, as university students for a few years, or as residents for a lifetime.

What draws so many to spend time in "the Queen City of the Ozarks"? For some, it's a place to call home, a neighborhood. And there are plenty of choices: from historic charmers like Pickwick—within walking distance of trendy restaurants, shops, and informal gathering spots—to newer planned developments, Springfield boasts a neighborhood to meet every interest.

Access to quality health care also brings people and businesses to a community. Springfield is home to not one, but two integrative health-care systems, more than most cities of equal size. Specialty care providers for home care, headache treatment, and hospice add to the comprehensive spectrum of available medical services.

All this and more make Springfield an easy place to live. ❖

Home of Springfield's largest nationally registered historic district, the city's Midtown neighborhood is a place of beautiful homes and structures, and the people who are devoted to keeping them in their original splendor. Located between the Central Business District and the Commercial Street Historic District, Midtown remains largely a residential neighborhood. Homes in the area consist primarily of one- or two-story balloon frame structures with Victorian architectural elements that, for the most part, remain as originally built. Streets are lined with mature trees, brick sidewalks here and there, and even a hitching post or two. Within the neighborhood's boundaries are other historical edifices as well, including city hall, a Carnegie library, and multiple university buildings. The area also hosts a variety of events year-round, including a Christmas homes tour, a Fourth of July parade, and concerts in the park. ❖

Photo by Thomas S. England

hoto by Thomas S. England

OXFORD HEALTHCARE: THE OZARK'S LEADING HOME CARE PROVIDER

As the leading home care provider in Southwest Missouri, Oxford HealthCare is dedicated to delivering a wide variety of quality services to clients of all ages—from newborns to seniors. Oxford offers nursing care, high-tech health monitoring, physical and speech therapy, bathing and personal care, housekeeping, meal preparation, shopping, transportation, and many more related services.

One call to Oxford provides access to every service, resource, and option available to help someone stay independent at home. Specially trained care coordinators help clients choose the services that best meet their needs, and services are provided by highly trained professionals dedicated to making a difference in the lives of people.

Oxford's focus on client care led to implementation of the most innovative technology in the home health care field. As the exclusive provider of the HomMed Health Monitoring System, Oxford has delivered twenty-first-century telemedicine to the Ozarks. HomMed features an easy-to-use medical device that produces an overview of a patient's health status by gathering vital signs and other health information in the client's home.

> One call to Oxford provides access to every service, resource, and option available to help someone stay independent at home.

Photo by Alan S. Weiner

◀ *Oxford nurses assist families by providing high-tech pediatric care in the comfort of home.*

This system allows potential problems to be identified earlier and helps prevent more serious illnesses, unnecessary hospitalizations, or emergency room visits. Oxford's innovative use of telemonitoring has set standards locally, regionally, and nationally.

Technology aside, Oxford's relationships with clients and their families are what make home care so rewarding. Leona, a longtime Oxford client, says, "I have the best caregiver in the world. She is respectful and punctual and very understanding. My services are excellent. She always makes me feel like life is worth living."

Whether patients are coming home from the hospital or just need some help to stay in their own homes, Oxford brings assistance and peace of mind to the client as well as the family. "I appreciate the way Kathy takes care of my mother," Carol says. "I know how much Mom looks forward to Kathy's visit. It helps me since I can't be there all the time."

This peace of mind is extremely important for Lisa, the mother of a pediatric patient. "Nursing care for a child with a disability comes from the heart. A child needs care and trust to develop a relationship, and we have that with Oxford," she says. "Oxford is dependable, and I appreciate the level of professionalism and communication I receive from them."

Since 1974, Oxford HealthCare has helped thousands of people of all ages in the Ozarks remain independent at home. Oxford employees are committed to those they serve and consider it a privilege to care for people in their own homes. ❖

Photo by Alan S. Weiner

Oxford employees provide ▶ for many needs in the home. This client also receives around-the-clock oversight using the HomMed Health Monitoring System.

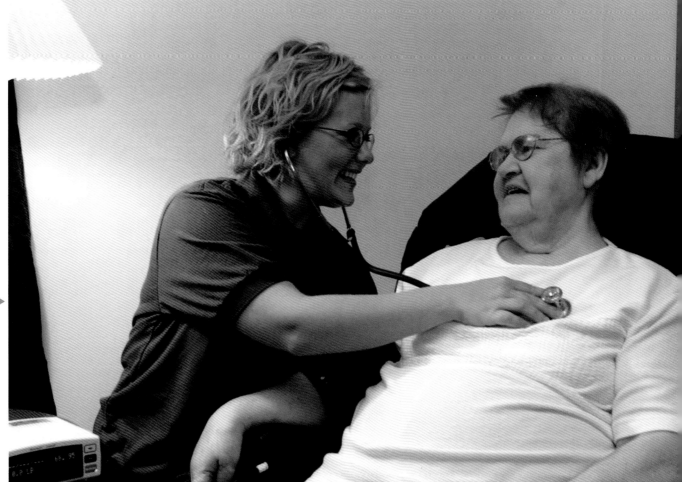

*e*Established in 1976 primarily as a ballet school, the Springfield Ballet continues its tradition of teaching dance to students from throughout the region. Students three to six years old may enroll in the school's preparatory classes, which teach the basics of movement, rhythm, and form. From there students move on to beginning, intermediate, and advanced levels. Everyone has the opportunity to participate in the ballet's yearly performances, one of which includes a special children's series of short, thirty-minute productions. Instructor and artistic director Marsha Warnke says that even for her students who don't become professional dancers, ballet provides a discipline that will serve them well in other areas of their lives. "But the main thing that makes the environment so special is that we're one big ballet family," she says. "We're not competition-based. I like to say, 'Love the art in yourself, rather than yourself in the art.' Ballet is something bigger than the individual." ✣

Photo by Lisa Means

Photo by Lisa Means

RIVERCUT 001
6
PAR 3
176
149
126
117

RIVERCUT DEVELOPMENT: MORE THAN A PLACE TO LIVE, IT'S A WAY OF LIFE

Wooded hills. Sweeping meadows. Gently flowing waters. Taken together, they make up the outdoor paradise that is one of the prominent features of Springfield's most distinctive residential communities.

When working on the initial design phase, the Rivercut Development Company's primary consideration was incorporating the beauty of the surrounding Ozarks and the nearby James River, while at the same time preserving as much of the natural surroundings as possible. Working in conjunction with V.T. Real Estate Development Group and V.T. Inc., the team borrowed components from their years of experience developing

"Rarely can you find a residential community within the city with such incredible natural views and such a peaceful environment."

successful hotel, resort, shopping center, and multiple family communities and combined them with their extensive experience in land conservation. The result is a community unequalled in beauty, amenities, and value.

Situated along the James River in southwestern Springfield, Rivercut Residential Community is known and desired for its natural waterfall, river access, a magnificent four-acre lake, a world-class golf course, and plentiful open space. As marketing director Angela Sylvester states, "Our residents come from all over the United States—some, only a few miles away, others from the

◄ *It's rare to find an urban residential community that incorporates so many natural elements, but Rivercut is a place where you are truly surrounded by nature. Even the golf course was designed to allow residents to enjoy the beauty of the land.*

coasts. One thing they all have in common is that they love the beauty of the Ozarks. Rarely can you find a residential community within the city with such incredible natural views and such a peaceful environment."

While similar communities boast of their common areas, there is nothing at all common about Rivercut. Recognizing the importance of preserving home values while also encouraging artistic expression, Rivercut's architectural guidelines are designed to inspire diverse yet complementary styles, including French Country, Old English, Craftsman, Old World, and Traditional. The designers also consulted extensively with arborists and conservationists to manage the community's growth and expansion. The resulting neighborhoods are not only beautiful but also integral to the area's aesthetic and protective of the natural surroundings.

Based on the idea that neighborhoods are more than just houses and streets, Rivercut features amenities that encourage a sense of sociability and community among its residents. Rivercut's exquisite clubhouse is the perfect spot for gatherings of all kinds, and the pool area is ideal on hot summer days and awesome sunset evenings. The natural beauty of the area inspires many activities, such as walking, biking, or jogging adventures. And the nearby James River offers plenty of opportunities to fish, drift along the water, or just relax by the shore.

Then there is Rivercut's magnificent golf course, which offers residents not only eighteen holes of challenging play, but also another way to enjoy the area's captivating beauty. As it winds its way through the development, the 7,000-yard, par-72 course is the perfect combination of terrain and setting. Designed by nationally ranked golf architect Ken Dye, the course features clubhouse facilities and a practice area hosting a Rick Grayson golf school.

With these amenities and more, it's clear that Rivercut is more than just a residential community. It's a way of life that accommodates diversity, preserves the value of one's investment, and protects some of Springfield's most valuable natural assets. ❖

Located along the James ▶ River, Rivercut Residential Community boast unequaled features, including a magnificent four-acre lake, a world-class golf course, and wide-open space.

Springfield's public spaces are not only designed for communal activities. They also provide peaceful spots for quiet reflection and concentration. For this local couple, Jordan Valley Park provides a scenic spot to engage in some early morning yoga.

City Utilities of Springfield: Making Life a Little Easier

As a locally owned utility company providing electricity, natural gas, water, telecommunications, and transit services to greater Springfield, City Utilities (CU) is in the business of making life a little easier.

But beyond delivering the essential comforts, CU understands that reinvesting in the community helps ensure an ever-improving quality of life. That's why CU and its employees contribute so much in monetary and hands-on support each year to activities that impact Springfield.

CU employees are leaders in volunteering their time and resources, including serving on boards and committees. Employee activities also help to develop the philosophy of "building a better

> But beyond delivering the essential comforts, CU understands that reinvesting in the community helps ensure an ever-improving quality of life.

tomorrow" through their work of promoting children's health, education, and mentoring.

CU makes a considerable impact on the area's economic growth as well. While its employees share talent with professional organizations, the company is involved in activities ranging from upgrading distribution systems ahead of demand to industrial park development.

Underlying CU's work is a strong commitment to environmental stewardship. From planting trees and preserving green spaces to promoting alternative transportation and renewable energy sources, CU continues to safeguard the landscape, helping to make Springfield a great place to call home. ❖

City Utilities' employee John Allen meets with customer Matthew Brandt at his home to review his service request. CU's customers enjoy the convenience of one bill, and dependable hometown services delivered with a personal touch.

Photo by Lisa Means

Originally an eleven-acre burial site for some of the soldiers who died at the Battle of Wilson Creek, the Springfield National Cemetery now serves as the resting place for more than fifteen hundred eligible veterans. Among the oldest graves are those marking the lives lost among the fifty-four hundred Union soldiers and twelve thousand Confederates who fought the historic battle on August 10, 1861. That year, delegates at the Missouri State Convention in Springfield debated the state's future, urging the passage of resolutions that would legalize slavery where it existed while opposing secession, which was favored by the governor. Although the battle, the war's first major conflict west of the Mississippi, was won by the Confederacy, it failed to strengthen the South's position. Ten years after the cemetery's founding, an inspection revealed that nearly seven hundred graves contained the remains of unknown soldiers. In 1999, the cemetery was registered on the National List of Historic Places. ❖

*t*hrough the Missouri Fox Trotting Horse Breed Youth Association, young equestrians can have fun and make friends while learning about horses and fox trotting. From seminars and trail rides to programs that foster self-improvement and leadership skills, the organization provides youth with opportunities to grow. ❖

DRURY UNIVERSITY: BEYOND ACADEMICS

At Drury University, students learn to explore new ideas and to think critically in preparation for the world beyond the classroom.

Founded in 1873 as a private, independent university, Drury University offers more than fifty undergraduate majors and academic programs, from traditional liberal arts programs in philosophy, art, music, and theatre, to professional programs such as architecture, business, entrepreneurship, communication, education, and the sciences. Drury also offers graduate programs in business administration, criminology, criminal justice, education, and communication.

> Drury melds a grounding in the liberal arts with professional studies, while emphasizing a student's place in the global environment.

Fifty years ago, Drury University was first in our region to offer graduate classes for working adults. Today, Drury's College of Graduate and Continuing Studies offers associate's, bachelor's, and master's degrees and certificates to nearly thirty-five hundred adult students on the main campus in Springfield and at seven program centers around the state.

To begin preparing for global participation, Drury students complete a unique core curriculum known as Global Perspectives 21. Students develop competency in a second language along with problem-solving and communication skills through GP21 studies that combine

◄ *Campus life at Drury puts students in the center of college activities, providing opportunities for developing friendships and for gaining an understanding of the needs of others.*

the humanities, sciences, and social sciences. Students gain a greater understanding and appreciation of other cultures and of the issues affecting people around the world, while earning a minor in global studies.

Drury students have access to a host of overseas study options, such as in Greece, England, France, and Spain, as well as short-term programs to China, Malaysia, Thailand, Lithuania, and South Africa. Nearly half of Drury's students study overseas. Some majors, such as business and architecture, require a study-abroad experience before graduation.

Through Leadership Drury, students learn to recognize the traits of a good leader, and are encouraged to assume leadership roles in areas about which they feel passionate.

A key to each student's experience at Drury is the relationship they build with faculty and staff members. Classes provide a mentoring environment where students receive the support they need to achieve high academic expectations. With a 12:1 student-to-faculty ratio and an average class size of nineteen, students are able to develop close relationships with their professors that extend well beyond the classroom. Through internships, club involvement, and campus employment, students benefit from the encouragement and guidance of Drury staff members as well.

One of Springfield's major employers, Drury employs more than eight hundred full- and part-time employees. Its annual operating budget of $55 million, with a total payroll of nearly $22 million, contributes to the local economy. Nearly 90 percent of the university's full-time employees live in the Springfield metro area.

More than three-quarters of Drury's faculty have obtained the highest degrees in their field, and many of them have been honored for their academic excellence.

Continued on page 236

Photo by Thomas S. England

Drury's F. W. Olin Library is ▶
the hub of intellectual life
on campus. A popular place
to study or read, the library
houses a collection of
176,000 printed items,
architecture databases, and
the ArtStor collection of
digital images. It is also
home to a special music
collection and a collection
on the John F. Kennedy
assassination.

Photo by Thomas S. England

Drury architecture students display models constructed for class assignments. The Hammons School of Architecture was the first accredited architecture school on a small university campus. Design-build projects, overseas study, and internships help make Drury architecture grads cutting-edge problem solvers.

Photo by Thomas S. England

Continued from page 235

The university's accolades include the following: listings in *U.S. News & World Report* "Great Schools, Great Prices" and "Best Master's Universities in the Midwest"; a *Princeton Review* selection as a "Best Midwestern University"; in the *National Survey of Student Engagement*, a record of comments by students about being motivated and challenged; recognized among "Institutions of Excellence in the First College Year" by the Policy Center on the First Year of College, noting exemplary efforts to help students transition from high school to college; as a *Barron's* "Best Buy in College Education"; and by *Time* magazine for its first-year programs.

The Drury experience takes place on a beautiful eighty-five-acre campus in downtown Springfield. It is an ideal setting for students to learn about the talents and strengths they have to offer the global community. ❖

Photo by Lisa Means

The Breech School of Business ▶ Administration develops leaders who are prepared to play prominent roles in a global economy. Drury offers six undergraduate business majors and an MBA program, and is home to the Edward Jones Center for Entrepreneurship and Innovation.

"On my honor I will do my best. . . ." More than words, the Scout Oath is a way of life for members of the Ozark Trails Council. Elementary-age boys begin as Cub Scouts and cross into Boy Scouting beginning in middle school, and continue through age twenty. In addition, Scout Exploring and Venturing are programs for boys and girls between ages fourteen and twenty. Life skills are learned every day by the more than thirteen thousand young Scouts of the Ozark Trails Council. ❖

Photo by Lisa Means

Photo by Lisa Means

With five high school football teams, Springfield offers plenty of Friday night gridiron action. John F. Kennedy Stadium, home to Parkview High School, is also the district's complex for homecoming games, marching band competitions, and other large events. ❖

The Springfield Little Theatre at the Landers offers a rich education program, with year-round classes for adults and youth in acting, musical theatre, dance, voice, and all things technical behind the scenes. The Summer Stages Program, designed for children ages four to eighteen, is a veritable sampler of all aspects of theatre, from marketing and production to costuming, set design, and performance. The Little Theatre also offers preprofessional training troupes for budding actors in elementary, middle, and high school. "The skills gained reach beyond theatre," says Lori Ann Dunn, education director. "We're equipping them to be successful in any career, and in life, by working with people, improving communication, and developing self-confidence." ❖

Photo by Rod Reilly

Photo by Rod Reilly

Photo by Rod Reilly

REGIONAL HOSPICE: SUPPORTING THOSE YOU LOVE WITH CARE

When treatment for terminal illness moves from searching for a cure to providing comfort and compassion, Regional Hospice has the answers patients and families need.

Regional Hospice offers a comprehensive program of services that include everything from pain management and comfort measures to patient and family education. Before hospice is needed, families may opt for the organization's complimentary intervention program.

This program provides information about the hospice process and helps families secure the support services they need while they make their decision about hospice care. When requested, the organization can also work with the family beyond the patient's last days, helping to provide closure at the memorial service as well as through the bereavement process in the time that follows.

> Regional Hospice serves twenty-five counties, bringing the support families need to make their loved ones' final days as peaceful as possible.

Care through Regional Hospice is provided by a talented and dedicated group of health professionals that includes a medical director, registered nurses and licensed practical nurses, social workers and case managers, and spiritual and grievance counselors. These professionals work in teams, pairing a set of caregivers with each patient, to provide a sense of familiarity and consistency at this most difficult time.

Whether at home or in a long-term care facility, Regional Hospice is available around the clock to assist patients as they end their struggle with conditions ranging from cancer to Parkinson's to Alzheimer's.

From offices in Springfield, Joplin, and Lebanon, Missouri, Regional Hospice serves twenty-five counties, bringing the support families need to make their loved ones' final days as peaceful as possible. ❖

▲ *Regional Hospice works face-to-face with families and patients to ensure that the final days they have together are peaceful and as stress-free as possible. The organization's intervention program offers families information about the hospice process before it is needed, and families can secure support services in the interim.*

The Springfield Regional Opera Guild is an essential part of the local arts scene. Members help in the office, organize cast parties for each opera, and create a number of interesting fundraising events, including the Hat Show Luncheon in September, Christmas Winter Wonderland in December, and the annual Garden Tour in June. Jean Wright, president of the guild, admires the water garden at the home of Darrel and Annette Matlock. Built with old barn wood and other recycled materials, this garden includes a koi pond, waterwheels, waterfalls, lilies, irises and other blooming water plants, and several aviaries filled with songbirds. "No matter whether you look up or down, there is something beautiful to see," Wright said. "We usually have five or six gardens on the tour, which is held on a Saturday and Sunday in the summer. Access to all the gardens on the tour is donated, so that every penny we raise goes to the support of the opera." ❖

Photo by Scott Indermaur

By employing a fully staffed team of baggage handlers and service providers, Springfield-Branson National Airport has succeeded in bringing additional routes to its airport, providing visitors and local travelers with access to key destinations around the country.

SPRINGFIELD-BRANSON NATIONAL AIRPORT — ACCESS TO THE WORLD

From humble beginnings at the end of World War II, the Springfield-Branson National Airport (SGF) has become one of the fastest-growing airports in the country—setting records in 2005 with a whopping 23 percent increase in total passenger numbers. A record like that doesn't just happen. It requires enthusiastic support from the community and a favorable business climate for the airlines. But there's one more important ingredient: imagination.

> If an airline doesn't have to hire more employees, it makes it more profitable to come to a smaller market like Springfield.

At nearly all airports, airlines provide the employees who load the baggage and service the airplanes. But in 2002, SGF imagination put a new twist on the business when it became one of the first airports to offer those services for the airlines. A master stroke, within three years it helped SGF win service to Cincinnati, Atlanta, Orlando, and Las Vegas. Why? If an airline doesn't have to hire more employees, it makes it more profitable to come to a smaller market like Springfield. By the middle of 2006, SGF had direct flights to ten major destinations: Atlanta, Chicago, Cincinnati, Dallas/Ft. Worth, Denver, Detroit, Las Vegas, Memphis, Minneapolis, and Orlando.

With the 23 percent passenger increase in 2005, the total number of passengers at SGF was 888,738. With the existing terminal bursting at the seams, SGF broke ground in 2006 for a new midfield terminal. The new facility will provide great customer service into the mid-twenty-first century. ❖

While growth for airports the size of Springfield-Branson National Airport is typically under 5 percent, this Ozarks facility set a record in 2005 when it experienced a 23 percent increase in total passenger numbers. Such rapid growth solidified the decision to break ground on a new airport, slated for completion in 2009. The new terminal's design is all about easy, hassle-free flying. From the parking lot to boarding areas, everything is on one level — no stairs, escalators, or elevators. Enhancing the airport's direct flights to ten of the nation's largest hubs, the new terminal features eight boarding gates, with room to expand to sixty. ❖

It was designed to emulate an Ozarks stream, complete with waterfalls, ripples, and a section that meanders in and out of walkways and steps. Of course, the fountain at Jordan Valley Park also provides immense enjoyment for visitors, especially young visitors, who love to play and relax in its jets. During its operational season, the fountain puts on a thirty-minute show at the top of every hour, from 10:00 a.m. to 9:30 p.m. Conceived as a "grand civic gesture," the 250-acre Jordan Valley Park offers Springfield citizens a beautiful outdoor spot for socializing and solitude, combining open space and buildings, water and meadows, playgrounds, and plazas. The park's primary indoor gathering place is located at the Creamery Arts Center, a city-owned building that is home to the Springfield Regional Arts Council, Springfield Ballet, Springfield Regional Opera, and soon, the Springfield Symphony. ❖

Photo by Alan S. Weiner

Who says dogs can't be civic minded? Recently more than one hundred dogs and their handlers raised one thousand dollars by participating in Dog Swim III at Fassnight Pool. The proceeds from the event were donated to the Cruse Dog Park Project. In case you haven't been keeping up with your doggy news lately, the Springfield–Greene County Park Board and the Citizens Dog Park Committee are developing a dog park to be located at what was formerly Loren Street Park. "A dog park is an enclosed, safe space for friendly dogs to play," said a four-legged spokeshound. "The park will operate on a self-policing honor system, and we dogs must have our owners with us at all times." ❖

Photo by Alan S. Weiner

Photo by Alan S. Weiner

Members of three families make up Pellham Commercial Realtors, a firm that began as the dream of a young boy and became one of Springfield's largest commercial real estate companies.

PELLHAM COMMERCIAL REALTORS: FROM CHILDHOOD DREAM TO FAMILY AFFAIR

As a farm boy in Fort Scott, Kansas, Galen Pellham was already dreaming of managing his own business. "I remember vividly playing at a rolltop desk on our back porch, taking notes on a pad, and then riding my bicycle, talking on a pretend telephone to clients."

That "business" turned into one of the area's largest and most renowned architectural/engineering firms in Springfield: Pellham-Phillips-Hagerman. The firm designed many notable landmarks including the Busch Municipal Building, Juanita K. Hammons Hall for the Performing Arts, OTC campus, James River Assembly, multiple theatres in Branson, projects for Silver Dollar City,

the Chateau on the Lake, and other hotels for John Q. Hammons throughout the country.

However, with groundwork already laid by his father, Galen's fascination with real estate as a second career took hold for both him and his family. Marleen, his wife, was already a commercial Realtor, so the transition became a natural fit for all. As in any industry, knowledge is power, so Pellham obtained the highly regarded CCIM designation. This in-depth knowledge, layered with twenty-five years of architectural experience and managing a large firm, gave Pellham the confidence to accomplish his vision of opening Pellham Commercial Realtors. Two of

> The future of Pellham Commercial Realtors promises new horizons by extending its borders to both local and international markets.

their children, Melanie and Christopher, were already working with them; daughter Amelia and her husband Kevin McAdams moved from Phoenix to complete the family venture.

Expanding the family affair are three sisters: Nicole Doran-Marsh and Michelle Doran, who work primarily in the Branson area, and Noelle Bonnette, who is in charge of leasing/property management. Three members of another well-known family are also part of Pellham Commercial Realtors: Sam Coryell Sr., Dan Coryell, and Sam Jr.'s wife Jennifer Coryell. The Coryells are one of Springfield's premiere apartment builders/owners.

In keeping with its mission statement, "To be the shining star in Commercial Real Estate, providing creative solutions with integrity to all parties," Pellham hired Ashleigh MacPherson, a UMKC law graduate specializing in land-use law. Ashleigh brings a sophisticated level of expertise to serve as the listing/contract coordinator. Further strengthening the firm is Susan Christy, an experienced broker-salesperson serving as the office manager, and Trip Rhodes, an investment broker.

The future of Pellham Commercial Realtors promises new horizons by extending its borders to both local and international markets. Renee Bowman, a resident of Bolivar, is marketing the area north of Springfield. Melanie Pellham recently spent three weeks in China with architects and developers to broaden Pellham's borders with international real estate. All these exciting endeavors inspire the company to continue to exceed clients' expectations by "providing creative solutions."

Keeping business and life in balance, each sales meeting begins by reading a chapter from *The Purpose-Driven Life*, and the motto of the company is from 2 Chronicles 20: "Do not be afraid or discouraged . . . for the battle is not yours but God's."

Pellham Commercial Realtors has grown from the Pellham family to become one of Springfield's largest commercial real estate companies in less than a year, and has truly become a family affair. ❖

Photo by Alan S. Weiner

Photo by Alan S. Weiner

◄me of the projects designed by PPH (Pellham-Phillips-◄germann). Many are notable landmarks in Springfield and Branson as well ◄as throughout Missouri and the nation.

Photo by Eric Franc

Located on Stan Musial Drive, the Missouri Sports Hall of Fame is filled with memorabilia and memories of all that is Missouri sports. Serving as both a museum to preserve the state's sports heritage as well as a source of inspiration for future generations, the museum contains displays commemorating a full range of sports and sports icons. From jerseys and helmets of the Kansas City Chiefs, St. Louis Rams, and St. Louis Cardinals football teams to trophies and racing suits from some of the state's top drivers, the hall is brimming with information. The Sho-Me Baseball Camp Theater features uniform apparel and autographed items from some of the sport's most notable names, such as Babe Ruth and Willie Mays. A six-foot bronze sculpture of Springfield native and golfing great Payne Stewart welcomes visitors to the museum's garden. Winner of eleven Professional Golfers Association of America (PGA) Tour events, including one PGA Championship and two U.S. Opens, Stewart was well-known for his lively and giving spirit and his artful golf attire, a throwback to the early days of the game. In October 1999, Stewart's soaring career came to an abrupt end when the private jet he was in lost pressure and crashed in South Dakota. ❖

Photo by Eric Franc

Photo by Scott Indermaur

Photo by Scott Indermaur

"Why do they act like that?" It's a question many parents often ask themselves of their children's behavior. In 2006, Springfield-based Community Partnership held a series of Caring Connection programs at two local elementary schools to answer just that kind of question. Established in 1998, Community Partnership brings together people and resources in twenty-one Southwest Missouri counties to help build stronger neighborhoods and families. "Our aim with Caring Connections is to get families to view schools as a hub for fun and for connecting with their children," says executive director Melissa Haddow. "So part of the program is to focus on family rituals. The other part is to model for these parents the kinds of behavior that encourages communication with their children and keep them from acting out." As part of the evening's events, families like Teresa Cruse and her children, Kailey, Cameron, and Braden, were treated to a Thanksgiving-style dinner, a meet-and-greet with Mr. Turkey, and a parent/child activity making picture frames. ✦

QUALITY WHERE IT'S MOST IMPORTANT: ST. JOHN'S HEALTH SYSTEM

With a history rooted in the mission of a worldwide charitable religious order, St. John's Health System naturally excels in personalized, compassionate care. Throughout its history St. John's has also been guided by visionary leadership, which has grown from a single facility into one of the nation's most integrated, state-of-the-art health-care systems.

St. John's Health System was founded by the Sisters of Mercy, a Catholic charitable order established in 1827 in Dublin, Ireland, to assist the city's working poor. When many of these laborers emigrated to the United States, members of the Sisters of Mercy followed. As America's urban economies grew, so too did the order, founding schools, hospitals,

and assistance programs throughout the country. One of those hospitals was St. John's, established in Springfield in 1891 by three Sisters of Mercy from St. Louis.

What began as a tiny four-room facility in downtown Springfield has grown into a 460-physician, 9,200-employee integrated regional health system that includes the original St. John's Hospital in Springfield; regional hospitals in Lebanon, Aurora, Cassville, and Mountain View, Missouri, and Berryville, Arkansas; St. John's Clinic, a home care division; and St. John's Health Plans.

Currently ranked fifteenth among America's Top 100 Health Systems, St. John's leads the way in bringing integrated services to those in need

> *Currently ranked fifteenth among America's Top 100 Health Systems, St. John's leads the way in bringing integrated services to those in need across the Ozarks.*

across the Ozarks. Specialties include women's health, neurosciences, cancer, senior health, pediatrics, cardiac care, emergency trauma, and sports medicine. The network also provides patients with the most up-to-date care in dozens of other medical, surgical, and dermatological services.

In Springfield, the 866-bed St. John's Hospital features a host of award-winning, state-of-the-art programs and services. In 2005, the hospital opened its new Emergency Trauma Center and Outpatient Diagnostic Center, facilities that are expansive and which rival the finest programs in the country. St. John's is designated as the region's only Level 1 trauma center for adult and pediatric patients, and provides the area's only burn unit.

St. John's Hospital is also renowned for the high quality of its pediatric care. The on-site Children's Hospital includes pediatric specialists and subspecialists, a Pediatric Intensive Care Unit, a Pediatric Intermediate Unit, and a Level III Newborn Intensive Care Unit, which has cared for sick and preterm babies for more than twenty years.

Accolades include recognition by *U.S. News & World Report* as a top urology center in the United States, two-time recognition as a quality respiratory care provider by the American Association of Respiratory Care, and the presentation by the Joint Commission on Accreditation of Healthcare Organizations with a Certificate of Distinction for Primary Stroke Centers.

St. John's operates from an abiding belief in the dignity and right of every human being to compassionate care that meets the highest standards of quality and performance. It's an approach to customer service that St. John's calls "Mercy Service," and it extends beyond the patient into the family as a whole.

Continued on page 252

Photo by Thomas S. England

Photo by Thomas S. England

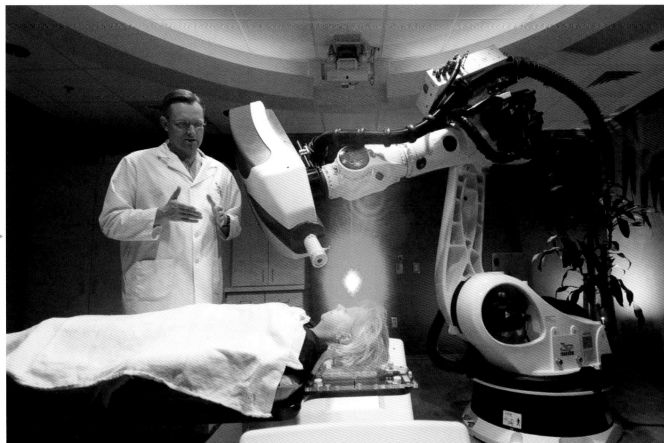

St. John's is the only ►
hospital in the region to
offer the state-of-the-art
Cyberknife, the most
accurate radiosurgical
device available for the
treatment of certain tumors.
St. John's is committed to
providing superior care to
patients by offering the
latest technologies.

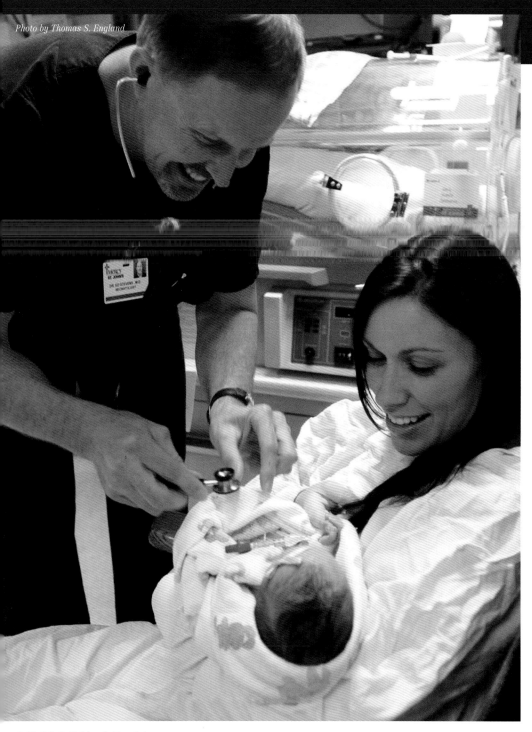

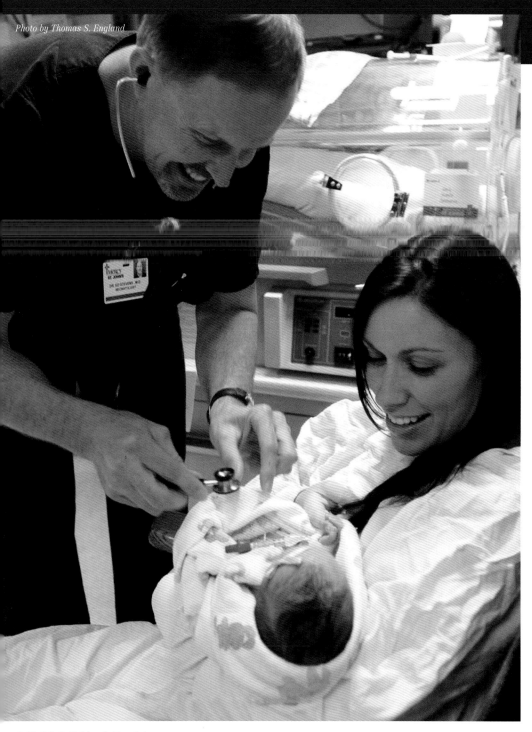

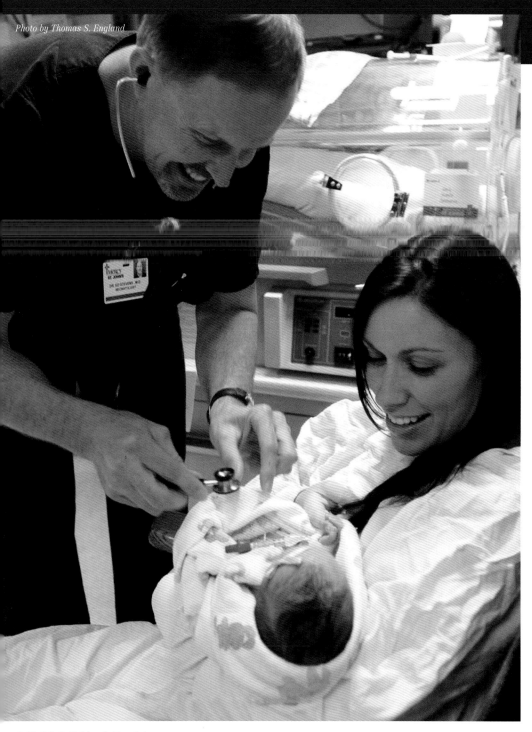

Photo by Thomas S. England

Photo by Thomas S. England

Continued from page 251

Stewardship likewise plays an important role in the hospital's service. As a not-for-profit hospital, St. John's remains guided by its founding organization's mission to provide care for the uninsured, indigent, and economically in need. In the fiscal year ending June 30, 2006, St. John's provided more than $12.9 million in charity care, $13 million in community outreach, $3.4 million in education and research, $1.5 million in donations, and more than $46 million in Medicaid subsidies. And its Foundation for Community Health provided aid and grants totaling more than $2.1 million.

Grounded in a history of service, guided by a dedication to high-quality performance, St. John's Health Care System is a vital provider of state-of-the-art, compassionate medical care for thousands of patients throughout the Ozarks. ❖

▼ At St. John's, providing spiritual care is an important part of the healing process and central to the hospital's mission. St. John's values the dignity of each human life and provides compassionate, personalized care to all patients.

▲ St. John's Children's Hospital includes pediatric specialists and subspecialists, a Pediatric Intensive Care Unit, a Pediatric Intermediate Unit, and a Newborn Intensive Care Unit, which has cared for sick and preterm babies for more than twenty years.

Photo by Scott Indermaur

In Springfield, romance doesn't just blossom in the spring. The embrace of stately trees, abundant in the traditional neighborhoods of central Springfield, their branches dressed in brilliant fall hues, seem to inspire this couple on their walk. ❖

An intimate moment shared with family and friends is made even more special by an interesting or unusual setting. Jennifer and Devin Glenn (far left), for instance, always knew they wanted to be married outdoors. They chose Jordan Valley Park as the scenic backdrop for their "I Dos." Jon and Alyssa Bormann (top and bottom) are among the many couples who have chosen Springfield's Pythian Castle as the spot to begin their lives together. In 1913 one of the oldest fraternal organizations in the country, the Knights of Pythias, built the castle in the spirit of the principles of the Knights' order—friendship, charity, and benevolence. The castle served as a home for widows and orphans and many years later as a U.S. Army hospital during WWII. Supposedly haunted, and certified as such by no less than three independent paranormal research associations, the castle is nonetheless a popular site for many special events, parties, and weddings. ❖

Photo by Douglas K. Hill

BUTLER, ROSENBURY & PARTNERS, INC.: TURNING VISIONS INTO REALITIES

Founded in 1978 by architect Geoffrey Butler, Butler, Rosenbury & Partners, Inc. (BR&P) has grown from one person to a multidiscipline design firm of architects, engineers, interior designers, and landscape architects. Their mission of "Your VISION. Our FOCUS." describes their company's promise to its clients and collaborators. This unwavering attention to clients results in innovative and unique solutions tailored to meet client needs.

The firm's staff of seventy-five is organized into four specialist studios: Business to Business, Retail & Entertainment, Civic + Community, and Hospitality. Supporting these market studios are three studios of structural engineers, interior designers, and landscape architects.

While the firm is active locally and has designed many of Springfield's landmarks, it is also designing hospitality, retail, and entertainment projects across the United States.

Longtime client Bass Pro Shops, for example, counts on BR&P to provide responsive, conscientious, and creative solutions to bring the retail giant's unique brand to each of its stores. The National Association of Store Fixtures

> Their mission of "Your VISION. Our FOCUS." describes their company's promise to its clients and collaborators.

and Manufacturers recently recognized one of the firm's latest Bass Pro projects, a new Outdoor World in Las Vegas, as the Specialty Store Over 25,000 Square Feet of the Year. The award recognizes the store's innovative merchandise displays with easy-to-navigate physical space for a more relaxed shopping experience.

The firm has also served as architect on some of the country's most noted hotels and convention centers, including dozens for Springfield-based John Q. Hammons Industries, another longtime client. Hammons's recently completed $54 million Embassy Suites Hotel and Convention Center in Frisco, Texas, was showcased in the April/May 2006 issue of *Hotel Design Magazine*, which ranks BR&P number thirty-six on its list of top hotel design firms in the United States.

Locally, projects such as the Juanita K. Hammons Hall for the Performing Arts at MSU, the Gillioz Theater restoration, the Jordan Valley Expo Center, the United States Courthouse at University Plaza, and many others reflect their level of creativity and care. Whether a client has been in the Springfield community for many years or is new to the area, BR&P is always ready to assist in creating environments best suited for the client's business and patrons.

BR&P is also expanding its operations in other locations. The firm recently opened a regional office in Phoenix, Arizona, and has begun an affiliation with a large design firm in China to provide resources for BR&P and to design projects in China.

Butler, Rosenbury & Partners is a committed community partner that provides outstanding professional design services locally, regionally, nationally, and soon internationally. ✤

Photo by Lisa Means

▲ *This three-story office building located in southwest Springfield is 149,000 square feet and serves as the operations center for a national company.*

◀ *Located in downtown Springfield on the edge of Jordan Valley Park, this ninety-two-thousand-square-foot facility with forty-five thousand square feet of exhibition space creates a great venue for conventions, meetings, and public gatherings.*

Photo by Lisa Means

The Battle of Wilson's Creek was fought ten miles southwest of Springfield on August 10, 1861. It was a bitter struggle for control of Missouri in the first year of the Civil War. More than twelve thousand Confederates and fifty-four hundred Union soldiers met on the hills bordering Wilson's Creek, and more than seventeen hundred lives were lost. Annual Wilson's Creek reenactments generally draw more than ten thousand reenactors and eighty thousand spectators. Three battle scenarios are enacted for the public: the prelude to Wilson's Creek, the Battle of Dug Springs—the attack on the Southern forces encamped on the banks of Wilson's Creek—and the Battle of Bloody Hill. Reenactments, which are equal parts theater, education, fellowship, and genealogy, are a good way for families to study history together. Wilson's Creek National Battlefield Foundation works with the park to preserve the site and to encourage understanding and appreciation for a valuable piece of history. ✣

Many of the fifth-grade students from Springfield area schools that visit the Gray/Campbell Farmstead in Nathanael Greene Park are amazed when volunteers Jane Sanders (left) and Delores Biggers explain how different life on the farm was in pre–Civil War days than in today's wired world. Clothes hand-washed with a pot of boiling water and a board? Wood hand-cut with a crosscut saw to run the granary? Wow, life wasn't easy. Every spring and fall the students come out for a hands-on experience to supplement their classroom study of pioneer days. The Gray/Campbell Farmstead includes the 1856 restored home of John Polk Campbell, nephew and namesake of the founder of Springfield. Other elements were added, including a granary from Diggins, Missouri, and a log house and barn from Hurley, Missouri, creating a replica of a typical Missouri farmstead. ❖

Photo by Rod Reilly

HEADACHE CARE CENTER: TAKING THE PAIN AWAY

It all started with a headache. Not your ordinary take-two-aspirin-and-it's-gone headache. It started with the debilitating headache of migraine that 12 percent of the American population suffers, and it resulted in a patient-centered, three-division organization with a single focus: improving health care for patients.

HeadacheCareCenter
CLINIC · RESEARCH · EDUCATION

It all began in 1996, when Roger Cady, M.D., founded a specialized clinic in Springfield for the diagnosis and treatment of people with disabling headaches and facial pain. Today, Headache Care Center is a nationally recognized referral center for physicians and patients, in large part due to its unique, interdisciplinary team approach that combines family practice, neurology, internal medicine, psychology, physical therapy, nursing, and education. "Our individualized approach

allows us to become partners with our patients to help them understand and gain control over headaches and their lives," says Cady.

Typically, many patients don't understand the process of migraine and are frustrated when their treatment no longer works. Because migraine is diagnosed from the patient's history, the new patient visit requires a thorough evaluation.

"Education begins with acknowledging that migraine is a real, neuronal, biochemical disorder. A migraineur is born with a highly sensitive nervous system that has a lower threshold to headache than the average person. Treatment is directed toward raising the headache threshold," explains internist J. Kent Dexter, M.D.

For those individuals who are disabled by headaches, Headache Care Center features a one-week, outpatient Intensive

> "Our individualized approach allows us to become partners with our patients to help them understand and gain control over headaches and their lives."

◄ *Headache Care Center, Clinvest,*
and Primary Care Network share
22,500 square feet of work space
in Chesterfield Village.

Program. Daily the patients see a physician, psychologist, physical therapist, and nurse. "As a treatment team, we evaluate patients from different perspectives to create the best strategy for them to manage their condition and get their life back," states neurologist Curtis Schreiber, M.D.

Photo by Scott Indermaur

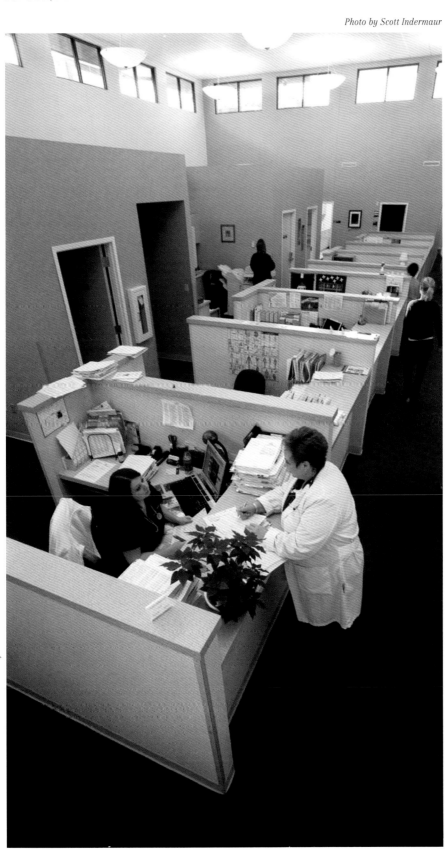

Photo by Scott Indermaur

The interior of the Headache ▶
Care Center is bright, roomy,
and dynamic—a positive
milieu for a change
toward health.

Dr. Cady has been a leading researcher in the field of headache and other disorders since 1990. As medical research expanded at Headache Care Center, the clinical research organization Clinvest was formed. Clinvest conducts medical research in the region of southwestern Missouri as well as nationwide. Regionally, Clinvest concentrates on the most effective therapies for headaches of all types, as well as hypertension, diabetes, osteoarthritis, fibromyalgia, gastrointestinal disorders, high cholesterol, and Alzheimer's disease. Clinvest research coordinators manage an average of twenty-five ongoing research studies, testing the effectiveness and safety of newly developed treatments. Nationally, Clinvest manages studies within a network of approximately two thousand primary care physicians.

In addition to medical and pharmaceutical therapies, Clinvest is involved in technology development, including a number of neurodiagnostic, neuropsychological instruments sponsored by the U.S. Department of Defense. They have been adopted by major medical centers and field hospitals for use in the care of military troops. "Knowledge gained through Clinvest ensures that the most up-to-date treatments are available to physicians and patients," adds executive

Continued on page 262

◄ Clinvest is a clinical research organization that seeks participants to volunteer for studies that assess the most effective therapies for disorders such as migraine, diabetes, fibromyalgia, irritable bowel syndrome, high cholesterol, Alzheimer's disease, and others.

▼ The Mental Efficiency Workload Test (MEWT) measures the effects of migraine, medication, concussion, fatigue, or other factors on cognitive efficiency. Neurobehaviorist and codeveloper of the test, Dennis Reeves, Ph.D., administers the MEWT to a research subject.

Continued from page 261

vice president of Clinvest Dennis Reeves, Ph.D. "Clinvest is another example of our integrated approach to health care."

PRIMARY CARE NETWORK™

Just as the Headache Care Center provides leading-edge clinical care, and Clinvest conducts and manages cutting-edge research, there is another important element to round out true comprehensive care: education of primary care physicians. Primary Care Network is a private, nonprofit foundation and the third division of a multifaceted company focused on patient health. Founded in 1997, Primary Care Network is dedicated to integrity and quality medical education and training to update physicians nationwide on new approaches and treatments for optimal medical care. "Right now we're presenting programs on more than thirty-five therapeutic areas all across the country," says Kenny Cox, executive vice president of education.

Practicing physicians are required to obtain Continuing Medical Education (CME) credits every year to maintain their medical license; thus, the need for educational programs is ongoing. Primary Care Network, accredited by the Accreditation Council for Continuing Medical Education of the American Medical Association, educates about twenty thousand clinicians a year. The CME education is tailored for primary care physicians, who provide the majority of medical care in the United States. Through a variety of formats, from Web-based to live programs, Primary Care Network is recognized for producing the most up-to-date, clinically relevant medical education to physicians. The ultimate goal is to optimize patient care for the welfare of individuals and communities.

Photo by Thomas S. England

Primary Care Network, a nonprofit foundation, is accredited by the Accreditation Council for Continuing Medical Education to provide CME programs nationwide to physicians. Roger Cady, M.D., presents information on the pathophysiology of migraine to health-care providers.

PATIENT-CENTERED CARE

Working in tandem, Headache Care Center, Clinvest, and Primary Care Network are poised to continue rendering a positive impact on the overall health of patients in Springfield, southwestern Missouri, and far beyond the state's borders. "Springfield has provided a wonderful home for our business, and we are proud to be a member of the community. Over the next ten years, we envision that our company will continue to expand and that health care will focus on patient-centered prevention," states Kathleen Farmer-Cady, psychologist and cofounder. ❖

Photo by Scott Indermaur

Through CME education, Primary Care Network documents patients' success stories and presents them to physicians across the country.

Photo by Alan S. Weiner

Photo by Scott Indermaur

For people like Krista Odaffer, Firehouse Pottery is a fun way to explore one's inner artist without committing to building a studio and purchasing supplies. This paint-your-own ceramic studio supplies blank ceramic items, colors, brushes, and space. All you provide is your imagination. When you're finished painting, leave your piece for the studio to fire and pick it up a few days later. Firehouse welcomes drop-ins Tuesday through Sunday (it's closed Mondays), and also takes reservations for birthday parties, showers, family get-togethers, and corporate and other events. And if you want to improve your skills even further, the shop offers monthly ceramic and glass fusion workshops. ❖

Joy Roan (left) and Abby Detweiler are among the many talented local artists who gather weekly at the home of Jeff and Alicia Brundege on the eastern edge of town. Jeff, a sculptor, and Alicia, a painter, offer their home as an "artist's enclave" where anyone can come to paint, draw, or sculpt every Tuesday. Some artists find the fellowship with other creative souls inspiring, while some are simply inspired by the creative atmosphere of the beautiful Brundege home—a work of art in itself. ❖

Generally bordered by Kearney and Chase streets, Washington Avenue, and the Kansas Expressway, Woodland Heights, located in North Springfield, is a part of town where people feel a sense of kinship. "It's been a good place to live," says Rebecca Tucker, seen here gardening with son Benjamin on a warm summer day. Tucker says that, while there are some rental properties in the area, most houses tend to be owned by residents who intend to stick around for awhile. "They like the neighborhood because they feel safe," she says. Of course, it helps that the area has one of the city's more active neighborhood associations, with monthly meetings that often turn to discussion of restoration projects taking place in the area's turn-of-the-century homes. The association is responsible for planting hundreds of trees in recent years, and its activities helped lead to the reworking of streets, sidewalks, and a park in an effort to reduce traffic and improve safety for residents and children at Reed Middle School, which is located in the neighborhood. ❖

Photo by Scott Indermaur

Photo by Scott Indermaur

Photo by Scott Indermaur

BKD Foundation Dedicated to Community Enrichment

Highly regarded as one of the nation's top-ten CPA and advisory firms, BKD has also earned a sound reputation for its dedication to community enrichment. Since its creation in 1999, BKD Foundation has contributed more than $2.3 million and countless volunteer hours firmwide to charitable causes supported by partners and employees in BKD's twenty-seven locations.

Community involvement means that volunteer time is as important as funding. BKD partners and employees actively pitch in and touch lives locally through the Boys and Girls Club, Habitat for Humanity, and Junior Achievement, among others.

Each BKD office has a foundation committee that meets periodically to select beneficiary organizations and initiatives in the local community. Past recipients include Breast Cancer Foundation, Developmental Center of the Ozarks, Southwest Missouri Humane Society, Junior League of Springfield, United Way of the Ozarks, Wilson's Creek National Battlefield Foundation, and the YMCA.

Personnel in local offices also contribute above and beyond the foundation's activities, with firm personnel serving on numerous civic and charitable boards. The BKD Matching Gift Program also provides financial support to the colleges and universities from which it recruits its personnel.

Whether helping to frame a home for Habitat for Humanity or donating monies to a health-care initiative, each year hundreds of BKD employees enthusiastically contribute to programs that strengthen and enliven their communities. ❖

> Each year hundreds of BKD employees enthusiastically contribute to programs that strengthen and enliven their communities.

▲ *Pictured (left to right) inside the reptile house at Dickerson Park Zoo are Dickerson Park Zoo development director Don Tillman, BKD professional practices partner Steve Rafferty, BKD partner Jason Rader, and former BKD managing partner Hearld Ambler. As longtime supporters of the zoo, Ambler and his wife Marge donated money specifically to help build the reptile house.*

Drury University's historic Stone Chapel (1880) is Springfield's oldest stone structure and is listed in the National Registry of Historic Landmarks. With its beautiful architecture and rich history, Stone Chapel is a popular site for wedding ceremonies and community events. ❖

Photo by Eric Francis

Photo by Thomas S. England

New student orientation at Drury University consists of four days of fun, friendships, and team building. Ensuring that students have a smooth transition to campus life is a priority at Drury. In fact, Time magazine highlighted the university's first-year program as one of the best in the nation. ❖

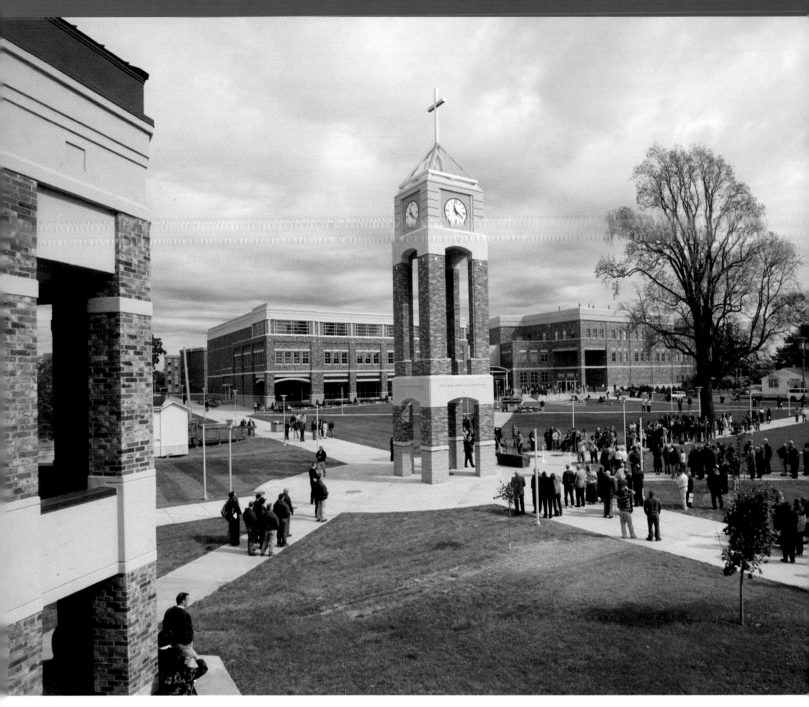

EVANGEL UNIVERSITY: BOLDLY CHRISTIAN, UNQUESTIONABLY ACADEMIC

From its beginnings as a former army hospital to its present-day role as a top coeducational Christian university, Evangel University boasts a history rich in innovation and inspiration.

The university traces its roots back to World War II when the land was occupied by O'Reilly General Hospital, a treatment center for wounded soldiers. During the war, the hospital earned renown as a pioneer in plastic and reconstructive surgery. Later, many of those doctors provided the foundation for Springfield's "Medical Mile."

In 1954 the federal government awarded parts of the O'Reilly property to various local organizations, one of which was the Assemblies of God, which built a new liberal arts college on its portion.

Since its establishment in 1955 with a freshman class of ninety-three students, Evangel University has served nearly thirty thousand students from every state and dozens of foreign countries. As a private Christian university of the arts, sciences, and professions, two thousand students annually enroll in eighty academic programs, with behavioral sciences, education, and business as its largest departments. In addition, Evangel offers eight graduate programs in psychology, education, and organizational leadership.

> As a private, coeducational Christian university of the arts, sciences, and professions, Evangel enrolls two thousand students in eighty academic programs each year.

◄ *In fall 2006 more than one thousand people attended the dedication of a seventy-five-foot clock tower, built in celebration of Evangel's fiftieth anniversary. The university has seen $40 million in development in the past ten years. At the right of the photo is one of two remaining WWII-era structures; this is the site of a new Administration Building.*

Owned and operated by the General Council of the Assemblies of God, Evangel University promotes high ethical as well as academic standards. As a community of scholars and students working together to fulfill the university's mission to discover, apply, and communicate truth, Evangel encourages the integration of faith, learning, and life. These are considered necessary for personal and intellectual discovery.

Evangel has benefited from the dedication of three learned and passionate presidents: Dr. Klaude Kendrick, who served from 1955 to 1958; Dr. J. Robert Ashcroft, who served from 1958 to 1974; and Evangel's current president, Dr. Robert H. Spence. With thirty-three years of leadership as of 2007, Dr. Spence is the longest-tenured college president in Missouri and one of the longest-serving in the nation.

Early in his tenure, Spence spearheaded the construction of two new residence halls and a 2,170-seat chapel. Since 1996 and under Spence's direction, Evangel has undergone an additional $40 million in campus development. Today most of the university's converted army barracks have been replaced by new, state-of-the-art educational facilities, including two three-story academic buildings, a fitness center, a student union complex, and a fine arts center. With student facilities complete, construction on new administrative offices commence in 2007.

Not only is Evangel University a great place to learn, it is also a great place to work. In 2005 and 2006, *Christianity Today* magazine named Evangel among the "40 Best Christian Places to Work" in the United States. Among its standout qualities are strong opportunities for growth, low employee turnover, and high levels of trust and commitment among students, faculty, and staff. Those qualities—combined with the steadfast integration of reason and faith, tradition and modernization—make Evangel University one of Springfield's most vital economic and academic resources. ❖

Photo by Lisa Means

The Evangel chapel faces ▶ *Glenstone Avenue and features a massive stained-glass window that is illuminated at night. The 2,170-seat facility is used for a variety of events that are open to the public. Attached to the chapel's south and west sides is the Barnett Fine Arts Center— home to Evangel's music, art, and theatre programs which also served as the rehearsal facility for the Springfield Symphony.*

Photo by Paul K. Logsdon

A certified nurse assistant joins a resident in the garden at one of Christian Health Care's many facilities. Whether it is skilled care, residential care, or the retirement community in Springfield, Christian Health Care facilities give seniors a new outlook on life by encouraging choice, wellness, and vitality. The Christian Health Care environment is a safe one that combines attention to both home and health-care needs and respects each person's desire for independence, dignity, and purpose. ❖

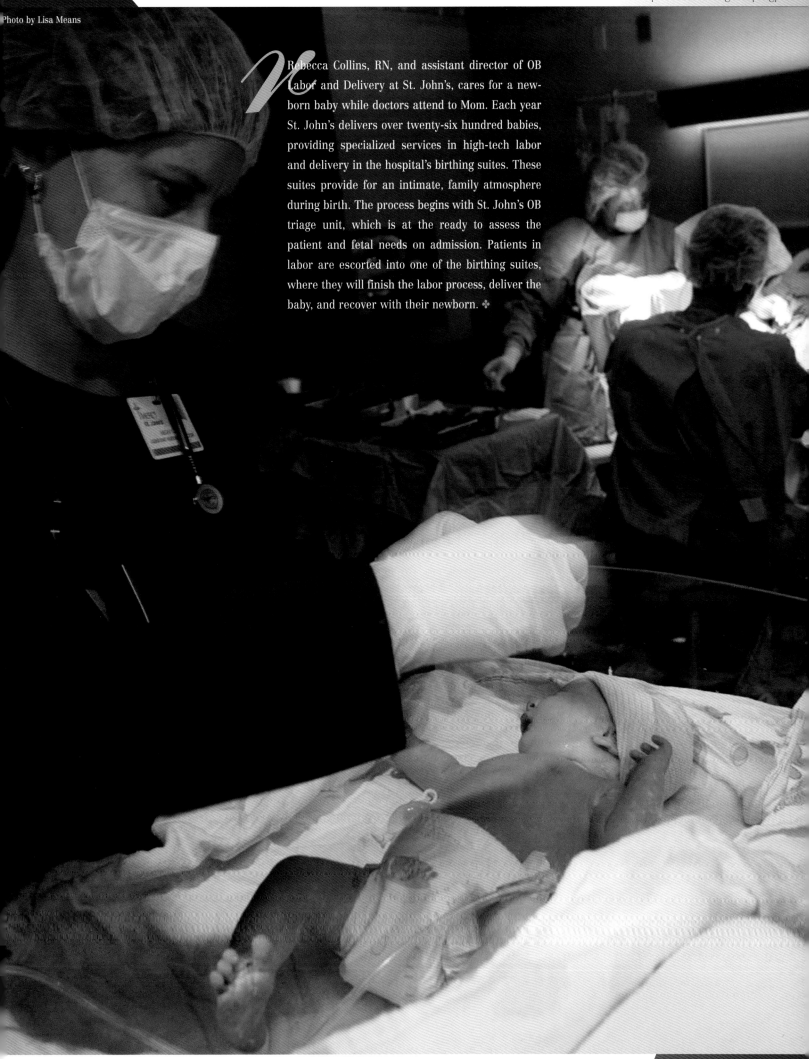

Photo by Lisa Means

Rebecca Collins, RN, and assistant director of OB Labor and Delivery at St. John's, cares for a newborn baby while doctors attend to Mom. Each year St. John's delivers over twenty-six hundred babies, providing specialized services in high-tech labor and delivery in the hospital's birthing suites. These suites provide for an intimate, family atmosphere during birth. The process begins with St. John's OB triage unit, which is at the ready to assess the patient and fetal needs on admission. Patients in labor are escorted into one of the birthing suites, where they will finish the labor process, deliver the baby, and recover with their newborn. ❖

When the winds subside after a tornado or the rains after a hurricane, the next thing people might see coming through their neighborhood is one of these colorful semitrucks. Based at Convoy of Hope World Distribution Center in Springfield, this large fleet of trucks can be ready at a moment's notice to deliver relief throughout the United States.

CONVOY OF HOPE: COMPELLED BY COMPASSION

The Southeast Asia tsunami. Hurricane Katrina. September 11, 2001. These were some of the worst disasters in recent history. Not only did they result in billions of dollars in damage and the devastation of millions of lives, they also challenged the resolve and resources of some of the world's most capable relief operations. One organization that rose to meet the challenge is Convoy of Hope.

A frontline, grassroots Christian relief organization based in Springfield, Convoy of Hope was itself born from tragedy. When he was a child, founder and president Hal Donaldson's parents were hit by a drunk driver, killing his father and temporarily immobilizing his mother. As a result, Donaldson and his three siblings experienced what it is like to go without. But thanks to the efforts of local churches and community agencies, the family recovered. That giving spirit stayed with Donaldson throughout his life and inspired him and his brothers to establish Convoy of Hope in 1994.

"We wanted to be part of a movement of compassion, encouraging everyone to do their part to help the suffering and the neglected," says Donaldson. "We hope to continue helping millions of people, but, more important, we hope to encourage others to reach out to people in need who cross their path."

Convoy of Hope provides its services through its divisions: U.S. outreach, U.S. disaster response, and international

> A frontline grassroots Christian relief organization based in Springfield, Convoy of Hope was itself born from tragedy.

outreach and disaster response. No matter the need or the location, the organization strives to provide its supplies and services as quickly and efficiently as possible. In 2005, the organization received more than $40 million in gift-in-kind goods and donations; 92 percent of all expenses were program costs.

"When people donate through Convoy of Hope, they can know those resources translate into bringing real help to real people," says Donaldson.

Since the organization's founding, it has mobilized a network of about two hundred thousand volunteers, representing twelve thousand organizations, to provide assistance to more than 15 million people in need. The organization also serves as a "channel of compassion" for various individuals, businesses, and churches that wish to provide relief services. And through its partnerships with various major companies, nonprofit organizations, and government agencies, it serves to effect long-term change in communities around the globe.

It takes not only determination but also organization to provide services to those in need. From its three-hundred-thousand-square-foot headquarters, warehouse, and distribution center in Springfield, Convoy of Hope's fleet of eighteen-wheel semitrucks makes daily transfers and deliveries of food and other supplies to communities in all fifty U.S. states and more than fifty countries. Through mid-2006, Convoy of Hope had distributed nearly 82 million pounds of food, water, and supplies.

Each year, Convoy of Hope conducts about forty U.S. outreach events, working with local partners to organize volunteers and create events tailored

Continued on page 274

ith Convoy of Hope, there is ▶ no such thing as drive and drop. After Hurricane Katrina, Convoy of Hope coordinated medical teams nd a number of distribution sites for disaster relief sponse. As people picked up water, ice, and food from Convoy of Hope, they could also receive basic medical care, including prescription refills. For their efforts, the medical team received an eryday Heroes Award from the American Red Cross.

▲ *During Convoy of Hope's international outreach events, such as this one in El Salvador, kids get to just be kids. They can enjoy carnival rides, play games, and participate in fun events like face painting. Like all outreach participants, they also take home a big bag filled with food and other essentials.*

Continued from page 273

to each community's specific needs. Events include job fairs, medical and dental screenings, grocery giveaways, haircuts, and more.

Internationally, Convoy of Hope sponsors a variety of initiatives to assist communities around the globe with their immediate or short-term needs. Its Family-2-Family program, for instance, provides tens of thousands of schoolchildren in South America and Africa with backpacks filled with school and hygiene supplies. Sustainable solutions that address poverty for the long term include the organization's Seeds of Hope program, which distributes seed packets and provides agricultural education to more than forty-five thousand impoverished families in countries like Venezuela, El Salvador, Zambia, and South Africa. Its life-changing Nurturing Hope program provides hungry third-world children with protein-rich meals while introducing their families to basic health-care and nutritional concepts.

Convoy of Hope's disaster-response efforts provide immediate relief wherever it is needed. Not only did the organization distinguish itself with quick responses to the tsunami and hurricane disasters, its credibility and effectiveness inspired local schools, businesses, and organizations to raise funds for continued assistance. And the efforts continue. In March 2006, Convoy of Hope's God Cares program was established to empower volunteers from across the United States to continue to reach out to the Gulf Coast communities. And because disaster knows no timeline or geographic boundary, Convoy of Hope remains active whether helping ice storm victims in Springfield, or reaching out to other victims halfway around the world.

▲ *With Convoy of Hope, each event is a chance to make a personal connection, like this one at an NFL-sanctioned event during the 2005 Super Bowl in Jacksonville, Florida. This volunteer knows that a hug, a smile, and the willingness to listen are just as important as a helping hand.*

"We were active in more than fifty countries around the world in 2005, responding to needs that never made the front page," says international director Kenton Moody. "So many times people comment that they didn't know Convoy of Hope does what they do. I think we are probably one of Springfield's best-kept secrets."

For millions of people at home and abroad, however, Convoy of Hope is no secret. Instead, it is a symbol of hope—actively and compassionately providing help no matter the cause, the location, or the need. ❖

This bird's-eye view of a Convoy of Hope outreach, at home in Springfield, illustrates the scope of the daylong event. Marvels of organizational skill, these events serve up to ten thousand guests. Volunteers meet on Friday night to receive their assignments, arrive on-site early Saturday morning, and hit the ground running in service to their honored guests.

Thanks to the generosity of its ▶ donors, Convoy of Hope provides relief to even the most desperate regions. One of its adopted cities is Mathare Valley, Kenya, which compares with Calcutta, India, in economic impoverishment. Now, the villagers have food, clean water, and seeds from which to grow crops, and its children have the uniforms, shoes, and socks that enable them to attend school.

An outdated lithotropic ▶ X-ray clinic that was donated to Convoy of Hope after Katrina is now the organization's Mobile Command Center. Other donors equipped it with generator backup and the latest in Wi Fi technology; It serves as both a storm tracker and a vital communications conduit

Photo by Alan S. Wein

How many times have you said to a friend that you should get together more often? In 1991, Mary Collette stopped saying it and just did it. She organized a weekly get-together of friends and colleagues that quickly turned into what she describes as an informal social networking group. Over the years, nearly one hundred women have cycled in and out of the gatherings. "Meeting like this allows us to catch up on each others' lives, to discuss our varied interests, to offer assistance and support." It's also a great way to welcome newcomers to the community. "Springfield is a very friendly, diverse place," Mary continues. "On any night with us you'll meet lawyers, teachers, restaurant owners, artists, and politicians." Because of its wide variety of food and drink and plentiful seating space, the Mud Lounge serves as their regular meeting spot Wednesdays after work. But every couple of months or so, the ladies meet for potluck at someone's house or attend a special event like a play, art opening, or fashion show. ❖

Each year the Springfield Museum of Art invites some of today's most talented watercolorists to exhibit their work in a summerlong exhibition known as Watercolor USA. First held in 1962, the show has grown into one of the most well-respected and competitive juried exhibitions of its kind in the country. "Back when we started, watercolor was underappreciated in the art world, so we were at the forefront of exhibiting the medium," says the museum's director, Jerry Berger. "Today, of course, watercolors are sought after by collectors and museums around the world." Established in 1946, the Springfield Museum of Art has since amassed an impressive permanent collection comprising primarily twentieth- and twenty-first-century American artwork. "The museum really is a little jewel," says Berger, who has served as director since 1987. "A community our size is very fortunate to have a museum of this caliber. And I consider myself fortunate to be able to add to the museum's collection, to put together great shows, and to exhibit them to our audience." ❖

Photo by Rod Reilly

Photo by Rod Reilly

...igor ● Post-Rehab Enhancement

CHRISTIAN HEALTH CARE: RESPONSIVE CARE IN SAFE ENVIRONMENTS

Sometimes, there comes a point when illness, injury, or simply the aging process lead to a time to make decisions about senior care. When that day arrives, people turn to Christian Health Care, an organization dedicated to giving seniors a new outlook on life.

Through Christian Health Care, seniors find three levels of responsive care, provided in safe environments, each encouraging wellness, vitality, and choice.

The first is Christian's skilled care, offering round-the-clock attention for seniors who are unable to live independently. On-call physicians, licensed nurs-

Whatever the choice, Christian Health Care offers a comprehensive selection of services geared specifically for seniors.

ing staff, and certified nursing aides assist residents with their daily care needs and medications while therapists work on rehabilitative issues designed to meet their individual needs. Additional provisions include meal planning and housekeeping services, medical care, and a regular calendar of recreational activities. Designed to help seniors get back as much independence as possible, Christian's skilled care is offered at nearly a dozen facilities in Springfield and communities throughout Missouri.

Next are Christian's Residential Care facilities, the perfect place for seniors who do not need full-time care

◄ Through Christian's rehabilitation services, therapists work to help patients regain their strength and endurance. In the therapy room, a physical therapist helps one patient with issues affecting his walking ability while an occupational therapist and a restorative aid work with other patients on upper-body strengthening and exercises.

but who prefer not to live on their own. Staffed with Certified Nursing Assistants who provide appropriate levels of care when needed, these facilities allow residents to perform their own daily hygiene but provide prepared meals, medication management, and activities both on and off site. Christian Residential Care is located in both Lebanon and Nixa, Missouri.

Each of Christian's skilled care and residential units is licensed by the Missouri Department of Health and Senior Services.

Rounding out the choices is Christian Health Care's retirement community in Springfield, which allows seniors to live independently. Complete with senior apartments, this community is ideal for those who are able to care for themselves but are more comfortable with close neighbors and emergency care nearby. Most apartments come equipped with kitchens that allow residents the freedom of cooking their own meals, while others include meal plans that give residents a chance to participate in a host of social and recreational activities.

Whatever the choice, Christian Health Care offers a comprehensive selection of services geared specifically for seniors. Among its offerings are physical, occupational, and speech therapy; peritoneal dialysis; respiratory care; intravenous therapy; specialty wound care; and transportation to and from physician and medical appointments. Christian can also address the special needs of seniors afflicted with Alzheimer's or dementia.

Each of Christian's facilities houses Medicare-certified beds for those who qualify. In addition, the care delivered by Christian's physicians, nurses, and therapists is complemented by caring health professionals, including care plan coordinators, dietitians, and social workers.

With the aging process often comes a need to make certain lifestyle choices. With Christian Health Care, those choices allow seniors to retain their dignity and independence. ❖

Photo by Rod Reilly

Photo by Rod Reilly

Christian Health Care's ▶ caring nurses love what they do, and it shows. Care at Christian is delivered in a safe environment that encourages wellness and helps seniors maintain a positive outlook on life.

Photo by Thomas S. England

Springfield was considered a leader in gifted education in Missouri when it formed Phelps Center for Gifted Education to address the needs of academically gifted students. Today numerous programs provide rigorous academic curriculum in a supportive environment for gifted students. ❖

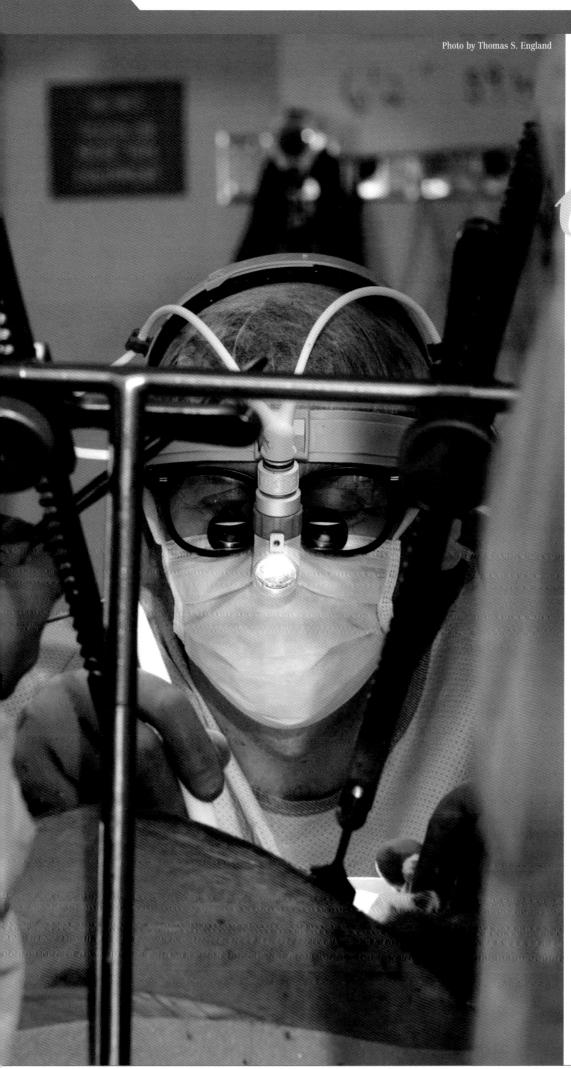

Photo by Thomas S. England

One of the advantages of living and working in the Springfield area is the outstanding level of health care, which features both the latest technology and world-class physicians. The CoxHealth campus is organized around five Centers of Excellence. In 2003, a $2 million gift transformed Cox Medical Plaza 1 into the Clarence R. and Edna M. Wheeler Heart and Vascular Center. This facility is totally dedicated to cardiac care, including education, noninvasive testing, surgical services, and an unparalleled team of specialists, including Dr. John Steinberg, who performs open-heart surgery in a state-of-the-art operating suite. ❖

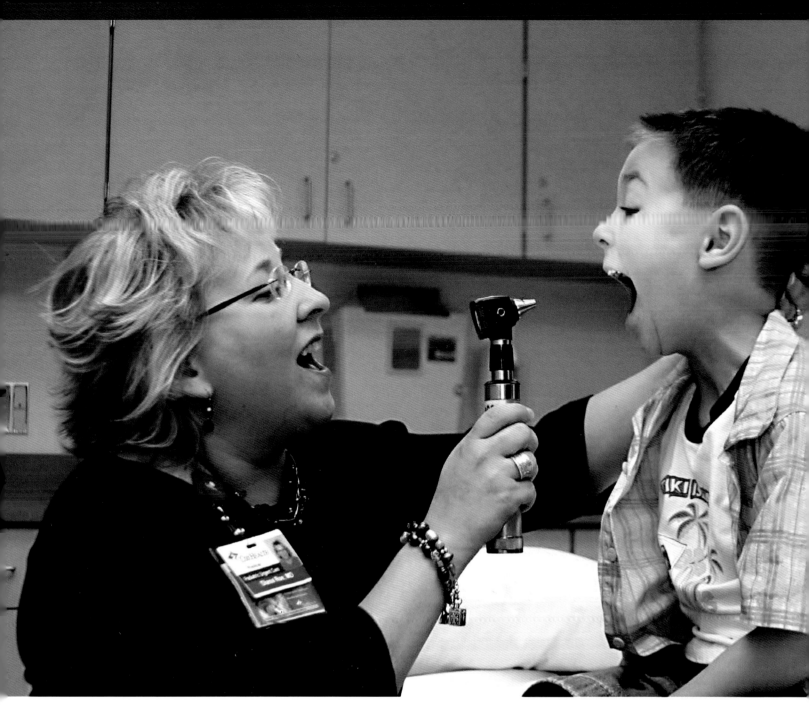

CoxHealth: Beginning a Second Century of Caring

A one hundredth birthday is definitely a milestone. Celebrating a century with plans in place for the next hundred years is even more unusual. However, for a hospital to accomplish that while maintaining roots in the same community and preserving its identity as a locally owned, public trust is nothing short of amazing.

CoxHealth came into being in 1906 when Ellen Burge donated her frame duplex on Jefferson Avenue as a Methodist hospital. It was named Burge Hospital in her honor. Eventually this site evolved into Cox North, and will greet its second century as CoxHealth Medical Park.

"What has made and continues to make us unique are the physicians, the staff, and the hundreds of volunteers."

From this humble beginning, CoxHealth has become a multihospital system, with a staff of more than nine thousand, making it the largest employer in Southwest Missouri.

Late in the 1940s, businessman Lester E. Cox led a series of capital campaigns, secured federal funding, and added more than $1 million to re-create a flourishing hospital. The hospital continued to grow with a series of expansions, upgrades, and new construction. In 1969, Burge was renamed Lester E. Cox Medical Center. Cox Medical Center South opened in 1985 and is now a major medical facility.

◀ *Pediatrician Dr. Diana Roe examines a patient at the new Pediatric Urgent Care Center at the Turner Center. The facility, which opened in September 2006, is the first urgent care center in Springfield totally dedicated to children.*

Although CoxHealth's growth has been spectacular, it is not just about bricks and mortar. "By all accounts, we are an outstanding medical facility," said president and CEO Robert H. Bezanson, "but what has made and continues to make us unique are the physicians, the staff, and the hundreds of volunteers—including our board members—who pour their hearts and souls into providing this community with the best health care possible."

For patient convenience, CoxHealth is organized around Centers of Excellence. These include the Bill and Ann Turner Women's and Children's Center, Hulston Cancer Center, the Meyer Center for Wellness and Rehabilitation, Wheeler Heart and Vascular Center, and the Martin Center for Diagnostic and Imaging Services.

"There are outstanding features of each center. For instance, the Meyer Center is the region's only medically based fitness and rehabilitation facility. The Martin Center focuses on diagnostic and imaging services, and Cox Walnut Lawn—which was formerly Columbia Hospital—houses skilled nursing, urgent care, outpatient services, and inpatient rehabilitation. These are all patient-convenient centers. In other words, patients coming for cancer care find everything they need in one location at the Hulston Center. Those being treated for heart problems find the same kind of individualized care at the Wheeler Heart and Vascular Center," Bezanson explained.

Children's health care and education is another important area at CoxHealth. "We are proud to have participated in the Children's Miracle Network since its beginning; 2006 marked our twenty-first year with CMN. Over the years we have raised more than $17 million, and all the funds raised here stay in the Ozarks to provide for children's services," said Bezanson. One of the programs funded through CMN is the C.A.R.E. Mobile. This clinic on wheels provides immunizations and preventive health screenings for children with limited access to health services. CoxHealth now has two such units.

Continued on page 284

Photo by Scott Indermaur

Photo by Gail Lurvey

Jeff Robinson, director of ▶ Radiation Oncology (right, kneeling), helps position a patient in the scanner in the BrainLab at Hulston Cancer Center. As part of an ongoing commitment to cancer care, the BrainLab is the first stereotactic radiosurgery program in the region.

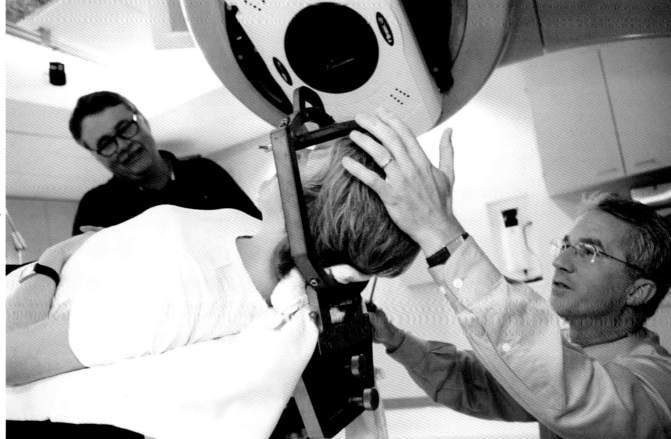

Photo by Thomas S. England

▲ *Nurse and educator Karen Madsen (in blue) works with nursing students from Cox College on the pediatrics floor of Cox South hospital. Students are exposed to many different aspects of nursing during visits to the hospital floors—everything from working with infants to reviewing computerized patient charts.*

Continued from page 283

Another outstanding service is Oxford HealthCare, which is the largest home health-care company in Southwest Missouri. Through the latest technology, patients can monitor themselves and transmit their findings to a central record-keeping unit where the information is evaluated. Directions are then relayed to the patient, a procedure that saves unnecessary trips to an emergency room. If a nurse is needed, one is dispatched to the patient's home.

"Our involvement with this community is not just within our four walls," said Bezanson. "We provide more than $84 million in community benefit services each year, including charity care, free clinics, and community outreach services. We support special fund-raising events, such as an annual golf tournament to support breast cancer, and our employees donate thousands of hours of their time to the community."

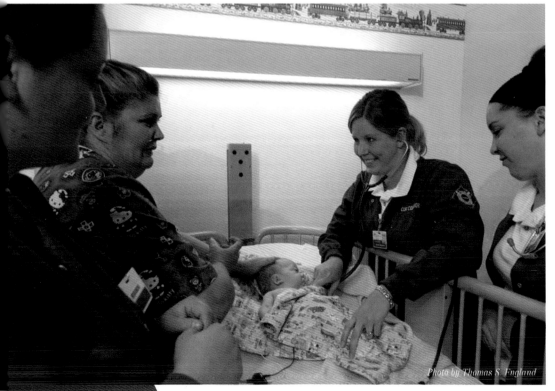

Photo by Thomas S. England

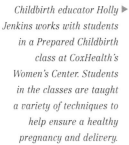

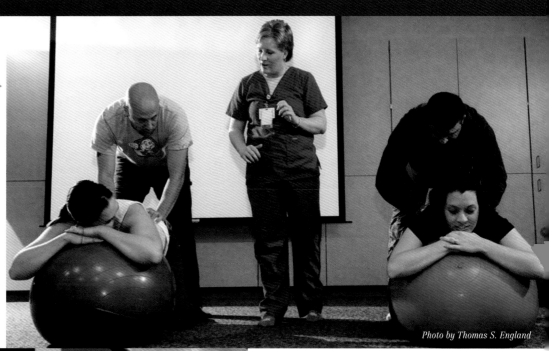

Childbirth educator Holly ▶
Jenkins works with students
in a Prepared Childbirth
class at CoxHealth's
Women's Center. Students
in the classes are taught
a variety of techniques to
help ensure a healthy
pregnancy and delivery.

Photo by Thomas S. England

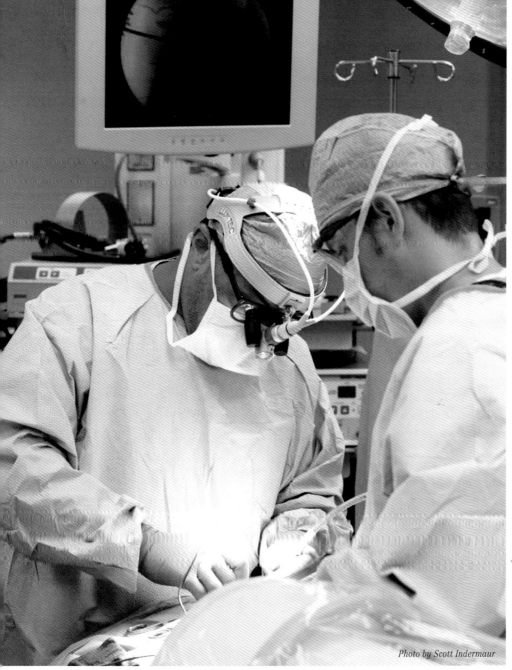

CoxHealth has won numerous awards, including recognition as one of the nation's Top 100 Integrated Health Systems. "We are also particularly proud that our fifty-five physician clinics are accredited by the Joint Commission on Healthcare Organizations," Bezanson said.

So what does the immediate future hold?

Within the next five years, a $55 million redevelopment project will transform the North campus into the new CoxHealth Medical Park. It will include a new Cox College, Behavioral Health Center, and Family Medicine Residency, with a twenty-four-hour urgent care center with radiology and laboratory support.

Statistics say CoxHealth's service area will increase to almost seven hundred thousand people by 2015. "Our roots run deep in Springfield, and whatever the future holds, we will be here to provide cutting-edge health care to this community," said Bezanson. ❖

◀ *Dr. Salim Rahman of Springfield*
Neurological and Spine Institute
performs back surgery at Cox South.

Photo by Scott Indermaur

Symbols of Parkview High School's success surround two speech and debate students preparing for competition. A National Debate School of Excellence, PHS leads Missouri in state awards and is home to national champions in Public Forum Debate. ❖

The residents of the Phelps Grove neighborhood say there is a lot to love about this area. Within walking distance of MSU, as well as entertainment and shopping areas, Phelps Grove offers moderately priced housing wrapped in the ambience of an established neighborhood. Residents love the abundance of sidewalks that run in front of charming bungalow-style homes built in the early 1900s. An added surprise is Phelps Grove Park, a part of the neighborhood and a favorite spot to play or take in one of the planned concerts. ❖

Photo by Lisa Means

Photo by Scott Indermaur

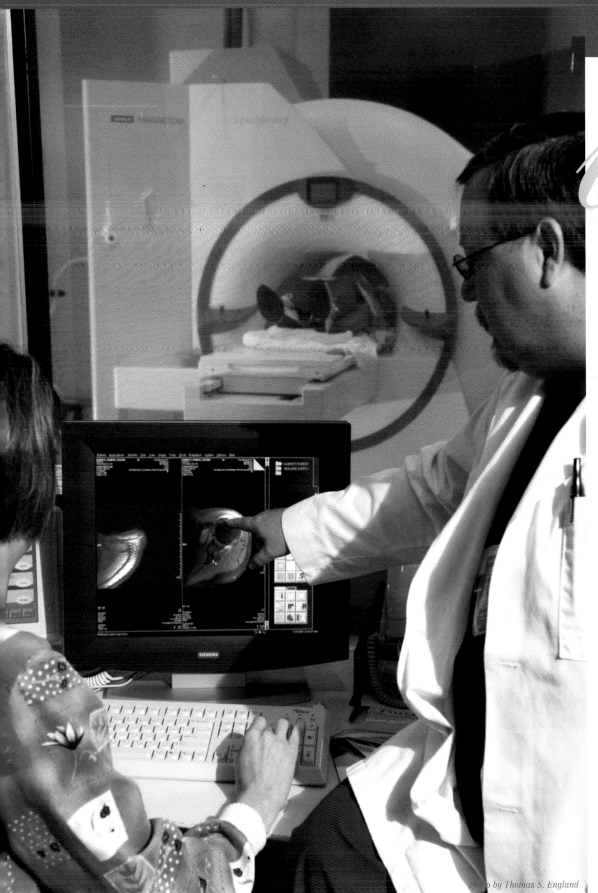

FERRELL-DUNCAN CLINIC: THE BEST IN MEDICAL CARE

When general surgeon Robert Duncan opened a practice with fellow surgeon Thomas Ferrell in 1945, the phone number was simple—just three digits. Some might also argue that the times were simpler as well. Though times have changed, with medicine becoming more advanced, and the Ferrell-Duncan Clinic now the state's largest independent multispecialty practice, one thing remains constant: the mission of providing Southwest Missouri residents with the absolute best of medical care.

> In keeping with its mission, Ferrell-Duncan Clinic has attracted physicians who are not only like-minded, but are at the top of their game.

Doug Duncan, orthopedic surgeon and son of Robert Duncan, reflects on his father's vision. "He said that he always believed that by establishing a workable philosophy of service and growth, and combining that philosophy with the proper selection of specialties, the patients and the primary care physicians in the community benefit. That's been the focus, as well as the advantage of a multispecialty clinic like Ferrell-Duncan," he adds. "The specialists view their role in the community as providing quality and timely specialty care for their patients, which ultimately facilitates the long-term medical management that is provided and coordinated by the primary care physician."

Photo by Thomas S. England

▲ *Medicine is both an art and a science, and the Ferrell-Duncan Clinic successfully melds the two with the latest technology to support quality patient care.*

In today's medical model, the role of the primary care physician has never been more important. That said, the role of the specialist is also critical, particularly as it relates to efficiently diagnosing and treating unusually complicated medical and surgical problems a patient may have.

"Specialties in medicine developed because of scientific advances and the ever-expanding body of knowledge about health, and the diagnosis and management of medical disorders and diseases," says Duncan. "In order to have comprehensive and up-to-date knowledge of these highly specialized methods, the physician, along with the support staff, have to constantly stay abreast of the body of knowledge they are expected to master," he adds. In the Ferrell-Duncan Clinic mission statement, the clinic pledges to use this knowledge "to deliver state of the art personalized healthcare in an ethical and efficient manner with the best available personnel and technology in a humanitarian, compassionate and responsive manner with respect for the dignity of the patient." "As a physician you are trained to have compassion and empathy. You have to address the medical conditions of the patients in your practice, but it is also important to focus on the whole person and what you can do to help," says Duncan.

In keeping with its mission, Ferrell-Duncan Clinic has attracted physicians who are not only like-minded, but are at the top of their game. Physician specialties include allergy/immunology, cardiology, cardiothoracic surgery, colon and rectal surgery, dermatology, electrophysiology cardiology, family practice, gastroenterology, gynecologic oncology, infectious diseases, internal medicine, nephrology, neurology, obstetrics/gynecology, orthopedics, otolaryngology, plastic surgery, pulmonology, rheumatology, general surgery, vascular surgery, urology, and vein and laser surgery. Essentially, there's a

▼ *Since 1945, the Ferrell-Duncan Clinic has grown with the Springfield community, always striving to meet its many health-care needs.*

Continued on page 290

Photo by Thomas S. England

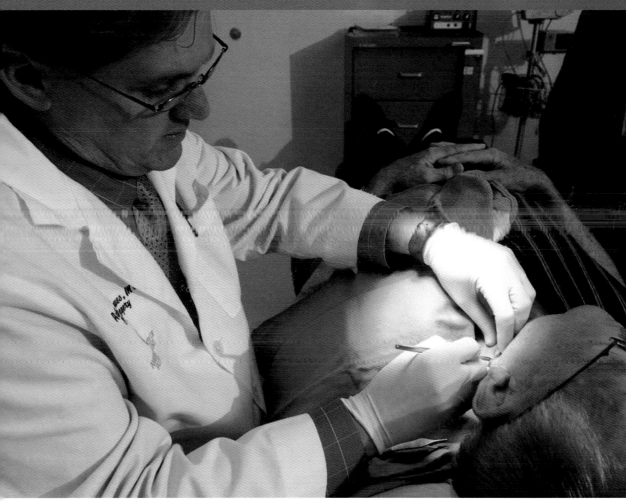

Continued from page 289

physician specializing in everything from head to toe for adult patients at Ferrell-Duncan.

Through the years, as the Ferrell-Duncan Clinic expanded by adding specialists, it outgrew the main clinic. Today the more than one hundred physicians are located in four state-of-the-art facilities in south Springfield and one in Bolivar, Missouri. In addition to the convenience of twenty-plus subspecialists practicing in these locations, comprehensive ancillary support services are available on-site. Such services include the expected—laboratory, radiology, screening mammography, ultrasound, medical billing services—and the unexpected—comprehensive audiology services, pacemaker assessment and reprogramming, outpatient IV therapy, outpatient injections, and immunizations. "Not only is it convenient to have comprehensive specialists and services located in one facility, it's essential for the optimal coordination of care. Patients and their physicians will agree: this is the way to assure quality care," says Charles McCracken, executive director. "Ferrell-Duncan has been an important cornerstone in the medical community of Springfield, and will continue to be so in the future." ❖

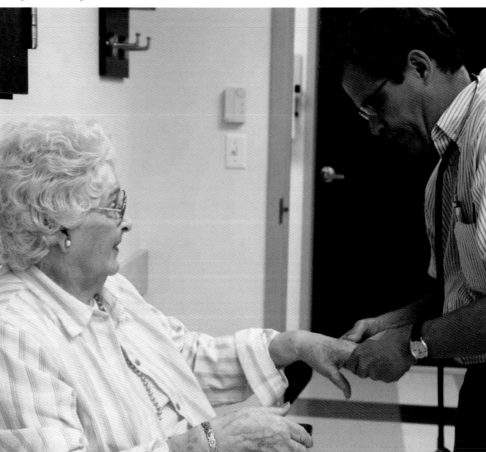

Headache Care Center's Migraines softball team's victories exemplify the mission of the center: to help individuals gain control of disabling headaches. ❖

Photo by Scott Indermaur

Dean R. Kinzer of Strafford, Missouri, enjoys a special treat from Andy's Frozen Custard. From sundaes and shakes to splits and "concretes," Andy's offers custard served up hundreds of ways. The creamy concoction is made fresh on the hour at Andy's using a special machine that produces custard with just the right content and at just the right temperature. Started in a lakeside shop in Osage Beach, Missouri, Andy's now operates three Springfield locations along with an ever-growing list of shops in Missouri and four additional states. ❖

Photo by Rod Reilly

A Southern Hills Neighborhood, nestled in southeastern Springfield, harbors many good memories for those who grew up there, and promises to do the same for newcomers. Developed in the 1950s, generations of families see it as a classic Ozarks environment surrounded by nature and filled with hospitality. Showcasing architectural styles from traditional colonials and ranches to contemporary, the development includes a variety of recreational areas, including three scenic lakes. The Galloway Trail, a thoroughfare for runners, walkers, and cyclists, winds along natural springs, charming homes, and tree-lined streets. The community sits conveniently adjacent to nearby shopping, dining, and entertainment. "We owned another house in the lake area and always loved the neighborhood because it is so convenient to everything," said Martha Rogers, pictured here with husband, Joe, enjoying their second Southern Hills home, built in 1990. ❖

Photo by Lisa Means

Photo by Lisa Means

Phelps Grove Park has a host of amenities, including a wading pool, rose garden, tennis courts, baseball field, grills and tables, play equipment, and even a physical fitness course. However, well-trained canines like Lily the basset hound and Nutmeg the beagle know that sometimes their friends just like to hang out. So they take Alesha and John Gonzales (right) to the park to relax and enjoy the sunshine. Of course, there are others who use the park for exercise, wandering leisurely through the forty-four acres near the charming, older neighborhood of Phelps Grove. ✣

Photo by Alan S. Weiner

Mary Collette participates in a Thursday night yoga group that has been meeting for approximately ten years. Their routine is to do yoga together in a space on the second floor of the historic Firehouse Number Two on Commercial at Boonville and then go to a member's home for a potluck dinner. This particular evening they met at Abbe Ehler's home in the historic Midtown neighborhood. In addition to Mary and Abbe, the group includes Christine Schilling, George Max Masses, Sonja and Brian Shipman, Chandler Carlson, and Thomas Ehler. ✣

Photo by Scott Indermaur

What started out over a century ago as the Springfield Creamery Company has become a distinctive part of Jordan Valley Park, the city's center of cultural activity. The building now houses the Springfield Regional Arts Council, host of workshops, classes, and gatherings for the area's cultural agencies. Among those who come to the center for its cultural activities are area youth participating in the Boys and Girls Clubs of Springfield, an organization dedicated to helping at-risk youth grow into productive adults. As part of the organization's art classes, boys and girls from the club made a trip to the Creamery, where members of comedy troupe the Skinny Improv performed at the Rotary Centennial Outdoor Classroom. Here, performers Anna Martin, Elijah Blaine Cunningham, Adam Hoelscher, and Jessica Landis improvise for the kids before giving them tips on how to make others laugh. ✣

People worldwide practice this ancient technique, but very few of them in the United States find their mayor leading the class. Mayor Tom Carlson—who has been actively involved in Springfield politics for at least twenty years—teaches an early-morning yoga class three times a week in the basement of City Hall. As both a businessman and a politician, Mayor Carlson knows the importance of keeping fit. In this busy world where we are constantly bombarded by the stress and strain of everyday activities, it is common knowledge that our minds and bodies need time to relax, rejuvenate, and unwind. ✤

Photo by Thomas S. England

▲ *Missouri State's compact campus provides a number of terrific views for students, faculty, and the many annual visitors. Shown here is the West Mall, with Strong Hall, the Avenue of Flags, and the Citizen-Scholar Statue in the Keiser Amphitheatre.*

MISSOURI STATE UNIVERSITY: "A COLLEGE WITH A CONSCIENCE"

Imagining and making Missouri's future. That is the goal of Missouri State University. The multi-campus statewide university takes the traditional mission of higher education—advancing knowledge—to a higher level.

Called "a college with a conscience" by the *Princeton Review*, Missouri State University is distinguished by its statewide mission in public affairs. The purpose of the mission is to develop educated persons while achieving five goals: democratizing society, incubating new ideas, imagining Missouri's future, making Missouri's future, and modeling ethical and effective behavior.

> The task of developing educated persons obligates the university to expand the store of human understanding through research, scholarship, and creative endeavor.

Integrated throughout the student experience, the curriculum, as well as faculty research, Missouri State's public affairs mission seeks to develop citizens of enhanced character. The task of developing educated persons obligates the university to expand the store of human understanding through research, scholarship, and creative endeavor and draw from that store of understanding to provide service to the communities that support it.

"The currency for the twenty-first century will be knowledge," says Missouri State president Michael T. Nietzel. "To be successful individuals will need to have education beyond high school; in many instances, graduate degrees will be essential. Higher education has never been more important, not only for the individual, but for the public good that is created as a result."

To accomplish its goal of helping make Missouri's future, Missouri State University students must be well-informed, confident, and conscientious leaders, prepared not just to take good jobs upon graduation but to make good jobs through the application of their knowledge and the pursuit of their ambitions. Missouri State cultivates these leaders through a breadth of opportunities and a depth of learning that comes from rigorous standards in the classroom, in research, and in extracurricular activities.

Founded as the Missouri State Normal School in 1905, Missouri State has grown in the last century to the comprehensive state university system of today, with more than twenty thousand students enrolled on its three campuses in Missouri. Missouri State University–Springfield is a selective admissions, graduate-level teaching and research institution; Missouri State University–West Plains is an open admissions campus serving seven counties in south central Missouri; Missouri State University–Mountain Grove serves Missouri's fruit industry through operation of the State Fruit Experiment Station.

In addition, the university, the second largest in the state, has a campus in China and continues to develop additional partnerships with other universities, such as the University of Missouri and New Mexico Tech, as well as private corporations.

"At Missouri State, we not only want to be known for our accomplishments, but also the way in which we conduct ourselves and do our business," says Nietzel. "Our goal is to be a model for others to emulate in our transparency, our stewardship, our inclusiveness, and all other aspects of our daily activities." ✣

Photo by Lisa Means

Rishi Patel, senior research scientist, inspects a calibration plate prior to coating silicon wafers with polymeric materials as part of the development process of fabricating novel sensor devices for utilization in public health and safety applications.

Photo by Alan S. Weiner

Photo by Alan S. Weiner

The center for community and recreational activities in Springfield since its establishment in 1913, the downtown YMCA continues in its mission to build healthy bodies, minds, and spirits. For nearly seventy years it served the housing and fitness needs of the city's young men until it merged with the local YWCA in 1982 to become the Ozarks Regional YMCA. Five years later it was renamed the G. Pearson Ward YMCA in honor of Mr. Ward's longtime sponsorship. Completely renovated in 1997, the Ward branch features two basketball gyms, a swimming pool, locker rooms, free weight room, Nautilus and cardiovascular equipment, an indoor track, and racquetball and handball courts. A variety of childcare, after-school, and family programs are also available to its membership. ✤

An Internet café, video game stations, iPod music stations, and a full-size gym for basketball and volleyball—they are all part of the Fusion Student Center at Central Assembly of God. The high-tech/high-touch center serves multiple purposes as the location for the church's youth activities and for SPIN, an after-school program for Pipkin Middle School. "It's a safe, healthy, and positive environment—a place where young people can hang out and connect with each other, and ultimately connect with God," says Cheri Stevenson, Central Assembly's associate youth pastor and director of SPIN. ❖

Photo by Scott Indermaur

Photo by Scott Indermaur

SPRINGFIELD PUBLIC SCHOOLS: A DISTRICT WITH DISTINCTION IN PERFORMANCE

As a society, we have become accustomed to having choices. We evaluate our options for cell phone and cable television services; we comparison shop before we buy a car or choose a bank. However, one of the most important decisions we make as parents is about our children's education. In Springfield, there are choices for that, too.

Springfield Public Schools is Missouri's largest fully accredited school district and has been recognized five years in a row as a "District with Distinction in Performance." That excellence results from the district's keen focus on ensuring all students achieve academically by offering choices that best fit students' differing educational needs and interests.

Flash Fact: Springfield has approximately twenty-four thousand students who attend more than fifty school sites.

Springfield's thirty-five elementary schools, one intermediate school, nine middle schools, five high schools, one gifted center, and one alternative education center offer an array of educational opportunities for all students.

High school students can enroll in the elite International Baccalaureate

> Springfield Public Schools has been named a "District with Distinction in Performance" five years in a row.

◄ An investment of $156 million in facility improvements is resulting in major renovations at several Springfield schools. Old and new complement each other at Central High School, originally built in 1893, where a renaissance followed improvements completed in 2002.

program or study broadcast media at a school that has earned five prestigious Robert F. Kennedy Journalism Awards. They can study music, compete in speech and debate, or play sports, all at schools recognized on the state or national level for outstanding achievement in these areas.

All five high schools also offer the A+ Schools Program, which provides financial assistance for eligible students to attend community colleges or career/technical schools in Missouri.

The Springfield community has invested more than $156 million in improving its education facilities through passage of three bond issues in six years. When these projects are complete, forty-eight school sites will have been improved—including total renovation of two high schools, construction of two new schools, and significant expansion or remodeling of other schools.

Flash Fact: Springfield Public Schools is the city's fourth-largest employer, with more than three thousand employees.

Operating under a philosophy of continuous quality improvement ensures that SPS makes efficient and effective use of its resources so every dollar spent has the maximum impact on classroom learning. Springfield's tax levy, set at $3.55 in 2006, per $100 of assessed valuation, is the lowest in the surrounding area and among the lowest in Missouri.

Flash Fact: Springfield teachers average about fourteen years of teaching experience, and more than 62 percent have advanced degrees.

SPS ensures a quality learning experience by recruiting and retaining highly qualified teachers.

Continued on page 302

Photo by Scott Indermaur

A volunteer force of about ► fourteen hundred supports Springfield students. Many, like Mayor Tom Carlson and city council members, are matched with a specific student for the school year. Each pair meets once a week to work on literacy skills.

Photo by Thomas S. England

Photo by Thomas S. England

Continued from page 301

The unique STEP UP professional development program supports new teachers and promotes professional excellence.

Flash Fact: Seventy-three percent of 2006 district graduates pursued some form of postsecondary education.

Community support of education in Springfield is evident in the number of volunteers and partners who donate time and resources to schools. A successful faith-based initiative recruits and trains volunteers to work one-on-one each week with elementary students who need assistance in reading and math.

As the district looks ahead to meeting the changing demands of educating students in the twenty-first century, it will rely upon a system of continuous quality improvement to guide its direction and decisions. This new culture challenges all stakeholders—students, faculty, staff, parents, and administrators—to be engaged in learning about and improving the educational system.

"I believe the best way we can work with our children is to take a planned approach to systemic improvement," said superintendent Norm Ridder. "It is often the system that gets in the way of our ability to perform at a high level in the classroom. Continuous improvement requires persistence and patience, but it promotes quality."

Photo by Thomas S. England

▲ *Extracurricular activities such as athletics, marching band, drama, and community service clubs offer Springfield students an opportunity to enhance their education by developing leadership skills and good sportsmanship.*

A focus on structured inquiry ▶ gives Primary Years Programme students the opportunity to reflect and take action as a result of learning. PYP is one of three international education programs offered in Springfield for grades kindergarten through twelve.

Photo by Thomas S. England

◀ *Glendale High School choir
students are fortunate to have
former Teacher of the Year
Kevin Hawkins as their
instructor. Another distinction
for the music department is
its designation as a Grammy
Signature School for
excellence in the musical arts.*

All these efforts translate into an outstanding educational experience for Springfield students, and it shows in their academic performance:

- In 2006, all five high schools met Adequate Yearly Progress in communication arts and math

- At all grade levels tested, Springfield students scored above state averages in communication arts and math on the 2006 Missouri Assessment Program tests.

- Springfield seniors consistently score above state and national averages on ACT composite scores. Springfield's graduating class of 2006 had an average ACT composite score of 22.6.

The district's strong academic performance and outstanding programs and services helped Springfield/Greene County earn a spot on the 2005 "100 Best Communities for Young People" as determined by the Alliance for Youth. ❖

Known for its educational excellence, ▶
*Springfield Public Schools is Missouri's
largest fully accredited school district.
Springfield students consistently
outperform their state and national peers
on standardized tests such as the ACT.*

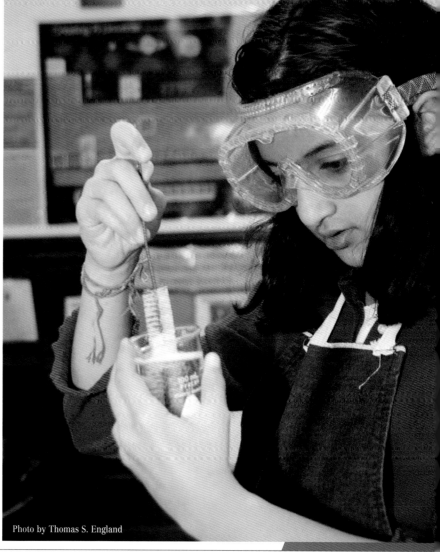

Photo by Thomas S. England

Hillcrest High School broadcast media students edit a news report for its nationally recognized *HTV Magazine*. The student-produced show has won five Robert F. Kennedy High School Journalism Awards and nine Pacemaker Awards in addition to numerous honors for individual students. ❖

Photo by Thomas S. England

Photo by Thomas S. England

The main campus of Ozarks Technical Community College in Springfield is one of five campuses and education centers across Southwest Missouri. The institution is proud of its reputation as "the community's college" and fulfills that role through a multitude of educational opportunities that enhance students' lives.

OTC's STRENGTHENING THE REGION THROUGH EDUCATION

Ozarks Technical Community College (OTC) continues to grow as an important resource for Springfield and the region, providing students and businesses with opportunities to advance their education and upgrade skills.

Founded in 1990 to fill the void of technical education in the area, OTC quickly grew into two campuses with three regional education centers. The institution now offers a wide range of educational opportunities, from associate degrees and technical certifications to noncredit courses that strengthen careers and personal lives.

Nearly ten thousand students attend classes each semester to take advantage of the day, evening, and weekend courses.

For students needing help with the fundamentals, OTC offers courses in general education, and in the basics of reading, writing, and mathematics. For those seeking a certificate or associate degree, OTC offers programs in the humanities, communications, math, and social sciences. And for people interested in a technical career, OTC's offerings range from culinary arts and computers to manufacturing and transportation.

The college services the entire community: local businesses and industries look to OTC to provide customized training solutions, from coaching to consultation services. Whether it is workforce readiness preparation for new personnel, skills enhancement for experienced professionals, or leadership development for frontline supervisors, OTC's programs can help improve productivity and performance.

Thousands in the community turn to OTC for its noncredit learning options in interests as diverse as flying, welding, music, foreign languages, and computers.

From general learning for the job seeker to skills improvement for the advancing professional, OTC's programs are helping to strengthen the region's workforce and enhance overall economic development.

In the future as educational needs continue to evolve, Ozarks Technical Community College will also change to meet the challenge. ❖

Photo by Scott Indermaur

The institution now offers a wide range of educational opportunities, from associate degrees and technical certifications to noncredit courses.

It's not only the fellows who get involved in Civil War reenactments. These two volunteers put in their time to represent the significant contribution women made during the conflict to help out. The six-hour Battle of Wilson Creek was one of the fiercest of the Civil War. John Ray and his wife Roxanna owned a house along the Wire Road, and during the battle she hid in the cellar with her children and slaves. The Ray House was used as a field hospital, which saved it from destruction. Like many women at that time, Roxanna assisted the doctors, helped tend the wounded, and cooked meals for all. Her children and slaves were kept busy hauling fresh water from the springhouse. The body of General Nathaniel Lyon was brought to the house, and Roxanna supplied a counterpane from one of her beds to cover the body before it was moved to Springfield. There another woman, Mary Phelps, prepared the body and then buried it in the backyard to protect it. It stayed safely hidden for approximately a month until General Lyon's family arrived from Connecticut to escort it home. ❖

Photo by Scott Indermaur

Photo by Scott Indermaur

Photo by Lisa Means

Through a wide variety of outreach ministries provided by more than four hundred places of worship throughout Springfield, staff and members of the congregations strive to better their lives and the lives of their community. National Avenue Christian (left and below left), welcomes the diversity he finds in his congregation. With Sunday school classes for all ages, choir rehearsals, Bible study, vacation Bible school, children's sermons, yoga classes, and an occasional all-church cookout, there is a place for everyone. First and Calvary Presbyterian Church (below) also has a long history of service in Springfield. Located near Missouri State University's campus, First and Calvary offers three Sunday morning worship services, adult and children's Sunday schools, and a series of active youth and adult ministry programs. Not only does St. Agnes Cathedral and Parish (far left, top) serve close to thirty-five hundred worshipers, its active outreach provides for the needs of thousands more in the community. "Part of our mission is to reach out to the poor and vulnerable," says Father Mike McDevitt. "So we are a typical Catholic church in the sense that even people who aren't Catholic know they can count on us for help." A few of its programs include holiday HUGS baskets (hats, underwear, gloves, socks) donated by parishioners, and participation in the Well of Life, a coalition of six downtown Springfield churches that provides rental, utilities, and grocery assistance to needy families.❖

Photo by Scott Indermaur

805

Originally from Minnesota, Kathleen Meek is now thoroughly acclimated to her new life in Springfield. She moved here in November 2005 with her husband, a Springfield native whom she met while they both attended law school in St. Louis. When searching for a home, the couple decided on this lovely Craftsman on Pickwick, located just down the street from where Kathleen's husband grew up. The best thing about living in the neighborhood, she says, is its friendliness. "We're close to everything," she explains, "and everyone made me feel right at home." She also likes that people are always out and about, walking with their kids and dogs, a big plus for their own pooch, Rosie.

From Pickwick to
Woodland Heights,
Walnut Street to
Midtown, each Springfield
neighborhood has its
own individual character.
They also share one thing
in common: a friendliness
that welcomes one
and all.

Photo by Alan S. Weiner

Photo by Alan S. Weiner

MURNEY ASSOCIATES, REALTORS: A COMMUNITY PARTNER

Back in 1997, Patrick Murney and a select group of management and sales associates saw something missing from their local real estate industry. The void, they decided, could be filled by an agency that operated with local management and that focused on the individual sales associate, thereby ensuring that the associate could provide the highest level of customer service and satisfaction in the marketplace today. This type of operation, they were certain, would create an agency that was more in tune with its community's real estate needs.

Turns out, they were right. In only three years, Murney Associates, Realtors® had grown into the number-one firm in Southwest Missouri, and today over five hundred Realtors® are part of the Murney Associates team.

From six area offices, Murney Associates provides residential resale, new construction, relocation, commercial sales and leasing, and development services to clients throughout the state.

Murney Associates' growth stems, in part, from its ability to anticipate developments in the industry and community, then sensing how those changes may impact clients and sales associates. This dedication to the local industry, combined with intuition, allows Murney Associates to continually improve the home buying and selling process.

The secret to Murney Associates' success springs from its service philosophy.

> Murney Associates' growth stems, in part, from its ability to anticipate developments in the industry and community.

*◄ Murney Associates, Realtors has sponsored
Hooked on Dance since its inception. The annual
event is one of Springfield's largest benefit galas.
Monies raised allow the Breast Cancer
Foundation of the Ozarks to impact the lives of
families facing breast cancer.*

Because Murney Associates understands the clear connection between satisfied sales associates and happy clients, the firm ensures that its associates have the best training, top-notch support, and the most innovative and efficient marketing tools available at their disposal. These tools enable associates to more readily match buyers with properties that fit their needs, which in turn saves the property owner valuable time and helps preserve their hard-earned equity.

Since its inception, Murney Associates has also been committed to taking an active role in events that impact its communities.

While being in real estate dictates taking a substantial interest in issues such as property values, taxes, school districts, and development and planning, Murney Associates' commitment to the community goes well beyond a business interest.

The company believes that giving back is a responsibility, and therefore supports a long list of charities and civic organizations through both funding and hands-on involvement. From organizations that focus on health-care concerns, to activities centered around churches and schools, to helping the hungry or homeless, to supporting arts and culture, there is seemingly no area of life untouched by Murney Associates' support.

Murney Associates has also earned a growing list of regional and national acknowledgments since opening its doors. Murney Associates has consistently ranked in the top forty of the nation's highest-producing independent real estate firms. The agency has been recognized for its rapid growth and has repeatedly been voted a local favorite by the people of the Ozarks.

Murney Associates intends to stay focused on the client and sales associate by staying in front of the curve and anticipating new developments that will allow the firm to deliver services more efficiently and continually improve the home selling and buying process. ❖

Photo by Lisa Means

Photo by Lisa Means

*Murney Associates, Realtors ►
has underwritten the St.
John's Sunshine 5K Run
ce 2003. The event attracts
thousands of participants
each year. The proceeds
from this event benefit the
Breast Cancer Foundation of
the Ozarks, an organization
providing resources for those
affected by breast cancer.*

Bobby Troupe wrote the song, but it's Nat King Cole's voice that most people associate with "Get Your Kicks on Route 66." The highway was the major path of migrants during the Dust Bowl of the 1930s. Better times in the '50s made it the Mother Road for vacationers headed to California. Mom-and-pop businesses vied with one another to attract attention, creating teepee-shaped motels, frozen custard stands, Indian curio shops, and reptile farms. Red's Giant Hamburg in Springfield was the first drive-through restaurant. Driving Route 66 through Springfield today, you can still see Melinda Court, which opened in 1944, and Rest Haven Court, which opened in 1947. Steak 'n' Shake continues to serve tourists and is a member of the Route 66 Association, which is working to have the road declared an official national landmark; in fact, Route 66 is beginning to show up on maps with that designation. The first sign for Historic Route 66 was posted in Springfield in 1991. Although a traveler can no longer drive all 2,448 miles of the original road, one of the best-preserved stretches runs between Springfield and Tulsa. ❖

Photo by Scott Indermaur

Photo by Scott Indermaur

Once a place simply to conduct business during the day, downtown Springfield is now a place to live, shop, and dine, as well as a place to be entertained day and night. Still in the middle of a revival, the downtown area has been the beneficiary of developers and supporters who have invested millions of dollars into residential, retail, restaurants, and entertainment facilities. ❖

Photo by Alan S. Weiner

Photo by Alan S. Weiner

Photo by Alan S. Weiner

Springfield Featured Companies

ACR Nally Marketing Group

2840 East Chestnut Expressway
Springfield, Missouri 65802
417.831.7672
www.acr-nally.com

Advertising Agency (p. 174)

ACR Nally Marketing Group is a full-service advertising and marketing agency representing clients from locally owned businesses to an international software company.

Battlefield Mall

2825 South Glenstone Avenue
Battlefield Road and Glenstone Avenue
Springfield, Missouri 65804
417.883.4111
www.simon.com

Retail – Shopping Center (p. 90–91)

Battlefield Mall is the Springfield area's premier shopping destination. The mall encompasses 1.1 million square feet of lease space, including both indoor shops and a lifestyle center with exterior entrances. It houses four department stores, over 150 specialty retailers, and a host of eateries.

Benjamin Franklin Plumbing

3378 South Scenic, Suite A
Springfield, Missouri 65807
417.823.8400
www.benfranklinplumbing.com/
springfield-mo

Plumbing Service (p.128–129)

Ben Franklin the Punctual Plumber® is more than a trademark; it is a way of doing business. The franchise in Springfield is owned by John Nicholson, and he and his staff believe that homeowners have a right to demand on-time service. Ben Franklin has the strongest code of ethics in the business, and the Springfield location proudly upholds that standard.

BKD Foundation

P.O. Box 1190
Springfield, Missouri 65801-1190
417.865.8701
www.bkd.com/about/BKDFoundation.htm

Nonprofit – Foundation (p. 266)

Established in 1999 to pool and direct firm resources toward local community programs, BKD Foundation is helping to enrich the people and charitable organizations within the areas served by the firm's twenty-seven office locations.

BKD, LLP

Hammons Tower
901 East St. Louis Street, Suite 1000
Springfield, Missouri 65801-1190
417.865.8701
www.bkd.com

Certified Public Accounting Firm (p.156–161)

One of the ten largest CPA and advisory firms in the country, BKD offers its clients an extensive scope of services delivered with a depth of expertise and integrity that makes them a standout in the industry.

Blackwell Sanders Peper Martin LLP

901 St. Louis Street, Suite 1900
Springfield, Missouri 65806
417.268.4000
www.blackwellsanders.com

Law Firm (p. 170–172)

With a practice that goes back to 1916, Blackwell Sanders Peper Martin has emerged as one of the Midwest's leading commercial law firms. From its offices in Missouri, Nebraska, Washington, D.C., and London, England, the firm provides clients with exceptional transaction and litigation services, no matter their location or jurisdiction.

BNSF Railway Company

3253 East Chestnut Expressway
Springfield, Missouri 65802
www.bnsf.com

Transportation – Railroad (p. 148–149)

The BNSF Railway Company is the product of hundreds of different rail lines merged into one of the country's most innovative and efficient transportation companies.

Butler, Rosenbury & Partners, Inc.

319 North Main Street, Suite 200
Springfield, Missouri 65806
417.865.6100
www.brpae.com

Architects (p. 256–257)

With the ability to understand and meet clients' needs for functional built environments, Butler, Rosenbury & Partners has earned the trust of their fellow community partners and citizens as well as some of the country's biggest names in the hospitality, retail, and entertainment industries.

Christian Health Care

1328 East Evergreen
Springfield, Missouri 65803
417.891.9939
www.c-healthcare.com

Health Care – Senior Care (p. 278–279)

Christian Health Care operates skilled nursing, long-term care, residential care, and independent living facilities that help seniors retain their sense of dignity and independence.

City of Springfield

840 Boonville Avenue
Springfield, Missouri 65802
417.864.1000
www.springfieldmogov.org

Government – City (p.62–63)

The City of Springfield embraces "citizen-driven, city-supported" planning for the future of Missouri's third-largest metropolitan area—a hub for health care, education, jobs, shopping, dining, entertainment, and recreation for a region of nearly four hundred thousand residents in the beautiful Missouri Ozarks.

City Utilities of Springfield

301 East Central
Springfield, Missouri 65802
417.863.9000
www.cityutilities.net

Utility (p. 230)

City Utilities is a locally owned utility company providing electricity, natural gas, water, telecommunications, and transit services to greater Springfield.

Commerce Bank

1345 East Battlefield
Springfield, Missouri 65804
417.869.5411
www.commercebank.com

Financial Institution – Bank (p. 124–126)

Commerce Bank is the principal subsidiary of Commerce Bancshares Inc. (NASDAQ: CBSH), a $13.9 billion holding company. Since 1865, Commerce has been meeting the financial services needs of individuals and businesses, and now operates across three states.

Convoy of Hope

330 South Patterson Street
Springfield, Missouri 65802
417.823.8998
www.convoyofhope.com

Nonprofit – Relief Organization (p. 272–275)

Through direct relief efforts as well as partnerships with concerned individuals, businesses, churches, and other charitable organizations, this grassroots, Christian-based relief organization is able to quickly and compassionately mobilize to bring hope to millions at home and abroad.

CoxHealth

3850 South National Avenue
Suite 510
Springfield, Missouri 65807
417.269.3000
www.coxhealth.com

Health Care – Medical Center (p. 282–285)

From its humble beginnings, CoxHealth has become a multihospital system providing the latest technology and world-class health care to the Springfield area. With a staff of more than nine thousand, CoxHealth is the largest employer in Southwest Missouri.

CU Community Credit Union

010 North Benton
Springfield, Missouri 65802

1017 East Republic Road
Springfield, Missouri 65807
417.865.3912
www.cupowerline.org

Financial Institution – Credit Union (p. 176–177)

CU Community Credit Union offers a full range of checking, savings, and loan options to over five thousand members in Greene and Christian counties from two locations in Springfield.

Dickerson Park Zoo

3043 North Fort
Springfield, Missouri 65803
417.833.1570
www.dickersonparkzoo.org

Attraction – Zoo (p. 16–17)

Dickerson Park Zoo, accredited by the American Zoo and Aquarium Association and recipient of the 1997 Edward Bean Award for Excellence, enjoys a positive place in the cultural fabric of the community, and by all indications, it will continue to be treasured as one of the city's beloved family traditions.

Drury University

900 North Benton Avenue
Springfield, Missouri 65802
417.873.7879
www.drury.edu

School – University (p. 234–236)

Drury University prepares students for global participation through its core curriculum, undergraduate and graduate studies, leadership training, and opportunities to be involved in the local community, local businesses, and activities around the world.

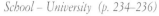

Empire Bank

1800 South Glenstone
Springfield, Missouri 65804
417.881.3100
www.empirebank.com

Financial Institution – Bank (p. 164)

Empire Bank is a community bank with full-service branches throughout the Ozarks. Since 1956, the bank has helped build a strong community through its products and its active involvement in the community and in economic development.

Evangel University

1111 North Glenstone Avenue
Springfield, Missouri 65802
417.865.2811
www.evangel.edu

School – University (p. 268–269)

A private, coeducational Christian university, Evangel University encourages its students to seek academic excellence through an integration of faith, learning, and life. The university supports more than eighty academic programs as well as seven graduate programs in psychology, education, and organizational leadership.

Ferrell-Duncan Clinic

1001 East Primrose
Springfield, Missouri 65804
417.875.3000
www.ferrellduncan.com

Health Care – Physician Group (p.288–290)

The Ferrell-Duncan Clinic is Springfield, Missouri's largest independent physician multispecialty clinic, with more than one hundred physicians practicing in more than twenty specialties. The clinic also has three satellite offices in Branson, Mount Vernon, and Bolivar.

General Council of the Assemblies of God

1445 North Boonville Avenue
Springfield, Missouri 65802
417.862.2781
www.ag.org

Religious Organization (p. 50)

From its headquarters in Springfield, the General Council of the Assemblies of God supports a Pentecostal organization of over 2.8 million worshipers in over 12,200 churches across the nation that are committed to a threefold mission of worship, discipleship, and evangelism.

Great Southern Bank

1451 East Battlefield
Springfield, Missouri 65804
800.749.7113
www.greatsouthernbank.com

Financial Institution – Bank (p. 180–181)

Great Southern Bank opened its doors in downtown Springfield in 1923. It is still a landmark there and operates thirty-seven branches in fifteen counties in the Ozarks, plus 170 ATMs and loan production offices in Northwest Arkansas, the Kansas City metropolitan area, Columbia, and St. Louis. The bank proudly serves more than ninety-one thousand customer households.

Guaranty Bank

1341 West Battlefield Road
Springfield, Missouri 65807
417.520.4333
www.gbankmo.com

Financial Institution – Bank (p. 144–145)

Established in 1913 as Guaranty Savings & Loan Association, and redefined and renamed Guaranty Bank in 2003, this financial institution is becoming a major commercial bank, offering corporate small businesses the same one-on-one service their residential customers rely on. With headquarters in Springfield, decisions are made locally, a plus for all customers.

Hamra Enterprises

1855 South Ingram Mill Road
Springfield, Missouri 65804
417.887.7677
www.wendysofmissouri.com

Hospitality – Food Service (p. 32–34)

Hamra Enterprises companies include Wendy's of Missouri, Panera Bread Bakery-Cafe in Chicago and Boston, Baymont Inn and Suites in Missouri, and Holiday Inn Express and Suites in Texas. The company also has commercial developments and other real estate holdings throughout Missouri.

Hawthorn Park Hotel

2431 North Glenstone
Springfield, Missouri 65803
417.831.3131
www.hawthornparkhotel.com

Hospitality – Hotel (p. 98–101)

The Hawthorn Park Hotel features two hundred guest rooms, ample meeting space, and above all, simple elegance and superior service. A complimentary twenty-four-hour shuttle is available for guest transportation between the hotel and the airport.

Headache Care Center Clinvest Primary Care Network

3805 South Kansas Expressway
Springfield, Missouri 65087
417.890.7888
www.headachecare.com
www.clinvest.com
www.primarycarenet.org

Health Care – Physicians Group (p. 260–263)

Headache Care Center, Clinvest, and Primary Care Network are three entities with one common goal: to provide patient-centered quality health care. Although based in Springfield, all three organizations have national reach.

Hiland Dairy Foods

P.O. Box 2270
Springfield, Missouri 65810-2270
417.862.9311
www.hilanddairy.com

Dairy (p. 22–23)

Hiland Dairy is the only locally operated dairy in Springfield and the largest dairy supplier in Missouri, Arkansas, Kansas, and Oklahoma. Founded in 1938, Hiland Dairy has earned the right to bear the Quality Chekd trademark for its consistent assurance of quality and food safety.

Husch & Eppenberger, LLC

1949 East Sunshine Street
Suite 2-300
Springfield, Missouri 65804
417.862.6726
www.husch.com

Law Firm (p. 132–133)

Husch & Eppenberger, LLC employs more than 275 attorneys in eight cities across the Midwest and Midsouth. For over eighty years, the firm has served individuals as well as local, regional, national, and international businesses, financial institutions, and charitable and governmental organizations.

John Q. Hammons Hotels

300 John Q. Hammons Parkway
Suite 900
Springfield, Missouri 65806
417.864.4300
www.jqhhotels.com

Hospitality – Hotel Developer (p. 94–95)

For over half a century, John Q. Hammons has been a leading innovator in America's hospitality industry. His business savvy and his generosity of spirit bring countless economic, civic, and cultural benefits to Springfield and dozens of other cities across the country.

Kraft Foods, Inc.

2035 East Bennett Street
Springfield, Missouri 65804
www.kraftfoods.com

Manufacturing Company – Food Products (p. 68–69)

Kraft is the second-largest food producer in the world. The company's history in Springfield began in 1939, when they produced process cheese. Kraft-Springfield has an economic impact of more than $88 million annually in Southwest Missouri, through wages and purchases of raw materials, utilities, taxes, goods, and services.

Larry Snyder & Company

4820 North Towne Centre Drive
Ozark, Missouri 65721
417.887.6897
www.lscinc.com

Contractor – General (p. 152–153)

Larry Snyder & Company offers complete construction services and specializes in commercial and industrial construction along with site development. Founded in 1978, the company builds in Missouri, as well as in other states throughout the Midwest and South.

Lathrop & Gage L.C.
1845 South National
Springfield, Missouri 65804
417.886.2000
www.lathropgage.com

Law Firm (p. 140–141)
Lathrop & Gage L.C. is a national firm steeped in the rich history of Springfield and the Midwest. Founded in 1873, it is the oldest law firm west of the Mississippi River. While it offers the depth and strength of a national firm, it is well known for its regional midwestern values and generous support of the Springfield area.

Law Offices of Dee Wampler
2871 East Battlefield
Springfield, Missouri 65804
417.882.9300
www.entrapped.com

Law Firm (p. 205–205)
With nearly fifty years of combined law experience between them, criminal trial lawyers Dee Wampler and Joseph S. Passanise provide their clients within nothing less than the best defense available.

The Maiman Company
3839 East Mustard Way
Springfield, Missouri 65803
417.862.0681
www.maiman.com

Manufacturing Company – Architectural Wood Doors (p. 192–194)
One of the nation's top manufacturers of beautiful and durable architectural-quality wood stile and rail doors is also an innovator in the wood flush door market. In 2002, the company introduced the first new commercial wood flush door product in thirty years, utilizing thermal-fused technology to produce a high-quality, economical, and ecologically sound flush door for a variety of applications.

Maxon's Diamond Merchants
2622 South Glenstone
Springfield, Missouri 65804
417.887.1800
www.maxonsdiamondmerchants.com

Retail – Jewelry Store (p. 38–39)
Since 1972, Maxon's Diamond Merchants has built a reputation for quality, integrity, and exceptional customer service. Rick and Jane McElvaine, co-owners and America Gem Society certified gemologists, are proud of the fact that Maxon's has been an official Rolex jeweler since the store first opened.

Missouri State University
901 South National Avenue
Springfield, Missouri 65897
417.836.5000
www.missouristate.edu

School – University (p. 296–297)
Missouri State University, the second largest university in the state, is located on 225 acres in the heart of Springfield. The West Plains Campus is located in the southwest area of the city. Missouri State's Springfield Campus is a selective admissions, graduate-level teaching and research institution offering more than 140 degree programs and options within forty-two academic departments.

Murney Associates, Realtors
1625 East Primrose
Springfield, Missouri 65804
417.823.2300
www.murney.com

Real Estate – Residential and Commercial (p. 312–313)
Murney Associates, Realtors, is the number-one firm in Southwest Missouri, with over five hundred associates and agents. From six area offices, Murney Associates provides residential resale, new construction, relocation, commercial sales and leasing, and development services to clients throughout the state.

Northrop Grumman Printed Circuit Boards
4811 West Kearney Street
Springfield, Missouri 65803
417.829.5200
www.ngpcb.com

Manufacturing Company – Printed Circuit Boards (p. 208–209)
A global leader in state-of-the-art printed circuit board technology, Northrop Grumman Printed Circuit Boards continues to meet a variety of increasingly sophisticated electronic communications needs for clients in the defense, telecommunications, computing, and medical industries.

Oxford HealthCare
3660 South National
Springfield, Missouri 65807
800.749.6555
www.OxfordHealthCare.net

Health Care – Home (p. 222–223)
Oxford HealthCare is the leading home-care provider in Southwest Missouri, delivering a wide variety of quality services to clients of all ages—from newborns to seniors. Since 1974, Oxford HealthCare has helped thousands of people of all ages in the Ozarks remain independent at home.

**Ozarks Coca-Cola/
Dr Pepper Bottling Company**
1777 North Packer Road
Springfield, Missouri 65803
417.865.9900
cocacolaozarks.com

Manufacturing Company (p. 104–105)
Ozarks Coca-Cola/Dr Pepper Bottling Company has been refreshing the Ozarks as a family-owned business since 1920 and was named Manufacturer of the Year by the Springfield Area Chamber of Commerce in 2006.

**Ozarks Technical
Community College**
1001 East Chestnut Expressway
Springfield, Missouri 65802
417.447.7500
www.otc.edu

School – Community College (p. 305)
Ozarks Technical Community College offers associate degrees, certifications, and noncredit courses that advance education and improve workforce skills. The college also offers customized training solutions for area businesses.

Paul Mueller Company
1600 West Phelps
Springfield, Missouri 65802
417.831.3000
www.muel.com

Manufacturing Company – Stainless Steel (p. 200–202)
Paul Mueller Company is a manufacturer of high-quality stainless steel equipment used in more than one hundred countries worldwide.

**Pellham Commercial
Realtors**
1531 East Bradford Parkway, Suite 301
Springfield, Missouri 65804
417.890.6868
www.pellhamrealtors.com

Real Estate – Commercial (p. 246–247)
Pellham Commercial Realtors is a family business that represents buyers and sellers in sales and leasing of commercial properties; markets and manages commercial properties, including retail, office, warehouse, and multifamily facilities; and provides financial analysis, master planning, and architectural/engineering services.

Postel Maps & Atlas, Inc.
240 North Marshall Street
Marshfield, Missouri 65706
417.859.7751 or 888.876.2627
www.postelmaps.com

Supplier – Maps and Atlases (p. 86–87)
Postel Maps & Atlas, Inc., supplies city, state, and county road maps and road atlases in folded, quick-view, and laminated versions to convenience stores, truck plazas, and department stores in Missouri and surrounding states.

Power of the Web.com
1722 South Glenstone, Suite M
Springfield, Missouri 65804
417.887.8984
www.poweroftheweb.com

Web Site Developer (p. 26–29)
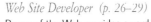
Power of the Web provides award-winning Web design and marketing strategies for clients at home in Springfield, as well as coast to coast.

Regional Hospice
1328 East Evergreen
Springfield, Missouri 65803
417.832.0577
www.regionalcarehospice.com

Health Care – Hospice (p. 240)
Regional Care Hospice provides end-of-life care for patients and their families with

services ranging from pain management and comfort measures to spiritual counseling and education.

Rick's Automotive, Inc.
2121 South Campbell Street
Springfield, Missouri 65807
417.887.2225
www.ricksautomotive.com

Automotive Services (p. 188–189)

Rick's Automotive opened in 1980 and has grown from a five-bay, three-employee operation to eighteen service bays and twenty-six employees. They serve an extensive clientele of walk-in customers as well as maintaining more than 110 fleets of various sizes. With a heavy emphasis on training and continuity, many of their employees have been with them for over twenty years, and they have more than four hundred cumulative years of technical experience.

Rivercut Development Company

6290 South Farm Road 131
Brookline, Missouri 65619
417.890.5200
www.rivercut.com

Real Estate – Developer (p. 226–227)

Springfield's newest community offers its residents unmatched beauty and value, with lots featuring breathtaking views of rolling hills, the James River, and the championship golf course. By incorporating the beauty of the Ozarks and the James River into the development, Rivercut is also ensuring their preservation for generations to come.

RPCS Inc.

336 South Barnes
Springfield, Missouri 65802
(417) 829-9220
www.pricecutteronline.com

Retail – Supermarket Chain (p. 108–109)

As one of Southwest Missouri's largest grocery chains, RPCS combines modern shopping conveniences like online ordering and delivery with old-fashioned customer service and dedicated community involvement.

The Signature Bank

4039 South Kansas Expressway
Springfield, Missouri 65807
417.889.2600
www.signaturebank.com

Financial Institution – Bank (p. 214–216)

The Signature Bank is the largest locally owned independent bank in the Springfield region. It was founded in 2004 by the merger of Signature Bank and THE BANK, both locally owned. Citing $847 million in assets in nine years, the Signature Bank continues to capitalize on its strengths: agility and flexibility. It has six retail locations in Springfield and a loan production office in St. Louis.

Springfield Area Chamber of Commerce

202 South John Q. Hammons Parkway
Springfield, Missouri 65806
417.862.5567
www.springfieldchamber.com

Chamber of Commerce (p. 184–185)

With nearly two thousand members, the Springfield Area Chamber of Commerce has helped Springfield become the state's third-largest city and earn the designation of "Missouri's economic engine."

Springfield Brewing Company

301 South Market Street
Springfield, Missouri 65806
417.831.8277
www.springfieldbrewingco.com

Hospitality – Brewing Company and Restaurant (p. 44–45)

Featuring some of the most advanced equipment in the world, Springfield Brewing Company is also the most unique brewery in southwestern Missouri, attracting both locals and visitors alike with award-winning beers, fine food, and an old-world pub-like setting.

Springfield Public Schools

940 North Jefferson Avenue
Springfield, Missouri 65802
417.523.0021
http://springfieldpublicschoolsmo.org

School – Public (p. 300–303)

Springfield Public Schools is Missouri's largest fully accredited school district and has been recognized four years in a row as a "District with Distinction in Performance." That excellence results from the district's keen focus on ensuring that all students achieve academically by offering choices that best fit students' differing educational needs and interests.

Springfield-Branson National Airport

5000 West Kearney Street
Springfield, Missouri 65803
417.869.0300
www.flyspringfield.com

Airport (p. 242–243)

The Springfield-Branson National Airport offers direct flights to ten of the nation's largest hubs and low-cost direct flights to major cities both east and west.

Springfield–Greene County Parks Department

1923 North Weller
Springfield, Missouri 65803
417.864.1049
www.parkboard.org

Government – Parks Department (p. 112–115)

The National Gold Medal Award–winning Springfield–Greene County Parks Department is committed to the goal of building a safe, accessible, comprehensive system of parks, trails, and open space that enhance the quality of life, preserve land, and connect the people and communities of the area now and for the not-so-distant future.

St. John's Health System
1235 East Cherokee Street
Springfield, Missouri 65804
417.820.2000
www.stjohns.com

Health Care – Health Care System (p. 250–252)
With roots in the community that go back to 1891, St. John's Health System has grown to include six hospitals, one health clinic, seventy physicians' offices, and some of the most compassionate, high-quality care available in the region.

Steiner Talent
2733 East Battlefield Road
#105
Springfield, Missouri 65804
417.889.9909
www.steinertalent.com

Entertainment – Talent Booking (p. 72–73)
"I admire talented people who are the best at what they do, and I love matching them up with people looking to hire top-notch entertainment," said Mark Steiner, owner of Steiner Talent, which books well-known entertainers Gig Salad, which represents local and regional acts; and Steiner People, a speakers bureau. Clients can view a talent roster for all three on-line.

TCSI/Transland
1601 West Old Route 66
Springfield, Missouri 65757
417.864.5710
www.transland.biz

Transportation – Trucking (p. 196–197)
TCSI/Transland employs hundreds of drivers and trucks in providing long- and short-haul loads, flatbed transport, intermodal transport, less than truckload, and special equipment services to all points of the compass.

TelComm Credit Union
2155 East Sunshine
Springfield, Missouri 65804
417.886.5355
www.telcommcu.com

Financial Institution – Credit Union (p. 136–137)
With five locations and a strong presence in southern Missouri, TelComm Credit Union is committed to using leading technology to stay ahead of members' needs; offer progressive, competitive, and convenient products; and prove that caring, personal service is not just a trend. It's a tradition!

UMB Bank
1150 East Battlefield Road
Springfield, Missouri 65807
417.887.5855
www.umb.com

Financial Institution – Bank (p. 166–167)
With nearly one hundred years of doing business in the Midwest, UMB Bank has built a reputation for sound banking principles, long-standing integrity, and steadfast commitment to customer relationships.

University Plaza Hotel and Convention Center
333 John Q. Hammonds Parkway
Springfield, Missouri 65806
417.864.7333
www.upspringfield.com

Hospitality – Hotel and Convention Center (p. 78–81)
University Plaza Hotel and Convention Center, located in Jordan Valley Park in the heart of Springfield, is Southwest Missouri's largest full-service hotel and convention center, offering thirty-nine thousand square feet of versatile function space on site, and 271 well-appointed guest rooms and suites.

Willow Brook Foods
P.O. Box 50190
Springfield, Missouri 65805
417.862.3612
www.wbfoods.com

Manufacturing Company – Food Products (p. 56–57)
Willow Brook Foods is a leader among deli, retail, warehouse club, and food-service protein manufacturers. Their production facilities in Springfield exceed high standards of excellence. Their mission is to provide customers with premium-quality products that meet the highest demands of safety and fit the needs of the consumer.

Many thanks for your support!

Springfield Editorial Team

Kimberly Fox DeMeza, Writer, Roswell, Georgia. Combining business insight with creative flair, DeMeza writes to engage the audience as well as communicate the nuances of the subject matter. While officially beginning her career in public relations in 1980 with a degree in journalism, and following in 1990 with a master's in health management, writing has always been central to her professional experience. From speechwriting to corporate brochures to business magazine feature writing, DeMeza enjoys the process of crafting the message. Delving into the topic is simply one of the benefits, as she believes every writing opportunity is an opportunity to continue to learn.

Rena Distasio, Writer, Tijeras, New Mexico. A full-time freelance writer since 2000, Distasio contributes articles and reviews on a variety of subjects to regional and national publications. In her spare time she and her husband and two dogs enjoy the great outdoors from their home in the mountains east of Albuquerque.

Grace Hawthorne, Writer, Atlanta, Georgia. Starting as a reporter, she has written everything from advertising for septic tanks to the libretto for an opera. While in New York, she worked for Time-Life Books and wrote for *Sesame Street*. As a performer, she has appeared at the Carter Presidential Center, Callanwolde Fine Arts Center, and at various corporate functions. Her latest project is a two-woman show called *Pushy Broads and Proper Southern Ladies*.

Amy Meadows, Writer, Canton, Georgia. Meadows is an accomplished feature writer who has been published in a wide variety of local, regional, and national consumer and trade publications since launching her freelance writing career in 2000. She also specializes in producing corporate marketing literature for companies large and small and holds a master's of arts degree in professional writing from Kennesaw State University.

Regina Roths, Writer, Andover, Kansas. Roths has written extensively about business since launching her journalism career in the early 1990s. Her prose can be found in corporate coffee-table books nationwide as well as on regionally produced Web sites, and in print and online magazines, newspapers, and publications. Her love of industry, history, and research gives her a keen insight into writing and communicating a message.

Thomas S. England, Photographer, Decatur, Georgia. England grew up internationally, graduated from Northwestern University, and began photography as a newspaper photographer in the Chicago area. He began freelancing for *People* magazine in 1974. Since then he has taken assignments from national magazines and corporations, specializing in photographing people on location. He lives in Decatur, Georgia, with Nancy Foster, a home renovator, and their dog Chessey. More of his photographs may be viewed online at www.englandphoto.com.

Eric Francis, Photographer, Omaha, Nebraska. Francis was born and raised in Nebraska. Early on, he honed his skills freelancing for local newspapers, magazines, and commercial clients. Francis now also works regularly for some of the nation's largest and best-known magazines, newspapers, and wire services, covering news, features, and sports. He continues to make his home in Omaha with his fiancé, Shannon, and their four children.

Scott Indermaur, Photographer, Lawrence, Kansas. Indermaur's editorial and corporate assignments have taken him from the smallest rural communities to the world's most urban environments. His gift lies in discovering the familiar in the exotic and the remarkable in the ordinary. Whether he's capturing a fleeting moment in history or cutting to the essence of a portrait, Scott tells the story in a language everyone understands. When not photographing, Scott, who along with his wife and son are all Tae Kwon Do black belts, also enjoys wonderful food and wine, meeting new people, traveling, music, and sailing. You can view his images and contact him at www.siphotography.com.

Lisa Means, Photographer, Dallas, Texas. Lisa graduated from East Texas State University in Commerce, Texas, and attended the University of London at Chelsea College. She worked as a staff photographer for DLM, Inc. before starting her own company in 1989. She freelances with both national and local magazines, direct clients, and advertising agencies across the country. Lisa's specialty is working with people on location. She lives with her son and their two dogs in Dallas, Texas. More of Lisa's work can be viewed on her Web site at www.lisameans.com.

Rod Reilly, Photographer, Atlanta, Georgia. Since 1979 Rod has used his training at Carnegie Mellon School of Design and Rochester Institute of Technology to create compelling environmental portraits on location of people as they live and work. His clients include Home Depot, Coca-Cola USA, United Parcel Service, Cox Communications, and McGraw-Hill. Starting his career as a staff shooter for Georgia Pacific, Rod has owned his own studio, Reilly Arts & Letters, for the last eleven years, and travels often on assignment. He is a member of ASMP and the father of three.

Gail Snyder, Writer, Woodstock, Georgia. Snyder is a writer and editor with twenty years of experience in corporate communications and publishing. She has edited or written articles focusing on corporate management strategies, published articles in a number of trade magazines and journals, and edited both fiction and nonfiction books. Gail enjoys explaining material to an audience in a way that reveals how any subject can be interesting. She earned her bachelor's degree in journalism from Georgia State University, where she went on to complete her master's in communications. Currently she works as a freelance and contract writer and editor.

Alan S. Weiner, Photographer, Portland, Oregon. Weiner travels extensively both in the United States and abroad. Over the last twenty-three years his work has appeared regularly in *The New York Times*. In addition, his pictures have been published in *USA Today* and in *Time, Newsweek, Life,* and *People* magazines. He has shot corporate work for IBM, Pepsi, UPS, and other companies large and small. He is also the cofounder of The Wedding Bureau (www.weddingbureau.com). Alan has worked in every region of the country for Riverbend Books. His strengths are in photojournalism.

The staff of the Springfield Area Chamber of Commerce, pictured outside the chamber office in the John Q. Hammons Enterprise Center, thank the dedicated business and professional organizations that sponsored this book, making its publication possible.❖

Photo by Lisa Means

About the Publisher

Celebrating Springfield—A Photographic Portrait was published by Bookhouse Group, Inc., under its imprint of Riverbend Books. What many people don't realize is that in addition to picture books on American communities, we also develop and publish institutional histories, commemorative books of all types, contemporary books, and others for clients across the country.

Bookhouse has developed various types of books for prep schools from Utah to Florida, colleges and universities, country clubs, a phone company in Vermont, a church in Atlanta, hospitals, banks, and many other entities. We've also published a catalog for an art collection for a gallery in Texas, a picture book for a worldwide Christian ministry, and a book on a priceless collection of art and antiques for the Atlanta History Center.

These beautiful and treasured tabletop books are developed by our staff as turnkey projects, thus making life easier for the client. If your company has an interest in our publishing services, do not hesitate to contact us.

Founded in 1989, Bookhouse Group is headquartered in a renovated 1920s tobacco warehouse in downtown Atlanta. If you're ever in town, we'd be delighted if you looked us up. Thank you for making possible the publication of *Celebrating Springfield—A Photographic Portrait.* ❖

BOOKHOUSE
GROUP, INC.

Banks ❖ Prep Schools ❖ Hospitals ❖ Insurance Companies ❖ Art Galleries ❖ Museums ❖ Utilities

❖ Country Clubs ❖ Colleges ❖ Churches ❖ Military Academies ❖ Associations

In a spirit of cooperation, Springfield, the state Department of Transportation, the Commercial Club, and Urban Districts Alliance worked to restore the 562-foot Jefferson Avenue steel bridge. The bridge was originally dedicated in 1902 and constructed to provide a safe walkway over the St. Louis and San Francisco Railway yards. There are thirteen sets of tracks just below the bridge, and train watching is a favorite pastime. The bridge links the Woodland Heights historic residential neighborhood on the north side with the Commercial Street shopping area to the south. This renovated six-block, mixed-use area is fast becoming the heart of a downtown restoration project.